The Final Word

Revelation simply explained

Steve Wilmshurst

First published in Great Britain in 2008

British Library Cataloguing in Publication Data
A record for this book is available from the British Library

EU GPSR: 6b Upper Water Street, Newry, Northern Ireland, BT34 1DJ

ISBN: 978–0–85234–669–3

Printed in UK

Evangelical Press, an imprint of 10Publishing

Unit C, Tomlinson Road, Leyland, Lancashire, PR25 2DY

info@10ofthose.com
www.10ofthose.com

13 15 17 20 18 16 14 12

Contents

Page

Preface

This book started life as a series of sermons at my home church, Kensington Baptist in Bristol. Kensington is the most encouraging and supportive of churches to preach in, and I want to acknowledge the help and kindness of all those who have urged me to 'write something on Revelation'! Thanks go to my ministry colleagues Andy and Mark for many interesting discussions (not always in agreement, of course!); to the teaching and wisdom of John Nolland and John Bimson at Trinity College, Bristol; to Christopher Ash, John Brand and David Field for various helpful and thought-provoking articles; to Susanna Taylor, for proof-reading; and especially to my family for their patience and general goodwill.

The title of the book is fully explained in the last chapter. But for now, let me simply recall the way the Christians in Smyrna recorded the martyrdom of Polycarp, their beloved leader, sixty years after Revelation was first brought to them with its special message for their own church. Pointedly, they described the year, not as the eighteenth of the Emperor Antoninus Pius, but in this way: '... when Philip of Tralles was high priest, when Statius Quadratus was proconsul, but Jesus Christ was reigning for ever, to whom be glory, honour, majesty and an eternal throne, from generation to generation, Amen.' He is the Father's Final Word. He was reigning then; he is reigning now; and one day all will acknowledge his eternal, universal reign.

Steve Wilmshurst
January 2008

Preface to the second edition

The simple objective of producing a second edition is to widen and prolong the usefulness of the book. (And yes, the irony of updating a book entitled *The Final Word* is not lost on me!) With this in view, I have updated illustrations that were no longer topical, tweaked the text in a number of places, added a few more explanatory notes and added questions for discussion and review at the end of each chapter. I have also tried to 'internationalise' it a little more, so that it is less limited to a western perspective. Revelation itself constantly presents us with a vision of the church united across 'nation, tribe, people and language' and it seems only right that a commentary on the book should attempt to reflect that unity.

Since the appearance of the first edition, I have taught Revelation and related subjects in a variety of places. I have enjoyed many vigorous discussions about aspects of my book with people holding different views; and I have continued to read and explore. Despite many attempts to convince me otherwise, and although I greatly enjoyed Sam Storms' *Kingdom Come: The amillennial alternative*, I have not shifted from my position on the millennium, mainly because I find the alternative paths of exegesis of Revelation 20 unconvincing. I hope my amillennial and other friends will continue to bear with me as graciously as they have done until now.

Something that has surprised and encouraged me is the number of preachers who have appreciated the book in sermon preparation. I really didn't expect that—but I'm grateful for it!

It is the encouragement of the many and diverse individuals who have commented appreciatively on the book that has convinced me that a new edition is worthwhile. So thanks go to all of them. This edition goes out with my prayers that we will all see more clearly the glorified Christ, the slain and victorious Lamb, the reigning and coming King.

Steve Wilmshurst
July 2014

Introduction: How to survive when the world is against you

The book of Revelation was written for a people under pressure—a people who knew all too clearly that the world was against them. Nearly all their early leaders, the apostles, had gone: most of them had been martyred. Although the gospel had spread throughout the Roman Empire, it had not taken it over. Persecution was looming and the law was against them. It is in that context of suffering and oppression that the Lord gives John the series of visions which he writes down in the form of this book. It is a survival manual, explaining how to survive when the world is against you. Even though it is a little harder for us to see, this is what we need to know in our day as well. In the West, we are not yet being openly persecuted, but, at least in the UK, that is the direction in which we are heading. Elsewhere, persecution is already rife. In any case, the world is against us and we have to know how to survive as believers on increasingly hostile ground. This is why Revelation is so vitally relevant for our day.

It is odd that when many people think about Revelation, they think of secrets or hidden messages. That is the opposite of what 'Revelation' means—which, obviously, is about things that have been revealed. For all its alleged difficulties, I remain convinced that Revelation is essentially not a difficult book to understand. Of course it has its tricky passages—it would be foolish to deny that. But the basic message can be summed up simply and wonderfully: Jesus wins, and as Christians we are safe with him! Even so, before we get into the text, it will nevertheless be helpful to look briefly at some key points of background.

The writing—who and when?

Tradition has always held that the human author of Revelation was the apostle John. This was certainly the view of the Church Fathers. The main reason for doubting John's authorship has been the very different style of Greek (including a lot of unconventional grammar) compared with the Gospel and letters which John wrote. Most of these differences can easily be explained, however, when we consider that this is a very different kind of writing from those other books. Add to that the fact that John must have written Revelation unaided, whereas he may have had some kind of literary assistant in the more peaceful circumstances of writing his Gospel and letters, as well as the number of significant words, phrases and themes used in Revelation which are strongly associated with John's Gospel, and most of the reasons for doubt evaporate.

John had spent most of his adult life as a church leader in what was known as the province of Asia, modern-day western Turkey. It seems almost certain that his home base was the city of Ephesus.

While some commentators have placed the book in the reign

of Emperor Nero, around AD 65, several factors point to a later date. One is that several of the letters to the churches, especially the one addressed to Ephesus, read as if the churches had been established for several decades at least. Another is the strong testimony of the Church Fathers, especially Irenaeus, who had been a disciple of Polycarp of Smyrna, who in turn knew John well. This testimony points to the reign of Domitian, near the end of the first century, and to its having been written somewhere around AD 95. At this point it seems that widespread persecution of Christians had not yet broken out, but in specific locations the rise of the cult of emperor worship and the pressure to conform to local gods and customs were placing severe pressure on the church. Under Domitian's rule, John, now an old man, was exiled to the island of Patmos, off the Turkish coast. It is a small, rocky island about eight miles by four, and the Romans used it as a labour camp. In spite of his age, John was probably consigned to hard labour in the stone quarries.

The writing—what kind?

The genre, or kind of writing, of Revelation is usually described as *apocalyptic*. This genre has its origins in the Old Testament, especially the later chapters of Daniel. The style continued to develop during the inter-testamental period. Many Jewish apocalypses were written within about a century before or after the birth of Christ; they are interesting from a historical angle, but even those which purported to be Christian never came close to being accepted by the church as inspired.

The most obvious common feature is the use of dramatic pictorial imagery. Apocalypses make frequent use of symbols, especially symbolic numbers, which came to have standard meanings—notably the use of seven to represent completeness, or perfection. Most of the symbols and images, especially in Revelation, draw heavily on the Old Testament, as we shall see.

The most important feature of apocalypses, however, is that they claim to reveal heavenly realities which are normally hidden from human view. Apocalyptic literature is often associated with frustration at God's apparent inactivity; apocalypses frequently contain the message that God is going to burst into history in a dramatic and unexpected way, despite all appearances that God's people are facing oppression and defeat.

Revelation does indeed fit into this category, but there is more to it than that. This book is also *prophecy*, as it claims directly in 1:3 and 22:7,19. That is to say, the heavenly truths about God's plans and purposes are here applied directly to God's people and their present plight. Revelation does not simply reveal what is going on in the heavenly realms, or what will happen in the last days: it tells us what to do about it!

Finally, the book is also in *letter* form. Not only in chapters 2 and 3, but very clearly in chapter 1, and again in chapter 22, we are reminded that this document was sent, firstly, to specific churches made up of real people living within a 150 mile radius of the place where it was written,[1] and, secondly, to all God's people, both then and since.

Still, the most distinctive style of writing in Revelation is apocalyptic, but you don't need a PhD in apocalyptic literature in order to read it! The key to understanding this book, along with the help of the Holy Spirit, is a good knowledge of the rest of Scripture. When people have gone wrong with this book—as many have—it has usually been because they have failed to tie it in properly with other parts of the Bible. There are hundreds of direct and indirect references to the Old Testament in these twenty-two chapters (the exact number is disputed, but it's an average of about one per verse), and so often the way to unlock the imagery of Revelation is to refer back to those passages.

How to read Revelation

Although the basic message of the book is quite straightforward, large parts of it are none the less controversial. Chapters 6 to 20 in particular have received widely (in some cases wildly) varying interpretations, some of which have become very influential and have even had a significant impact on American foreign policy in the Middle East. A quick tour of the four main schools of interpretation is therefore worthwhile. Depending on your church background, you will probably have been exposed to one or more of these.

The first way of reading the middle chapters of Revelation is *'futurist'*. This means that all the events recorded here will take place in the future, in the final months and years before the return of Christ. They belong to the end of the age. This view is very popular among evangelical Christians today, especially in Africa and North America. It is the view that inspired the *Left Behind* series—twelve books, with accompanying movies and many spin-offs, which have sold tens of millions of copies and are set in the last days of the earth. These books understand many of the images in a very literal sense, such as water that literally turns to blood, or a literal 144,000 Jewish evangelists—though no literal four horsemen or literal dragon!

In spite of its popularity, I firmly believe that the *Left Behind* series has got the picture wrong. This school of thought is not nearly sensitive enough to the way that apocalyptic imagery works. Moreover, if all these signs are confined to the future, then most of Revelation has been irrelevant for the last two thousand years. All we can do with it is skim through it, say, 'That's interesting,' and shut it again. The Holy Spirit does not give us any part of the Bible just so that we can do that.[2]

The second way of reading these chapters is the exact opposite—it is called the *'preterist'* school. This says that the events we read about in Revelation 4 to 19 have actually *already* happened. They all took place in the first century, in the period up to the Jewish War and the fall of Jerusalem in AD 70, soon after the book was written (so preterists favour the earlier date of writing). In particular, the beast whom we meet in chapter 13, with his famous number 666, is really a code for the Emperor Nero. Again, that would make the book very meaningful for people in the first century, John's own persecuted church, but it is hard to see the relevance or value for *us* of a coded account of events which took place two thousand years ago.

A third way of understanding Revelation is the *'historicist'* school. As you might guess, this is the idea that Revelation is a continuous story which corresponds to the whole of history between Jesus' first coming and his glorious return. So, as history rolls on, at any given point we can say, We are now up to 'chapter *x*, verse *y*'. It sounds good—until you actually start looking at all the different ways that people have tried to line up events in Revelation with events and dates here on earth. For a start, everyone who does this always works it so that the end is just about to happen in their own time, then matches up all the rest of the prophecy to events that have already happened. It just doesn't work.

The final way that people read Revelation is known as *'idealist'*. This view says that the others have got it all wrong; there are no real events in here at all, and the whole book is really only about the overall way God works in human history. It is to do with principles, or 'ideals'. But it is clear that some specific events *are* referred to here, especially towards the end, where the descriptions very explicitly relate to the unique events of the return of Christ, the final judgement and the new heavens and new earth. We are dealing with more than just general principles.

The fact is that all these four theories are partly right. Yes, the climax of all these events does lie in the future, and they do lead up gloriously to the Lord's return. Yes, it is absolutely vital to start with the first readers of the book in the time of John himself. We shall fail to understand it correctly unless we try to hear this prophecy as they would have done in the first place. That is true of every Bible book. But it does not finish with them: the message is for us as well. Yes, these events are unrolling through history all the way from the time of John until Christ returns in glory. But Revelation does not run in a straight line through history, as if we could tick off each horseman, each trumpet, each scene as it appears here on earth. It is more as if we are looking at the same scene from many different angles, one at a time. Each series of seven judgements leads up towards the same climax—the return of Christ to judge the earth.

So we need to read this book carefully, and most of all we need to tie it in with the rest of Scripture. Jesus himself speaks about his return in Matthew 24; we can look at what he says there. The Old Testament prophets speak time and again of the Day of the Lord, the day when God will judge the whole world. Scripture does not contradict Scripture, so when Revelation gets tricky we have the rest of the Bible to shine a light on it. But this book was not written for us to speculate over while we put our feet up. The churches to whom it was first written didn't have the luxury of doing that. It is here to help Christians to survive in a hostile world, and that is how we need to study it. This book is not for theologians to fight over; it is for ordinary believers to keep fighting the real fight.

For further reading

There are many, many commentaries and other books about Revelation! Some of these, of course, are more helpful than others. Michael Wilcock's *The Message of Revelation* in the 'Bible Speaks Today' series is excellent and very accessible. It is particularly helpful for seeing the 'big picture' of the book. Much larger (and more expensive!), Greg Beale's 'New International Greek Testament Commentary', *The Book of Revelation*, is comprehensive, masterly and detailed, though it needs a knowledge of Greek to get the best out of it. A little shorter and taking a slightly different line, I appreciate Robert Mounce's *The Book of Revelation* in the New International Commentary on the New Testament series.

I have also found helpful Leon Morris's *Revelation* in the 'Tyndale New Testament' series, Simon Kistemaker's *Revelation* in the 'New Testament Commentary' series and Gary Benfold's *Revelation Revealed*, which takes a similar approach to the present book. I have borrowed unashamedly while disagreeing with all of them at some point or other! William Hendriksen's very useful *More than Conquerors* should also be mentioned here. Finally, and with a wider focus than Revelation alone, Wayne Grudem's *Systematic Theology* has excellent chapters on the return of Christ and the end times, including a full chapter on the millennium; whereas most of the commentaries I have just mentioned take an amillennialist line, Grudem adopts the classic premillennialist position, but, as always, he is very fair to those who take a different view.

Revelation in outline

1:1–20	Prologue: the man at the centre of history
2:1–3:22	Letters to the seven churches
4:1–5:14	The vision of heaven
4:1–11	The throne of God
5:1–14	The scroll and the Lamb
6:1–8:5	Seven seals: suffering
6:1–8	The four horsemen: suffering on earth (Seals 1 to 4)
6:9–11	The martyr church (Seal 5)
6:12–17	The day of final wrath (Seal 6)
7:1–17	The crowd of the redeemed
7:1–8	144,000 on earth
7:9–17	The multitude in heaven
8:1	The seventh seal is opened: silence
8:2–5	The prayers of the saints
8:6–11:19	Seven trumpets: warning
8:6–13	Warnings in nature (Trumpets 1 to 4)
9:1–12	Torment for the unrepentant (Trumpet 5)
9:13–21	The day of final battle (Trumpet 6)
10:1–11:14	God's Word
10:1–11	The angel and the scroll
11:1–14	The two witnesses

11:15–19 The seventh trumpet sounds: the kingdom has come
12:1–14:20 Signs of cosmic conflict
12:1–17 The woman and the dragon
13:1–18 The first and second beasts
14:1–20 The redeemed and the lost
  14:1–5 144,000 in heaven
  14:6–13 Three angels: the time has come
  14:14–20 The harvest of all the earth
15:1–16:21 Seven bowls: God's wrath
15:1–8 The seven angels prepared
16:1–9 Judgement in nature (Bowls 1 to 4)
16:10–11 Judgement on the beast's throne (Bowl 5)
16:12–16 The day of final battle (Bowl 6)
16:17–21 The seventh bowl is poured out: 'It is done'
17:1–20:15 The triumph of Almighty God
17:1–18 The woman who is Babylon
18:1–24 The fall of Babylon
19:1–21 The victory of Jesus
  19:1–10 The Hallelujah Chorus
  19:11–21 The Word rides out to war and victory
20:1–6 The millennium
20:7–10 Satan's last throw
20:11–15 The final judgement
21:1–22:5 The new heavens and the new earth
22:6–21 Epilogue: Come, Lord Jesus!

Part 1

Prologue: The man at the centre of history

(1:1–20)

1

The First and the Last

Please read Revelation 1

It seems that everyone loves a conspiracy story. Whether the event is the death of JFK or of Princess Diana, the Apollo moon landings, or even the tragic outrage of the Twin Towers, there is always a ready market for theories that involve undercover government agencies, mysterious figures lurking in unexpected places, bizarre coincidences and, especially, official cover-ups on a grand scale. The bigger the supposed cover-up, the more respectable the organization that has managed it and the longer the truth has been successfully concealed, the more popular the theory is likely to be. And when the truth finally emerges—assuming that it ever does, or that there is any truth to emerge at all—the greater will be the delight.

All this, of course, explains the monumental success of a book like *The Da Vinci Code* (published in 2003). The book works on two levels. On one level, it is a thriller, the familiar genre of page-turner, with each short chapter ending with a fresh cliffhanger. Throughout the book you are pursuing a mystery, and only on the final page is the answer fully revealed. But it is on the second level that it really catches the attention of the reader, with its claims to unlock deep secrets and unmask the truth. Inside the front cover is inscribed the claim that although the work is a novel, all the descriptions of artwork, architecture, documents and secret rituals are *true*. The fact that the alleged cover-up concerns no less a subject than the origins and founder of Christianity, the notion that the culprit is the mighty Roman Catholic Church and the idea that this conspiracy has been running for two thousand years all combined to make this book the phenomenon that it is. Never mind that it is not great literature, never mind that, if you know even a little of the history of the early church, the story has holes big enough to drive a tractor through—this tale is compelling. People are still hooked by the big conspiracy story, still fascinated by keys which claim to be able to unlock the mysteries of the world.

But the greatest exposé of them all is not to be found in some modern blockbuster, but in the book that I hope you have open in front of you now. The book of Revelation (Greek *apocalypsis*) does precisely what it says: it *reveals* a story, a great, sweeping narrative that embraces the whole of history, and above all it reveals a person, the Lord Jesus Christ, who is the First and the Last. John is in exile on Patmos, and one day he sees a series of amazing visions which he is told to write down and send out to seven churches, including his home church, Ephesus. The point of all this is explained right at the start: it is to show us what is going to take place—to *show* us, not to confuse us! It is expected that we will understand what is going on!

The man who is coming back (1:1–8)

The focus of the book is not some long-suppressed secret, not some great conspiracy that has kept the truth underground for two millennia—quite the opposite. It is no secret at all.

The focus of this book is the man Jesus Christ—the man who is coming back. Look at verses 1–2. It is all about him and it all belongs to him. This is not 'the Revelation of John', as some have titled it, for John merely saw and recorded. It is truly 'the revelation of Jesus Christ'. Jesus' story doesn't end with Easter—certainly not with the cross, not even with the resurrection. After his resurrection, Jesus doesn't simply fade away or disappear. He ascends to his Father and he is enthroned in heaven—we shall see much more of that heavenly throne-room scene in later chapters. But this is the point: history has not finished with Jesus. It never will; history really is 'his story'.

The word 'soon' here may refer to the fact that all times are 'soon' to God (see 2 Peter 3:8–9), but equally it suggests that the events that John is about to see will start to happen immediately, rather than being reserved for the end of time. Furthermore, verse 1 makes it clear that God both knows *and determines* the future—contrary to what some Christians are teaching in our own days.

The opening verses give us our first glimpse of the great themes of the book, as Jesus Christ is introduced—not as someone who can be dismissed as an irrelevant figure from the distant past, but as a character who is *now*, the man we cannot ignore. As early as verse 3, there is a call to respond. This verse contains the first of the seven blessings to be found throughout the book. The blessing, we note, is not for those who manage to solve Revelation's puzzles, or to construct clever charts of the end times, but for those who heed and obey the Word of God that is found here. As if to reinforce this message, a very similar blessing appears in the final chapter (22:7).[1]

We should also note that the book is described as 'prophecy', a word with a wider meaning than simply 'predicting the future'. In the context of Scripture, it refers to speaking words which God has given. These are not merely John's personal speculations.

Look now at verses 4–6. John is told to write 'to the seven churches in the province of Asia', or western Turkey, as we know it today. There were more than seven churches in that region, actually—the New Testament mentions several others, including Colosse—but the seven symbolize completeness. The seven churches, which will be named later on, are here to represent the whole of God's people; this message is not confined to a select few, but is for everyone to hear, as verse 3 makes clear.

The message comes from the Three-in-One God himself. It comes from God the Father, 'him who is, and who was, and who is to come', the one revealed in the Old Testament as the 'I AM', the one who *is*, past, present and future.[2] It comes from God the Holy Spirit, the 'sevenfold spirit before his throne' (see NIV footnote)—seven again standing for completeness, but probably also stressing his presence in each of the seven individual churches. Unusually, God the Son, Jesus Christ, is mentioned last, no doubt in order to lead into what John will now say about him. *This* is the man at the centre of history. He is 'the faithful witness', the one whose words and character are utterly reliable as he reveals the true nature of God to us. He is 'the firstborn from the dead'. He is risen himself, for death could not hold onto him, but, more than that, he is the 'firstborn', meaning that there will be many others who rise from death after him. Christ's resurrection is just the beginning, the guarantee of our own. And he is 'the ruler of the kings of the earth'. He is the King of Kings and, whether they acknowledge it now or not, everyone who holds power on the earth will one day be made to realize that.

With these staggering claims, then, Jesus Christ is introduced. In a world full of deceit and lies, he is in fact the one source of reliable truth. In a world that is dominated by death and that fears it more than anything else, he is the one who has overcome death and can do the same for us. In a world full of tyrants and many other abusers of power, he is the true ruler who holds the ultimate power. We can see what a huge encouragement this would be to the scattered little churches of Asia Minor, under such pressure from the mighty empire. What an encouragement this is too for persecuted Christians today, in North Africa and the Middle East, in Iran and Pakistan! Their Lord Jesus is the real ruler, and every authority will one day be giving an account to him. This is quite an introduction!

But Jesus Christ is not just the central character; he is the one who gives us our own place in the story. The great story of history is about him, but he offers us the chance to take our own little, mixed-up stories and make them part of his own (1:5–6). This majestic character, this leading player, offers us a place in his story. He offers us his love, by setting us free from the sins which condemn us, all the accumulated rubbish of our own private stories, all that we regret and all that we ought to regret. He offers us freedom from all of that by dying for us, by shedding his blood for us. This King has been slain to purchase his own subjects; he is the Lion who is also the Lamb, as we shall see in chapter 5.

This story, then, is not a puzzle that we have to solve. It is not some enticing mystery, or a thriller which we can put down once we reach the final page, amusing us for a while but leaving us untouched. No, this is a drama for us to join. As chapter 5 will show us, the script is written, and Christ is centre stage. Our lives take on meaning and purpose only as we join this drama, as he makes us 'a kingdom and priests to serve his God and Father'. What is this 'kingdom'? It is the extent in time and space where Christ's kingly rule is freely accepted and acknowledged. For now it is limited, even hidden, as many of Jesus' own parables teach us, but the day is coming when the kingdom will be universally recognized and enforced. We are also 'priests', those who represent God and speak his words to the world (a pale reflection of what Christ himself has done) and who intercede with him for the world.

There is a sense of urgency, for the story is moving on (1:7). This is the man who is coming back! In themes which are drawn from Daniel 7 and Zechariah 12, John paints a picture of the day when Jesus Christ will return to the earth where he once walked. The 'clouds' that accompany him represent the majesty and authority of the Son of God. He will come so that *everyone* will see him. Some will be excited, thrilled to see the Jesus they have loved and longed for, the one 'who loves us and has freed us from our sins by his blood'. Others will be devastated when he appears, realizing in that dreadful moment exactly what it means to have rejected the Son of God. All over the world there will be people mourning when Christ returns to claim what belongs to him.

This theme will be greatly expanded as the book unfolds, but this section concludes with a solemn affirmation by God, the 'Alpha and the Omega', the almighty A and Z of all creation (1:8). This is the weight of authority which lies behind the book. Now the visions begin, and now comes the first of many messages of strength and support for God's embattled people.

The Lord among the lampstands (1:9–20)

In Britain, when British politicians talk about the church, they like to applaud us for our 'values'; but they stop at that. They rarely mention Christ, let alone suggest his uniqueness. It is as if a Christian were simply someone who has decided to adopt a set of values—which are, in any case, 'shared by all the major world religions', as it's sometimes expressed. That is how our culture, our world, wants to understand Christians. It cannot cope with what the *Christian* faith really is. It is safer to lump us together with all the world religions and call it 'faith'. Thus

Prince Charles can say he wants to be defender of '*faith*', so that he does not have to suggest that there is only *one* faith that is worth defending.

With that in mind, look at verse 9! John is quite clear as to why he has been sent to Patmos. It is certainly not because he has 'religious values'. The Roman soldiers did not come knocking on his door in Ephesus saying, 'John, we understand you are a man of faith and you have values which are shared by all the world's major religions—so we are consigning you to hard labour on Patmos'! John is on Patmos 'because of the Word of God and the testimony of Jesus'—the very same message that this book itself will bring (1:2). In other words, he will not stop talking about Christ. He refuses to keep quiet about that name. At a time when it is dangerous and difficult to be an outspoken Christian, John is precisely that.

He is not the only one. He addresses his readers as his companions in 'suffering', in the 'kingdom' and in 'patient endurance'. Christians everywhere are suffering; they must all be patient and endure, because they belong to the kingdom of God. Being part of the kingdom of God means that the kingdoms of this world may well not like us. There is a conflict between the two. It will not be our values that offend them; it will be the Word of God and the testimony of Jesus.

So here on Patmos John's visions begin. Here, 'on the Lord's Day'—on Sunday, that is—it seems that he has the chance to be alone for a time (it is very unlikely that any believers would have been allowed to organize a regular meeting in such circumstances!). No doubt he is thinking about the people that he loves back in Ephesus; he is longing to be back in the meeting they will be having at this moment, probably gazing out to sea, straining to catch a glimpse of the mainland thirty miles away, when something very unexpected begins to happen.

John says he was 'in the Spirit' (1:10), which may mean that he went into some kind of trance. But the visions he is given are not the sort of mystical religious experience that people sometimes talk about. One of the strongest features of this passage is that the amazing vision is accompanied by so many *words*. It is the same throughout Revelation—in almost every case, even when the visions are at their strangest, we are given at least some explanation. We are expected to understand what is going on.

Here, at the beginning, John is twice instructed to write down what he sees (1:11,19); verse 19 in particular embraces the whole of the rest of the book,[3] reiterating the message of verse 1 that the future is already fixed as far as God is concerned, and that it is in his hands. This is not a book that John ever intended to write, but it *can* be written down! The language he uses may be very strange—only some of that comes over in translation, but at times it is *very* strange—yet it is still human language that makes sense. This is God speaking to us, not through vague sensations or mystical religious feelings, but through words with a meaning. John is to write it all down and send it to the symbolic number of seven churches, which although they represent the whole church of Christ, including us, are also the *real* churches of Ephesus, Smyrna and the rest. Before the next vision begins in chapter 4, each of these churches is sent its own individual letter.

The vision begins with a voice speaking, a loud voice like a trumpet call (1:10). Verses 12–16 describe what John sees. The heart of the vision is a human figure, majestically dressed in a sweeping robe. As the description unfolds, it is the stunning brilliance of the scene that dominates all. It is well worth pausing to imagine it. He sees a head and hair that are pure white. Here is dignity; here is wisdom. We speak of eyes that sparkle, eyes that flash, but these eyes *blaze* like flames. If white hair suggests great age, it is old age with no loss of dynamic power. The feet are like some hot, glowing metal, its exact nature unknown; the face is like the full power of the midday sun; a sharp sword emerging from his mouth is the powerful words that he will speak. And as he does speak, his voice is, literally, 'as the voice of many waters'. The pounding of the sea that John has come to know so well in his island prison is drowned by the voice of this awesome figure.

As is so often the case, the key to understanding these visions is found in the Old Testament, and in this case in one of the visions already alluded to in Daniel 7 (see 1:7). The figure of one 'like a son of man' recalls Daniel's picture of the one who comes 'with the clouds of heaven' into the presence of Almighty God, the Ancient of Days. He is given authority, power and majesty, so that everyone will worship him, and a kingdom that will never end. That name, 'Son of Man', is one that Jesus Christ took for himself. John's vision is of Jesus Christ, the same Jesus who walked the earth, the one who was spat upon and hung up to die on the cross; this same Jesus, risen from death and ascended to heaven, is the figure who appears to John on Patmos. Even today, the man Jesus Christ is in heaven. He is glorified; he is awesome—but in the vision he is still recognizably human, with hands and feet, face and hair. He is still the Son of Man, God in human flesh. This is the Christ the world has to reckon with.

John reacts to what he sees with sheer terror (1:17). Remember who this is, collapsing to the ground! This is John the apostle. He well knows who is standing in front of him. Sixty years ago he was living with this man. He camped out in the countryside with him, ate and drank with him, went fishing with him. On one occasion they went up a mountain, along with a couple of others, and there was a vision of Jesus then, shining and glorious. Yes, he remembers that they were afraid *that* day. John has followed him to the cross, looked on as he died, met him after he rose from death, watched as he ascended into the clouds. John knows Jesus better than anyone; he was Jesus' closest friend when he was on earth, and since then he has spent his whole life following him. But even John falls flat on the ground when he meets the glorified Christ—like a dead man.

It is not that John is naturally hysterical, nor even that he is especially sinful, to be so disturbed by Christ's appearance. It is simply the way that every human being would respond. If we had a brief glimpse of the glory and the purity of God revealed like this in Christ, we too would collapse in terror, because in that moment, like John, we would become horribly aware of our own sin and of his purity, his majesty, his greatness. I would see what I am like; I would see what God is like—and I would react just like John.

So John lies there at the feet of Christ, and there he hears his words: 'Do not be afraid.' *Why* should he not fear? Again, it is not that John's reaction was wrong in some way. No, it was fully appropriate. Look at what Christ says about himself (1:17–18). He is 'the First and the Last', echoing the words of God himself in verse 8—he is the Lord of time, the one who is there from before creation to the very end of days. He is the Lord of history, the one with authority. He was dead and now is alive again, living for ever and ever. He has triumphed over death. Already for John, sixty years have passed since Jesus' resurrection. Today that has become almost two thousand years. In the light of eternity, that is the blink of an eye, but from then until now Christ holds 'the keys of death and Hades'. 'Hades' here does not refer directly to hell; it means more generally the home of the dead—and Christ has the keys to that place.

These are awesome statements, yet Christ makes them to reassure John, not to terrify him even more! The message is that John need not fear, because, with all his authority, Christ Jesus speaks to him as his friend. John is the friend of the man who is running the show from beginning to end, the man who has power over death, who can lock us *out* of death. If Jesus speaks to us as a friend, we have *nothing* to be frightened of—not physical death, because that will be followed by resurrection, and not what the future on earth may hold, for the Lord of time and history is our friend. But we can also plainly see that anyone who is *not* a friend of Christ has a great deal to fear from this vision. Those keys can lock someone into death as well as out of it. The man who is the First and the Last is the man who will pass the final verdict on you and me. He has the authority to do that—and he will.

Did you notice what John sees first in the vision? Surprisingly, it is not that glorious, dazzling figure that he notices first; it is 'seven golden lampstands' (1:12). And Christ is holding in his right hand seven stars (1:16).[4] Now look on to verse 20. Think what that vision would mean to the persecuted churches to whom John is writing. Think of the comfort of knowing that they were held in his right hand! But then think what it means to us now. Why is the church significant? Why is the church important in the world? It is not because it is ruled by important leaders like popes and archbishops, nor because it has money and buildings, nor because politicians are sometimes polite to it! We matter simply because the risen, glorified Christ is with us. The churches, shining our apparently feeble light into the darkening world, are actually lamps around the feet of our Saviour. We matter because he holds us in his right hand, the best and safest place we could possibly be.

If you are a Christian, do you see what our Lord is like? Have you taken in the vision that John saw of the Lord, King Jesus in his majesty? He is beautiful. He is dazzling. He has all the power over *all* that you dread. He holds the keys of death and Hades; and he holds us firmly in the grasp of his right hand.

To discuss or think about

1. Look at the three titles of Jesus Christ in verse 5. How would they encourage a persecuted Christian then, and how can they encourage you?
2. Verse 7 affirms the return of Christ in majesty. What impact is that truth having on your life right now?
3. Spend some time contemplating John's vision of the risen Christ. How does it challenge you? How does it help you?

Part II

Letters to the seven churches

(2:1–3:22)

2

Firm as a rock?

Please read Revelation 2–3

The scene is a specialist's office in the heart of a busy hospital. You have been sent here because something is not right—those odd twinges, those unexpected headaches. The tests have all been completed; the examinations are all done; and today you have come to hear the answers. You feel fearful, dreading what the doctor might say. The verdict could be very painful. Yet at the same time, you also feel confident. You know that you are in the safest possible hands. The walls of the office are lined with the doctor's qualifications and the awards he has won. This is the leading specialist, the top man in the field. If there is anyone you can trust with your health, even with your *life*, it is surely this man. And now he leans across the desk and begins to speak. 'Well', he says, 'I have some good news and some bad news for you.' He pauses. Now what do you do? The tension is almost unbearable. You *could* say, 'Right, thanks very much, it has been nice meeting you!' and rush out of the room. 'When all is said and done,' you say to yourself, 'perhaps it's best *not* to know after all. I'll go back home, and carry on the way I am, and hope for the best.'

Now we might have some sympathy for that point of view; it is not sensible, but at least it is understandable! But what if the illness is not physical, but spiritual? What if you are refusing to hear the Holy Spirit's verdict on the condition of your heart? That is exactly what the seven churches are faced with in chapters 2 and 3 of Revelation: a probing examination by an authority who is more wise, more skilled, more direct than any medical specialist—in fact, he is infallible. In these seven short letters the Lord Jesus Christ speaks into the heart and life of each of the churches. He gives them a clear diagnosis; he sets out their prospects; he explains what it is they need to do.

But the analogy with the doctor breaks down at this point. The specialist may like you, or he may not. But the Lord Jesus *loves* the churches, and where there is sickness he passionately longs for their healing. More than that, while human doctors can often do a great deal to help, there will always be a limit to what they can do. But there is no spiritual sickness that Christ cannot heal. There is nothing in our hearts that is beyond the Lord's power to put right. Even when the disease seems to be terminal, here in these letters we shall see that there is always hope for the Lord's people. But first they have to listen to the diagnosis. As we read these seven letters, that is just what we need to do. Of course, they are not addressed directly to us here and now. But as we study them prayerfully, the Lord will show us the answers to the questions: 'What does the Spirit say to *my* church? What does he find in *my* heart?'

We shall look at these seven letters over our next two chapters. The Lord has a lot to say about the churches, and rather than look through one letter at a time, with all the repetition that would involve, we shall take a more thematic approach.

Each letter is addressed to the 'angel' of the church, and there have been several suggestions as to who that might be: the pastor (but it doesn't sound very biblical to identify a church so closely with one individual); a 'guardian angel' (if a church has such a thing); the church's 'essential spirit' (too vague to be meaningful); or, perhaps the most likely, simply 'messenger' (which the word can also mean). It is hard to be sure, but it doesn't matter too much—what is clear is that ultimately each letter is aimed at the church itself.

It is clear too that the letters follow a definite pattern. Each one begins with an introduction, where Christ describes himself in a specific way, drawn from an element of the vision that so overwhelmed John in chapter 1. Then there is commendation and rebuke—the true verdict on the church's state of health. That is followed by a warning or command, a promise and the closing formula: 'He who has an ear, let him hear what the Spirit says to the churches.' It would be easy to let these final words slip past us, but in fact it is this command that assures us that these words are for us as well—not just for the few dozen in Smyrna or Sardis then, but for the millions of us who have read them in the centuries since.

The locations of the seven churches

Before we get any further into the letters, let's take a quick tour of the places where these churches were located. The order in which they are listed is not accidental. Many commentators have tried to match the characteristics of the seven churches with seven stages of church history, from the apostolic era until now, but I have never found that approach very convincing. Apart from the fact that it assumes that we are in the final stage today (which may or may not be the case!), it also seems a very parochial point of view. It requires, for instance, that we are now in a 'Laodicean stage'—i.e., a very unhealthy one. But while that may be true in the West, is it true of the church in the world at large—in China, for instance, or Brazil? Such schemes don't really work (and we shall find many more examples of that as we move through the book!).

There are, however, two ways in which the order makes sense. One is that there is a certain symmetry about the verdicts on the churches: for instance, only the first and last are threatened with extinction. The other is simpler: the order follows the natural route of a traveller making a tour of the churches, starting with *Ephesus*, which was the site of John's home church, as well as a sea port, and therefore a very natural place to start. At the end of the first century AD, Ephesus was the biggest city in the province of Asia, with a population running into hundreds of thousands and dominated by the Temple of Artemis (or Diana), one of the wonders of the world, with its swarms of prostitute priests. Paul himself spent years in Ephesus and founded the church, which was probably thus the oldest of the seven (most of the other cities were no doubt evangelized from here) and also had the proudest heritage. Before much longer, Ignatius would write to Ephesus on his way to martyrdom in Rome. He had heard of them as a church so well-taught that it was impossible for any heresy to gain a hearing there. Clearly, this church had heeded Paul's warnings in Acts 20, but there are vital things it had forgotten as well.

Smyrna (modern-day Izmir) was also situated on the coast, but about forty miles further north. Ruined in antiquity, it 'rose from the dead' centuries later, in 290 BC. It was noted as a centre of emperor worship, with a fine temple built around the time of Jesus. As the letter suggests, it also seems to have been a place where Jewish opposition to the church was especially fierce. This is the church which Polycarp would lead for many years until his martyrdom by the Romans in 155, when it is recorded that the Jews eagerly helped to gather wood for his burning. It is likely that Polycarp was a young man in the congregation at

Smyrna—and possibly already a leader there—when the letter of Revelation 2 arrived.

Further north again, a messenger would reach *Pergamum*, the seat of government for the province and prominent as a religious centre. Among many other temples, including those which crowded onto a hill behind the city, there was the earliest temple of all for state-backed emperor worship. Most likely this cult lies behind the reference to Satan's 'throne'.

Moving east and inland along one of the major trade routes, we come to *Thyatira*. It was a small town (though it gets the longest letter!), but well off because of its commerce and noted for its numerous trade guilds. It seems these guilds were strong enough to make it difficult to survive economically without belonging to one; their idolatrous feasts would be hard to avoid. For a Christian to be faithful in this environment was a struggle indeed; the temptation to compromise would have been severe.

The same road led on south to *Sardis*, a city with an astonishing history. It boasted an all but impregnable citadel, but twice in the past complacency had led to its capture by stealth. A call to 'wake up' here is highly pointed! Sardis was wealthy and comfortable, a spirit which seems to have infected the church as well.

From Sardis our messenger would move east to *Philadelphia*, known for geographical reasons as the 'Gateway to the East'. Although it was a prosperous place, it had seen upheaval in the form of devastation by an earthquake in AD 17. For some time afterwards the inhabitants were reluctant to return to their homes for fear of aftershocks. A house that one will 'never again have to leave' would be an appealing prospect in such a town.

Finally we reach *Laodicea*, almost due east of our starting point. There were two other notable churches nearby in the Lycus Valley, Colosse and Hierapolis, but they are not addressed. Laodicea was one of the world's richest commercial centres, famous for its medical school, where an effective eye-salve had been developed, as well as for its textile and banking industries. Its wealth was such that it actually refused the help it was offered for rebuilding after an earthquake in the previous generation. All it lacked was a good water supply; instead, it relied on the tepid, unpleasantly lime-rich water which reached it from the nearby hot springs. Of all the seven letters, the one to Laodicea is the sharpest in its allusions to the city and its surroundings!

So much for the cities—now for the message. Whatever these churches think of themselves, the Spirit of Christ gives them, and us, the infallible view. The strengths and weaknesses he finds in them really fall into two groups. We shall look at one of these groups in this chapter and the other—which is all about image versus reality—in the next. But first, what are the churches doing as they relate to the demanding challenges of the world around them? Are they as they should be, firm as a rock?

Doing the job

If the Lord had wanted, he could have whisked us off to the glory of heaven (which this book describes so vividly) the moment we were saved. But his chosen way of working is very different. His choice is to build his church here on earth as the primary means of proclaiming salvation and demonstrating what it means to live for Christ. Chapter 1 ended with the picture of individual churches shining like lamps, illuminating a dark world and driving away the shadows. The first of the seven letters starts in the very same way, with the picture of Christ walking among the lampstands (2:1), and that in itself is a challenge, as we move from the vision of the glorified Son of Man into the gritty reality of everyday life. The first thing he says to the church at Ephesus is: 'I know your deeds, your hard work and your perseverance' (2:2). A church is meant to do the job (Ephesians 2:10)—to do good works, prepared in advance by God, and thus to portray his character to the watching world. The close link to the image of the lamps reminds us that it is through our deeds that a church's true identity is clearly seen.

This is basic. It sounds obvious, yet there have been times through history when it has been forgotten. The church is not here on earth simply to engage in contemplation and perform her liturgies, regardless of whether anyone ever hears them; nor is she to lead a life of quiet passivity, wishing the world would simply leave her in peace, as she waits for Christ to return. This requirement may also sound tedious and exhausting; indeed, anyone who has been committed to an active church is familiar with the problem of exhaustion! Perhaps that is why both Ephesus and Thyatira (2:19) are commended in the same breath for their perseverance; they have kept going when the temptation is to give up. At Sardis, on the other hand, Christ declares the church's deeds incomplete (3:2)—surely an understatement given the condemnation which follows!

The letters do not go into great detail about these 'deeds', though they certainly include the activities that we shall look at in a moment, but from the rest of the New Testament we know very well what they should be: serving one another with a depth of commitment that the world does not know; providing a model of the wonderful new order of the kingdom of God, with the freedom and justice that Jesus proclaimed; and, through and alongside these, the clear, Spirit-empowered proclamation of the gospel of salvation in Christ. These are the 'deeds' which Christ commends in Ephesus, Thyatira and Philadelphia (3:8) and misses at Sardis. This is, quite simply, the essential mission of the church, and it underlies everything else. We are here to work. We should expect to be busy!

Guarding the gate

If simply 'doing the job' can be thought tedious, the next area is positively unfashionable, and never more so than in our own time. To 'guard the gate' means to protect those inside it from marauders, as Paul instructed the Ephesian elders to do in Acts 20:28–31. And here it is the Ephesian church which seems to be doing best. The marauders are those who slip into a church to spread false teaching and thus, like wolves among sheep, do disastrous damage to the flock. This church is commended for refusing entry to false apostles (2:2)—they understand that such men are dangerous and must be kept out at all costs. To do so they have had to test them, for false teachers do not generally wear badges proclaiming their identity. They are also commended for hating the practices of the mysterious Nicolaitans (2:6)—hating the heresy, not the heretics, we should note.

We do not have Nicolaitans today, but we certainly have teachers who try to deflect us from the Bible's teaching in many areas. To mention just a few current issues, they may deny the truth of God's all-pervading sovereignty, or dilute the wonderful reality of Christ's death as our substitute, or claim to offer, here and now, more of the blessings of the coming age than the Bible gives us any right to expect.

Plenty of people today have given up believing that there is any such thing as truth, still less one *single* truth that has to apply to everyone. Even within many churches, the whole idea that we should 'guard the gate' against impostors and false teaching is laughable. And yet, time after time, the New Testament, in fact the whole Bible, commands us to do just this: to watch out for anyone and anything who will lead us astray. This is not because we are to be obsessively pedantic about our theology, ticking off doctrines like train-spotters at the end of a platform somewhere, but because our God is the God of *truth*, because there is only one way in which we are to be saved and one written Word by which we are to live, and because false teaching destroys God's people. Paul doesn't call them 'savage wolves' for nothing.

It may well be that the promise for Ephesus is linked to their intense and repeated battles with falsehood, for they are told that their destiny is to rest in God's garden city and enjoy the fruit of the tree of life (2:7), a beautiful image which anticipates the description of the new Jerusalem (22:2,19). We face similar battles and we look forward to the same reward. May we be as passionate for the truth as the church at Ephesus.

But such hard-edged determination is absent from the third and fourth churches to be addressed, Pergamum and Thyatira. They, like many churches we know today, are happy to be tolerant. There is much that is positive in each of these places, but they are compromised by their willingness to allow false teaching and gross immorality within their ranks. We have to admit that these errors are hard to identify. Like Ephesus, Pergamum has been involved with the Nicolaitans (2:15); unlike Ephesus, she has let them in. We can only guess that they are linked to the group connected with Balaam (2:14), but even that does not help us very much. Balaam is famous for his talking donkey—not what is in mind here!—and, more importantly, for his refusal to curse the Israelites at King Balak's behest. But he is also implicated in the immorality that took place at Peor (Numbers 31:16). It may well be—and this approach would be typical of Revelation—that the group at Pergamum have never even heard of Balaam and that the Spirit is invoking his name to point out to the church the seriousness of what they are tolerating.

In any case, the appalling fact is that the group is now operating from *within* the church. At least, it should be appalling to us and it certainly is to the Lord; verse 16 warns of swift retribution against the offenders if there is no repentance. The 'sword of my mouth' has already been mentioned at the start of the letter (2:12) and no doubt refers to the word of truth, an appropriate weapon against the false teaching at Pergamum (and see 19:15, where Christ is seen riding out at the head of heaven's armies to defeat the nations at the end of the age).

At Thyatira the problem seems to centre on one individual, named here as 'Jezebel' (2:20), but in this case too that is likely to be a symbolic name, recalling Ahab's godless wife in 1 Kings. This 'Jezebel' has set herself up as a teacher with a message that is leading believers ('my servants'—these are not the impostors themselves) into immorality. It has been plausibly suggested that there may be a connection with the very strong trade guilds in this city. 'Jezebel' may have been teaching the church that it was acceptable to take part in the idolatrous celebrations which were an essential element of belonging to these guilds. This could also explain the allusion to 'Satan's so-called deep secrets' (2:24)—the 'secret' being the idea that physical acts cannot pollute a soul that is pure. This teaching showed itself in the Gnostic heresy which was beginning to appear at this time and which also majored on 'secret knowledge'. Whether or not this theory is right, 'Jezebel' has been encouraging compromise with the world and the church has been cheerfully accepting it. But once again the warning is sharp (2:21–23). In Thyatira the opportunity for repentance has already been given and now it is passing; the punishment for continuing in such sin will be severe.

Appropriately for a letter which challenges impurity so thoroughly, the message to Thyatira features a running theme of Christ's authority and splendour. It appears in the opening greeting, is emphasized in the repeated warnings and culminates in the promise to share his authority over the nations in the age to come (2:26–27).[1] But the ultimate promise is of himself, for he is the Morning Star (2:28; see 22:16).

The retribution linked so directly to this toleration of

error and sin in the churches shows us that the Spirit takes this matter extremely seriously. We may be shocked by the warnings—especially by the very graphic expressions used for Thyatira—just as we are shocked by the story of Ananias and Sapphira, struck dead for their deliberate deception in Acts 5, or even by Paul's apparent severity over the case of the 'immoral brother' in 1 Corinthians 5. If we are shocked, it is because we do not share our Lord's passion for the purity and holiness of the church he loves and for whom he died. By the end of the book we shall have contemplated the beautiful image of the church as Christ's bride, and he will not have his bride dirtied and compromised by deliberate sin.

The practical implications of this are very straightforward: local churches must take the purity of the fellowship very seriously. Leaders are to guard the gate; in other words, they must watch over their flock in order to protect them from false teaching and to guard against immorality of any kind—it is their God-given ministry to do so. Where people persist in leading believers astray by their words or actions, they must be put out of the church. Even if no one else takes church discipline seriously, let us all be determined that our own church will do so! Failure in this area is one of the most disastrous weaknesses of the church in the West today. As a result, we see churches everywhere happy to compromise with error and to look tolerantly on evil behaviour. Against this background, it is not surprising that church organizations struggle to take a clear stand on the great moral issues of our day, such as the Bible's position on homosexual practices or the ethics of the beginning and end of life.

There is, however, one caveat to make. We should also remember that the problem with holding a firm line against error is that it so easily becomes unbalanced and slides into lovelessness. As we shall see, this is the great problem with

Ephesus, where their zeal for the truth is not matched by the zeal of love.

Defying the enemy

Not all opposition comes from within, or from attempts to infiltrate a church. While we must guard the gate, there is also the enemy who is *outside* the gate, and this enemy must be defied. Indeed, the example of Pergamum shows us that Satan, the great Enemy behind all our enemies, uses these two major strategies to destroy the churches. The first operates by seduction, appealing to our desires and ambitions. If that does not work, he still has his second line of action: to attack us head-on through persecution. More specifically, these are the two strategies of Babylon, which throughout Scripture stands for rebellion against God. Babylon is fiercely opposed to God's people and becomes a major theme in the later chapters of Revelation, especially 17 and 18. These are the two strategies which Daniel and his friends faced in the earthly city of Babylon, which first attempted to seduce them by giving them power and privilege, and then attempted to kill them when they resisted the seduction.

But at Pergamum the first of these methods has already succeeded, even though the second has not. At Pergamum they have faced and survived opposition (2:13—note the double reference to Satan). The heartland of emperor worship will not easily tolerate a group that declares its allegiance to another Lord. In this case it has even resulted in martyrdom. At both Philadelphia and Smyrna the opposition arises from the Jews. As sometimes happens elsewhere in Revelation (notably in chapter 11), the old language of 'Jews versus Gentiles' is adapted here to express the opposition of the world to God's own people. These opponents really are Jews in the literal sense—they belong to synagogues (2:9; 3:9)—but they can no longer claim to be God's people because they deny Christ and oppose one of his churches. Thus they have forfeited the cherished name of 'Israel'.[2] But it is the name of *Christ* which is so precious to the believers of Smyrna, Pergamum and Philadelphia (3:8).

In Smyrna, meanwhile, persecution is still on the rise (2:9–10). Already they face 'slander'; a specific, though limited, period of much more virulent attack ('ten days') now approaches.[3] The warning, couched in words of wonderful, warm encouragement, reminds them that the Lord is in control even of times like these—a reminder which will be clearly broadcast to the whole church several times in the book and is one of its most vital themes (6:10–11; 11:7–12; 12:17; 13:10; 14:12). That is why the church in Smyrna should not fear—not out of empty bravado, but because they know who is really in charge. However feeble they may feel, with him they are both wealthy and strong. How this letter must have encouraged them again sixty years later when Polycarp and others were martyred!

It is noticeable that the two healthiest churches, those of whom no criticism is made, have both faced serious opposition. Both Smyrna and Philadelphia are given special promises connected with their faithful defiance. Smyrna's enduring believers are promised 'a crown of life' (2:10) and reminded that the 'second death' cannot hurt them (2:11—see 20:6,14 for the fearful explanation). Christ has already reminded them that he is the one who has conquered death for ever (2:8). Even if their faithfulness costs them their physical life, they are eternally secure. When the church in Smyrna later reported the death of their pastor Polycarp, they said, 'He was crowned with the crown of immortality.' I am sure they had verse 10 in mind when they wrote that.

For Philadelphia, the church of little power in a city of insecurity, the promises emphasize safety and permanence (3:10–12).[4] There will even be a respite from trouble. The door is open—almost certainly this refers to the opportunity for further service, for effective mission. It has been opened by the Lord Jesus himself, so that no one can shut it (3:7–8), for those who bear the name of God and of his own city. More than any of the other six letters, this one anticipates the great themes which will be opened up later in the book: vindication for God's suffering people (6:10), the name of the Lamb on the foreheads of the saints (7:3–4; 9:4; 14:1; 22:4), the new Jerusalem which comes down from heaven (chapter 21), and the promise of Christ's personal return (chapter 22).

Meanwhile, the closing promise to suffering Pergamum (2:17), though obscure (at least seven theories are in circulation to explain the 'white stone'!), is certainly personal. Both elements of it relate to something revealed only to the recipient, as if to assure believers of the personal relationship they will enjoy with Christ if they remain faithful against every kind of enemy, both internal and external.

There are two churches, however, which show no evidence of conflict and no sign of hard work. It is not surprising that these are the two which face the severest condemnation—Sardis and Laodicea. Whatever else there is to say about them, it seems that they pose no threat at all to the world or to the enemy of souls. In a sense, that is the worst criticism that can be made of a church—that it bothers no one. There is no enemy to defy, for no enemy is bothering to attack. There is no gate to guard, for the church is so thoroughly compromised that there is no visible difference, let alone a clear boundary, between it and the world. There is no work being done, for the church has lost sight of what she is here for. If your church looks anything like that, almost certainly it is high time to get out.

Firm as a rock? How do our own churches measure up to the standard? Would the Spirit of Christ approve of *our* deeds, or find them incomplete? Would he see us guarding ourselves carefully against error and immorality (and doing so in a spirit of love!) or quietly letting it go? And where there is opposition—which even in the West is now on the rise, for in a sense we all live 'where Satan has his throne'—are we able to face the worst with confidence in the Lord who reigns over every earthly power? It would do us good to imagine what persecution would be like—the economic pressure, slander, prison and death which threatened the faithful churches of Asia—and ask ourselves what our true priorities are in this life. The persecuted churches of today have much to teach us.

To discuss or think about

1. In your own church, is the 'gate' effectively guarded against false teaching? If so, is the guarding combined with genuine love?
2. If we believe that preserving gospel truth in our churches really is important, what steps does a church need to follow to do so? And what desires should such action spring from?
3. If persecution is slight or rare where you live, how do you think your own church, and your own faith, would cope if it became far worse? And if persecution is familiar to you, how do the letters to the churches encourage you?

3

Good image or good heart?

Please read Revelation 2–3

Detective novels come in all shapes and sizes. But, however different the plots, and whether the style is racy or staid, they all arrive at the same point in the end. The point of a detective story is always to find the villain. The tale invariably concludes with the unmasking of someone with a fine reputation, someone whom no one would ever guess could be a murderer (murders, of course, make for the most gripping stories!). The better the plot, the more unexpected is the final twist. But, from Scooby-Doo to Sherlock Holmes, we are always left with a fine name ruined, an image thoroughly shredded.

Of course, this dismantling of an image is not confined to fiction. It happens all the time in the real world too; in fact it is the speciality of many journalists, who often take self-righteous delight in destroying reputations. Whether it is Watergate, where investigative journalism eventually brought down a president, the many drugs scandals in sport worldwide, or the indiscretions of celebrities, we are all too familiar with the pattern of a fine public image brought down in ruins. The truth is that one's public image—and for that matter, one's opinion of oneself—is often sharply at odds with reality, and when the truth is revealed it is often a shock.

Far more probing and far more accurate than any journalist's investigations, however, is the Word of God. This living Word that is 'sharper than any double-edged sword' stops at nothing in seeking out the truth; under the gaze of Almighty God nothing remains hidden (Hebrews 4:12–13). Every human heart and every individual is subject to that searching Word, and very often it reveals that the image we cling to so fondly is a long way from the reality. This theme of image and reality runs strongly through the letters to the seven churches. In the previous chapter we looked at what the Spirit has to say about the actions of these churches—the question of whether they are standing firm and remaining faithful. Now we follow the Spirit's penetrating gaze into the very heart of the churches to measure the gap between what they claim and what they really are. As we do so, we must remember that the same gaze is always penetrating our own hearts, and we must keep asking what he will find there.

Clinging to a reputation

There are two churches which stand accused of living on a false reputation. In one case, Sardis, it is a reputation with outsiders. In the other, Laodicea, the problem is what they claim for themselves.

A good reputation with outsiders

The Lord introduces himself to Sardis as the one who holds the seven stars, the churches, in his hand—a reminder of his authority—and 'the seven spirits of God' (3:1). This rather unexpected expression simply means the Holy Spirit in his fulness—seven being the number of completion as well as perfection—and it is there to remind this almost-dead church that the only true source of life is the Spirit himself.

But now comes the punchy headline: '... you have a reputation [literally, 'a name'] of being alive, but you are dead.' Outwardly, this church is known as being alive: it would seem to outsiders, to visitors, that all is going well. Presumably there are signs of activity and organization; perhaps there are good numbers, competent leaders—all the evidence that most people would look for in making a judgement about the life of a church. The stunning complacency which characterized the town in previous years has clearly infected the church as well; otherwise how could it be content with its condition? It certainly seems that they believe their own publicity at Sardis. We are familiar with churches which look as if they are dying, especially if we judge success by numbers. Sardis, by contrast, looks very much alive, but to someone who can look at the *inside*, to one who sees the heart, it is dead.

What is it that reveals this 'deadness'? We are given certain clues in the following verses. Verse 2 says that their deeds are incomplete in God's sight. We have already noted that the Sardis church faces no opposition; presumably this is because it poses no threat. Its people are compromised—an impression strengthened by the suggestion in verse 4 that most of them *have* 'soiled their clothes'. Instead of appearing distinctive, their lifestyle is just as polluted as the world around them. They do not stand out in any way. They can continue with their churchy activities while their everyday life blends in perfectly with the normal life of the town. As a church, they are dead—or at least dying, for verse 2 does offer a ray of hope. There is still the chance to 'strengthen what remains'. So verse 3 urges them to return to their starting point in the gospel, presumably looking back a generation to the days when the church was founded. As long as it is still possible to remember what they received and heard, hope remains. The warning is to repent, or else face the unexpected visit of Christ. This is not a reference to his Second Coming, but to the discipline the church can expect to face for its disobedience.

Just one thing saves this church from the threat of extinction. Not everyone has fallen into sinful ways—verse 4 shines the spotlight on a small group who have maintained a clear witness to their Lord. Given the state of the rest of the church, their stand is all the more commendable. The Lord says that 'they are worthy'. There is a tendency with some evangelicals to feel that God can never really be pleased with us: our sinfulness is so deep and far-reaching that he will never finish pointing out our faults! One of the wonderful features of these seven letters, though, is that over and over again the Lord finds things to commend in his people. In this case it is a message of huge encouragement to anyone today who is struggling to be a clean and pure witness in a dark world, especially when even their own church no longer supports them in doing so. If that is you, then the Lord says you are *worthy*; and your destiny is to walk with him, dressed in the white that stands for righteousness. At the same time, the example of Sardis is a fearful warning to churches that are looked on as successful. We should always ask what such a reputation is based on—especially if the church is our own!

The believers in Sardis, like those in the other churches, are offered a promise if they are faithful (3:5). Remember that 'he who overcomes', or 'the victorious one', is not a title for some kind of super-Christian. In Revelation especially, 'overcoming' is effectively another word for being a 'believer in Christ'.[1] Given the book's setting in a time of persecution, it is simply assumed that faith in Christ will lead to victory over Satan and the power of sin. The promise to such believers in Sardis is wonderful: the risen Christ tells them that they will not lose their place in the book of life. The church as a whole may die—in fact, that seems the most likely outcome—but true, faithful believers never will. The church may die, but *their* names will ring out in heaven. Dressed in white (a picture which will be expanded in chapter 7), they will be accepted for ever by their heavenly Father.

A false view of themselves

However its members may think of themselves (probably very highly), the church at Sardis maintains a good outward reputation in sharp contrast with the inward reality. At Laodicea it is the church's view of itself which is the big problem. The people's own verdict is summed up in 3:17: 'I am rich; I have acquired wealth and do not need a thing.' They demonstrate amazing complacency. The verdict of Christ is starkly different: the condition of this church is embarrassingly bad, yet the people in the church fool themselves that they are well off. Very likely it is the prosperity of the town itself which has removed any sense of dependence on their Saviour. But material prosperity does not equate to spiritual riches, as the sad state of the church in the West confirms. The end of verse 17 gives us a picture of a church which has nothing in itself and nothing to offer the world outside—and again, there is no sign that it is making any impact whatsoever on that world.

In the case of Sardis the prescribed remedy is simply to 'remember', 'obey' and 'repent' (3:3). For Laodicea, the picture is filled out a little more, but the essential message is the same: only Christ has the solution to their problem. The first step is to recognize and admit the problem, and the second is to turn to him for help. As long as there is any life at all in the church, there is still hope, for in Christ there are all possible spiritual riches. Thus verse 18 tells the Laodicean church to obtain wealth, dignity and health from Christ to deal with their poverty, disgrace and sickness. Though we could link each of these items directly to spiritual realities (especially the white clothes of righteousness in Christ), they are probably selected mainly for the references to Laodicea's famous commercial successes—its banking, textile and eye-care industries. The familiar features of their own town are called on to provide powerful illustrations of the resources they have in Christ, if they will only turn back to him. The alternative, as we shall see shortly, is the end of their smug church.

At Sardis, at Laodicea, and to some extent in Ephesus too (given the fault we are about to examine), the churches are living on a false reputation. Good organization, hard work and a glorious past can all conceal terrible deadness in a church. The letters to the churches suggest that the signs of that deadness are a lack of impact on the world outside, so that it feels no threat from what we are doing, and a complacent unwillingness to admit our own weaknesses. Laodicea warns us vividly of the way material comforts so often sap believers' spiritual energy. If it is hard for the rich to enter the kingdom of God (Luke 18:24)—and most members of Western churches must be counted as rich—it seems to be equally hard for them to be faithful citizens once they are in it. A good reputation may be easy to obtain, but in the sight of God it is quite worthless.

Taking the temperature of love

The loveless church

We saw in the previous chapter that the church in Ephesus is praised highly for being faithful to the name of Christ, even in adversity. They have beaten off the attacks of false teachers and have kept going without flagging. It might be said that this too is a church with a fine reputation—certainly that is how Ignatius sees it less than twenty years later on his way through Asia to Rome. No doubt also its great history, especially its long association with Paul, Timothy, and now John himself, has added to its high status among the churches. Unlike Sardis and

Laodicea, this high reputation is not unfounded and there really is much that is good in the Ephesian church.

But there is one crucial flaw, and it undermines all the rest. After all the praise, the criticism bursts like a bombshell: 'Yet I hold this against you: you have forsaken your first love' (2:4). The next verse follows this up with a warning to repent just as clear and strong as the one issued to Sardis and Laodicea—or perhaps even stronger, since it is directly linked to a warning that the church is in danger of being extinguished altogether. This will not happen by accident, or because the church simply fizzles out; the warning is of a deliberate judgement from God (2:5).

How can it be that such a fine church is sent such a harsh message? Apart from the fact that a well-taught church should know better, there are two reasons. One is clear from verses 4–5. They have not 'lost' their first love, as if in some careless moment it has fallen out of their pocket; they have 'forsaken' it, or abandoned it. They have fallen from the height on which they used to stand. Thus the call to repentance is coupled with a command to return to doing what they did in the first place. Ephesus has been given so much over the years. For them, this command must recall the heady days of Acts 19, when, in the time of Paul's ministry, the power of the Holy Spirit brought mass repentance and public renunciation of sin. It was probably in the years immediately after this that missionaries from Ephesus planted most of the other six churches,. Thirty years later, the intense activity and faithfulness remain, but the fire of love has gone. It is sadly possible to be loyal without being loving.

The second reason speaks for itself. Love for Christ, for the church and for the world outside (probably all are included, but the first is the key to the others)) is simply so important! No other failing would be taken so seriously that in the sight of Christ it cancels out all the church's hard work. Love is the most basic response of the saved sinner to his Saviour. It comes even before obedience, for it is the only true motive for obedience. Love for fellow believers and for the needy world follows close behind our love for him. If we are at all like Jesus, we will love—him first, then others. The verdict on Ephesus is that this essential foundation is missing. The church has moved away from the love it used to have.

Of all the failings the Spirit points out in the seven churches, this is surely the one that must hit home to us the hardest. We are used to working hard in our church life. Anyone who is bothering to read this book is probably already committed to the life of a local church (and if you are not, you certainly ought to be!). Perhaps we would receive just the same praise as the Ephesians for our perseverance and determination—even for our discernment of error. But would we also receive the same searing criticism that there is no love, or very little, in all our busy activity? We should note that even Thyatira, a mixed church if ever there was one, is commended for its love (2:19). The message to Thyatira shows that hard work and love do not have to be strangers to each other. But in Ephesus that is just what they have become. Is the same warning hanging over my church or yours—that, for all our proud history and heritage, the Lord could come and remove the lampstand from its place? If the same lack of love is found in us, either personally or in our churches, there is only one remedy: to repent and return, to go back to where we started, even if that means going back twenty, thirty or forty years.

The lukewarm church

Ephesus is not the only church that is accused of a lack of love. Although the word is not used, it is lovelessness that so clearly lies behind the desperate condition of Laodicea. The final letter opens with Christ's description of himself as 'the faithful and true witness' (3:14), one who will accurately portray the plight of the faithless church. And now the words, 'I know your deeds,' sound their most ominous ring. Whatever Paul wrote to this church a generation ago (Colossians 4:16) has clearly been ignored or forgotten. Here verses 15–16 famously allude to the town's unpleasant, foul-tasting water supply, describing a church that falls uselessly between the heat of true spiritual life and the coldness that has never been awakened. It is not that spiritual deadness is ultimately a better condition to be in than half-heartedness (as has sometimes been suggested). But it can certainly be much harder to bring to life people who have heard the gospel and become hardened to it than it is to reach people from right outside the church. As a body, the Laodiceans are lukewarm, tepid, undrinkable! The Lord's verdict is unforgettable: they make him truly sick. Spiritual warmth comes only with heartfelt love, and that is entirely lacking in Laodicea. The complacency of the church described in verse 17 suggests that they are looking only at surface appearances—and they like what they see—but in their hearts there is no love to be found. Their position is the exact opposite of the church at Smyrna, who knew they were poor but are assured by Christ that they are truly rich (2:9). Which of these churches would we rather be? Entangled in the comforts of the materialistic West, our response may not be as clear as we would like to think!

So Laodicea too is under threat, and yet here too there are still grounds for hope. Verse 19 calls for serious repentance. And if the picture of the sickly water is striking, so too is the image in verse 20 of the Lord knocking at the door—not now of the church, but of individuals, for the promise which follows is for individual believers ('anyone'). Astonishingly, the Lord who has felt so sickened by the state of the church is willing to come in and eat the main meal of the day with anyone who will let him in. Loving fellowship can be restored as easily as that. However far we have fallen, however we have failed to live the life that the

Lord calls us to live, above all however faint our love has faded, still the offer stands. If it was true for the believers in the disaster zone that was the Laodicean church, it must surely be true for us. The offer is there for us to take.

The offer is followed by the promise (3:21). Even in Laodicea, Christ considers that there will be overcomers! This most failing of churches is offered a promise that anticipates the glorious vision of heaven's throne-room which immediately follows in chapter 4. Living with Christ here and now will be followed by living and reigning with him eternally. Thus the seven letters end on a note of amazing hope. Failing, faithless churches can be brought back from the dead. Believers who have compromised can be restored, if they will only repent. We dare not live on image and reputation, but for all those who overcome the future is as bright as it could possibly be, even though it lies the other side of persecution and suffering.

To discuss or think about

1. What would the Lord say to you about the state of your heart: your love for him, your fellow believers and the outside world?
2. Looking back over all the praise and rebukes delivered to the seven churches, which are the most relevant to you? Are you moving forward: in love?; in a genuine zeal for the truth?; in a humble and realistic view of yourself?; in a longing for the purity of your own church—and so on?
3. Is there one church that you (or your church) can identify with more than any of the others? If so, how will you respond to the message given to that church?

Part III

The vision of heaven

(4:1–5:14)

4

The plot is not lost

Please read Revelation 4–5

Have you ever seen one of those really bad amateur dramatic performances—the kind of show where the hero doesn't just fluff his lines, but actually forgets when to leave the stage and stands there looking lost until someone appears to hustle him off? A show which lurches from one disastrous scene to the next, so much so that the story becomes completely impossible to follow? A show which leaves you with the overwhelming impression that the players have totally lost the plot? Unfortunately, it is not just badly performed plays which can make us feel like that. That sense of the plot being lost, that feeling of undirected chaos, can also be a picture of our lives. We have the sense that we are simply lurching from one disastrous scene to the next. There is a conflict here, a calamity there; one scene where life begins to look more hopeful, then another when our highest hopes collapse in ruins.

Whereas at the end of a bad play you can simply walk away

and vow never to return, that is not so easy when the stage is the whole world. In Shakespeare's famous lines:

> All the world's a stage,
> And all the men and women merely players:
> They have their exits and their entrances;
> And one man in his time plays many parts.[1]

But what if the plot has been lost? What are the actors supposed to do then? What if the script has been thrown away, there is no storyline, and all we can do is improvise until the end of time?

Revelation speaks to exactly this problem. It was written to people who were worried that the plot had been lost. In the sixty or so years since Jesus had risen and ascended, much had happened. The church had spread over huge areas of the Roman world. But all was not well—or at least so it seemed. The church was expecting that Jesus would come back soon, that he would return to earth as he had promised, but there was no sign of that happening. Meanwhile the very last of the people who had known him on earth, providing a living link with Jesus Christ, were dying. Instead of the church sweeping all before it and bringing down the Roman Empire, it was persecuted. The author of this book, the apostle John—probably the last of the original inner circle of disciples—had been banished to hard labour on a remote island. What was going on? What had happened to the storyline? Like us, those early Christians needed reassurance. These two chapters provide just that.

Revelation 4 and 5 form a dramatic scene in two parts, which assures us with absolute certainty that the plot is not lost. Something that we shall notice, as so often in Revelation, is that John has to strain the bounds of human language and imagery to describe what he is seeing. The scene set before him is so staggering, so far outside the limits of what human beings normally encounter, that it becomes all but indescribable. But we shall try to explore the vision that he sees.

The scene is set (4:1–11)

'After this I looked' (4:1), and similar expressions, will become a repeated refrain. What John will see takes place in 'heaven'—meaning not the sky, not some physical location 'up there', but the place where spiritual realities can be clearly seen, where you can get behind the scenes of the apparently meaningless drama which takes place on the earth we know. The voice that John has heard before, the voice of Jesus (1:10), ushers him in through a door into this world of heavenly reality. We notice that he is viewing by invitation, not as the result of some self-induced trance.

He is told that he will be shown 'what must take place after this'. This is where his questions are going to be answered. This is where the true story is going to be told. Apparently there *is* a plan after all—this is no mere forecast but 'what *must* take place', and John, with Spirit-given insight, is about to see just how it unfolds. Unlike Paul (2 Corinthians 12:2–4), he is to tell what he sees. His record of it makes up the remaining nineteen chapters of the book!

The vision which immediately follows is breathtaking, awe-inspiring, almost impossible to describe; but John does his best.

1. The throne (4:2–6)

First, in the centre, he sees a 'throne ... with someone sitting on it' (4:2), but the one seated on it is never described, nor even named, almost certainly out of reverence. His appearance is like that of precious stones (4:3); the 'jasper' here may be what we know as diamonds, but anyway the impression is one of shining brilliance, of value beyond calculation, of majesty. The emerald rainbow encircling the throne is enigmatic (an all-green rainbow?) but certainly calls to mind God's faithfulness to his promises (Genesis 9:12–16). Emanating from the throne are fearful sounds and sights (4:5) that recall God's appearance in majesty at Sinai (Exodus 19:16–19). In front of the throne there is something that looks like an expanse of crystal-clear glass (4:6). In John's day, ordinary glass would have been anything but clear; it was more like a sort of cloudy brown bottle-glass. Glass that was 'clear as crystal' would be staggeringly expensive, so again this is an image of infinite value as well as stunning beauty. While commentators have suggested various 'meanings' for the glass sea,[2] the effect of this beautiful crystal expanse is to place a gap between the throne and all that surrounds it. God's throne is assigned its own unique space.

So the very first impression the vision makes is to show us that there is someone in charge. John's first readers were being threatened with the might of Rome. They were being told that the emperor was their lord and that they had to worship him. But now John sees the *real* throne. It is not in Rome, just as today it is not in London, Washington or Beijing. Whatever seems to be going wrong in the world, however little we can understand about what happens to us, God is still sovereign, still on the throne. If the world's story is a great drama, here is the wonderful truth: the Director's chair is still occupied.

2. The beings around the throne (4:4,6–8)

There is more to be seen. As we would expect, God's majestic throne is the focal point of it all. Gathered around the throne there are two ranks of living beings (4:4).

There are many significant numbers in Revelation, but the figure here of 'twenty-four' is not a difficult one to understand. At the end of the book there is a description of the new heavenly city, with its twelve gates and twelve foundations. On the gates are the names of the twelve tribes of Israel; on the foundations are the names of the twelve apostles; and these twenty-four around the throne are twelve plus twelve, the representatives of all of God's people before and after Christ, gathered together in heaven in the presence of God. Here we need to bear in mind something that becomes even more important as we move through the sequences of 'sevens' further on in the book: these visions are not consecutive in time. The fact that John may actually be seeing *himself* in this inner circle does not create a problem for him, even if we think it does for us!

Within that circle are the 'four living creatures' (4:6–8). The descriptions sound bizarre to us, but, as with so many of John's visions in this book, they contain strong echoes of what the Old Testament prophets saw. Although there are some differences from the four cherubim which accompany the divine presence in Ezekiel 1 and 10, it seems reasonable to identify these creatures as the same beings. It is also reasonable to say that these four rather terrifying creatures represent all created beings in the presence of God.[3] That is suggested by the resemblance of each to a more familiar living being and by the number 'four', which often represents the world of nature. But here, in the presence of God, creation does not debate, nor does it analyse what it sees; rather it worships him (4:8) in a song that echoes the seraphs' cry of God's holiness in the vision of Isaiah (Isaiah 6:3). From their position so close to his throne, they declare his uniqueness, both of character and of eternity. Then they are joined by the twenty-four elders in declaring the praises of God (4:10–11). This is the due response and the highest possible activity of all God's creatures, angelic or human—to direct their adoration and blessing to their glorious Creator.

Such, then, is the vista that meets John's eyes. This is the spiritual reality, an apparently timeless scene, with the Almighty God on the throne at the focus of creation's worship. It is awesome, so that it defeats our imagination. Yet from our point of view—and, indeed, from John's as well—there is still something missing. How does all this connect with *us*? We are living out our struggling lives here on this chaotic, suffering earth. Yes, this vision of the heavenly throne-room is amazing and majestic, but if God is really in charge, how does that work out down here on earth—whether for the troubled churches of the late first century or for the confusion of the world that we know?

Moreover, John has been promised that he will see what is going to happen in times to come, but so far that has not happened. So we move on to the second part of the scene in heaven as we go into chapter 5. In many ways, it is a repeat of the first part—there are many parallels—but chapter 5 sees the appearance of two new and vital elements of the drama.

The drama unfolds (5:1–14)

1. The script (5:1–3)

The first is the script of the play! Look at verse 1. This is what we have been waiting for. The scroll contains what John has been promised he will see. Chapter 6 will reveal what happens when the scroll is eventually opened. From the context, it is clear that it contains the plans of God for the story of our world. It is nothing less than the whole plot of history. A scroll was not made like a book, but by gluing together sheets of papyrus reed into a single sheet, long and narrow, which was written on and then tightly rolled up. It was much easier to write on one side than the other, because of the grain of the original reed. But, unusually, this scroll is written on *both* sides, which is a way of telling us that it contains the full story. Resting on the open palm of the one on the throne is not just a summary of the plot, but the complete script of God's plans and intentions.

But there is a problem. The scroll is sealed up with seven seals. This is hard to visualize, but it seems from what follows that we are to imagine seven sections which can be unsealed and read one at a time. John does not find it possible to be fully consistent in describing his visions! But now someone has to break open these seals. The question is asked: 'Who can do it?' (5:2–3). John makes it clear that it is not a question of strength, but of who is 'worthy' for the task, of who has the *right* to open the scroll and set God's plans moving. It is like a lock without a key. So who holds the key? Who can open the scroll? John's reaction is utter misery when it seems that there is no one—not just because it looks as though he will never see what has been promised, but, more importantly, because God's plans for the world are stalled until the scroll is opened.

2. The hero (5:6–14)

But help is at hand. Just when it seems too late, the second vital element appears. The hero of the drama is finally about to appear on the stage. Verse 5 announces him. Both these titles, 'Lion of the tribe of Judah' and 'Root of David', though unusual, allude to the hopes of the Jewish nation for the coming of their King. In the language of the Old Testament, they both look ahead to the one who will fulfil the nation's long-disappointed hopes, the distant descendant of the patriarch Judah (Genesis 49:9–10) and David, their greatest king. That is exactly what he now comes to do again. Just when it seems that the show cannot go on, just when it seems that there is no future, the hero steps forward. John looks around for the Lion, but, in an amazing twist, what he sees is 'a Lamb' (5:6). The Lamb appears at the throne, the focal point of the scene. This is not some external agent putting in an appearance, but one who is familiar with the very throne of God!

There is no doubt what the picture of the Lamb represents. For the Jews, a slain lamb meant sacrifice. Lambs were slaughtered at every Passover feast, and at many other times as well, as an offering for people's sins. This Lamb has been slaughtered, yet here he is very much alive again, risen from death. Just as the one on the throne is never named as God, so the Lamb is never directly named as Christ, but his identity is obvious. His sevenfold horns and eyes stand for his complete authority—a horn is a biblical symbol of power (see Daniel 7; 8)—and universal knowledge. Jesus Christ, the Son of God, is the one who has the right to open the scroll and set God's plans in motion. As he takes the scroll from the hand of God, there is a new outbreak of praise and worship in heaven. The living creatures and the elders fall down and give him praise. Until this moment, until the Lamb appears, the praises have been spoken. But now heaven bursts into song! (5:9–10).

Their song makes clear the Lamb's qualifications to open the scroll, to hold the key to the locks of history. Verse 5 has already told us that he has 'triumphed'; John's later visions will reveal how he has triumphed over death, over the power of Satan and his allies, over the godless and rebellious realm of Babylon. Now the *means* of his triumph is the theme of the song: it was on the cross that the Lord Jesus, the slain Lamb, bought his people with his own blood, purchased us for God and gave us a destiny in his new kingdom (see 1:5–6). Here we find our rightful role as his servants and as priests with the permanent privilege of access to his presence.[4] That is worth a new song! Indeed, it *demands* a new song, for the appearance of the slain, resurrected and glorified Lamb brings about the most radical change imaginable. The death of Jesus Christ stands at the heart and centre of this world's story. It is his death that gives this world a future and gives us—a people gathered from the four corners of the earth—a hope and a destiny. Here is the vital connection between the astounding scenes in heaven and the life that we live here on earth. The missing plot is in the hands of Jesus Christ, and through his death, the pivotal point in history, God's purposes can begin to unfold.

This vision closes with the whole of creation—first the massed ranks of angels innumerable, and then every being in heaven and earth—joining in with the jubilant song of the living creatures and the elders around the throne. Step by step, the song moves out from the vicinity of the throne to be shared by every created being. Without exception, they now worship Jesus Christ as they worship God himself. There is no distinction. God the Father is the author of the plan; God the Son rolls it out. Naming him as 'the Lamb' places the cross of Christ at the heart of their praises. The angels are no more than spectators in the redemption of humanity; fallen angels were never offered salvation, as we were! But the angels delight to observe and to praise God for every sinner who repents. Above all, they delight to worship their God and the Lamb.

Here on earth, we need to feel the power of the song. Most of us live in pluralist societies which applaud the worship of anything and everything, so it is vital that we grasp the uniqueness of this hymn of praise. This is not one scene among many, as if many gods or great men were each to receive eternal praise from their followers. In heaven, in eternity, there is room only for the praise of *one* God, one Lord.

Such is the first of John's visions of heaven. With this first glimpse we perceive the true spiritual reality that lies behind the world that we see with our ordinary human eyes. At the centre of it all, at the point of origin of any meaning and purpose there is in the world, is not an empty space, as many people think, not some sinister supercomputer with us as helpless sub-programs, but a throne with one seated on it, and a Lamb who was slain and who lives again. At times, when we look out and see the turmoil in the world—senseless slaughter and natural disasters taking thousands of lives—it certainly seems as though the plot is lost. At times in our own lives, when we face relationships that break down, betrayal, our fears for our future, our disappointments in other people, our shame in ourselves, it seems that there is no script at all. Yet the plot is not lost. It is in the hands of the Lamb of God, Jesus Christ. There is a plan and a purpose in the world, a great unfolding story.

Struggling with our sense of meaninglessness and frustration, we must do what John did—look at the Lamb on the throne. When we feel valueless, that not a soul would miss us if we just dropped out of sight, we must see our worth in the wounds of the one who died for us, who stands in the centre of heaven's throne. He died the death that won the praises of heaven and unlocked the whole of history, and he did it *for us*. But the ultimate question for every human being must be: 'Have you found your part in the script, or are you still trying to write your own?'

To discuss or think about

1. Read the two chapters again and notice how much changes (and what stays the same!) when the Lamb appears. What does this tell us about the place of the Lord Jesus at the centre of God's purposes?
2. Think how the scene of the heavenly throne-room would have encouraged John's first readers, living in an oppressive and seemingly all-powerful empire. Pray for persecuted Christians you know of who face a similar threat.
3. Are there areas of your life that you feel are out of control—that the 'plot has been lost'? How does this vision, with its clear view of God's sovereignty, help you to trust him in those areas?

Part IV
Seven seals: suffering
(6:1–8:5)

5

Suffering and the end of the age

Please read Revelation 6

Anyone who wants to be in government (at least in a democracy!) has to be able to answer the hard questions, the ones that people care about most. Now Christians say that the real power in the world is held not by politicians, but by God. He is the one who is really in charge, and there is one question which Christians are very often asked about God, perhaps the hardest question of all. Some people ask it to trip us up, but for many it is a desperately serious and painful question. It is the question about God and suffering: why does he allow it? This world is full of suffering and evil on all levels, from world events such as wars, famines and natural disasters, through to the smaller-scale but equally tragic pain of crime on our streets, the hidden violence in people's homes, the agony of seeing a loved one die painfully, or even a child bullied at school. If God is really in charge, why doesn't he do something about it?

There was a British prime minister who was said by one of his critics to act as if he was 'in office, but not in power'. He was the prime minister, but he seemed strangely unable to influence events or to sort out the big problems. That is the way some people think of God. He is in office, but not in power. He cannot or will not *act*. The vision of the scroll in Revelation 5 surely raises this question. God is sovereign; he is still sitting on heaven's throne, and through Jesus Christ his plans for the world are going into action. But if this is true, why is there so much pointless suffering? This is not just a debating question—except, perhaps, for people who have never suffered, who have never seen anyone they love suffering. It is one that we have to answer if the Christian faith is worth anything at all. A faith that collapses at the first sign of trouble is no good to anyone. If we believe in God, and if we recognize that there is a great deal of evil in the world, we have just three options:

1. God cannot do anything to stop the suffering. He is not all-powerful: he is in office, but not in power.[1]
2. God is responsible for the evil himself—he does evil deeds directly.
3. God actually uses evil events within his own good purposes.

C. S. Lewis, who wrote the Narnia stories, was a Christian thinker and philosopher of the mid-twentieth century. Later in life he fell in love and married, but then his wife contracted cancer and eventually she died. Lewis kept a record of the way he grappled with the appalling pain of this time as he tried to understand it in the light of a God of love. But is that what he is? As Lewis struggles, tortured, he writes like this: 'Not that I am (I think) in much danger of ceasing to believe in God. The real danger is of coming to believe such dreadful things about him. The conclusion I dread is not "So there's no God after all", but "So this is what God's really like. Deceive yourself no longer."' A little later, in desperation, he writes of fearing that we are really like 'rats in a trap. Or, worse still, rats in a laboratory.' 'Sooner or later,' he writes, 'I must face the question in plain language.

What reason have we, except our own desperate wishes, to believe that God is, by any standard we can conceive, "good"? Doesn't all the *prima facie* evidence suggest exactly the opposite? What have we to set against it?'[2]

If you have ever felt like that, you are certainly not alone. This chapter gives us part of an answer to the problem of suffering, although it is not the answer that everyone would choose. In Revelation 6 we see what happens when the seals begin to be opened and God's plans go into effect. We don't *hear* the scroll's words being read aloud; instead we *see* them acted out. This scene is sometimes thought to focus directly on the suffering faced by the church in the world, but apart from the fifth seal (6:9–11) there is little evidence of that. The church is most certainly involved in suffering, raising the serious question of whether she will survive it at all. That question is answered in chapter 7, but in chapter 6 the suffering in view is universal, as we see the effect of the first six seals being opened. In a pattern that will be repeated with the trumpets in chapters 8–9 and the bowls in chapter 16, they are grouped 'four plus two' with a further delay before the seventh.

The meaning of disaster—Seals 1 to 4 (6:1–8)

In this section, four times a seal on the scroll is broken open; four times one of the living creatures around the throne calls, 'Come!'; and four times a horse and rider appear. These are the four horsemen of the Apocalypse, one of the most well-known images in the whole book, which have inspired literature—even science fiction—and artwork, some of it very fanciful indeed. We must remember that the images are just that; John is struggling to put into words the indescribable visions he is seeing. Up to this point, we have already found imagery drawn from several Old Testament books, especially Daniel, Isaiah and Ezekiel. There are visions of coloured horses somewhat similar to these in Zechariah 1 and 6 and, though there are also significant differences, the meanings of these four are clear enough: they are messengers of God.

The first seal (6:1–2)

The first seal is opened; the first of those living creatures thunders 'Come!' and a white horse appears. Logically, the summons must be addressed to the rider and his horse, not to John, who is already present.[3]

Some have argued that the rider on the white horse is Christ, on the grounds that the similar rider in chapter 19 certainly *is* Christ. On this interpretation, John is seeing a vision of the gospel spreading across the world in the face of all opposition. But this is surely a strange way to read it. This rider may be the first, but he is still only one among four. Is Christ to be regarded as one among four—especially when all the other three are harbingers of such evil? Moreover, John has not yet seen the vision of chapter 19 and he would therefore have no reason to interpret this earlier vision in the light of the later one! It can also be argued that armed conquest is an unexpected way to visualize the worldwide spread of the gospel of Jesus.[4]

It makes far more sense to understand the first rider as a member of the group. John sees the horseman riding out as a victorious conqueror, armed for battle and wearing a crown—a picture of aggression, conquest, imperial power. White was the colour of the horses in the Roman Empire's victory parades, but, on the other hand, the bow was not known as a Roman weapon, and the vision is clearly not limited to a single empire. The picture is of earth's strongest powers going to war. It is the aggression of Attila the Hun, of Tamburlaine, of Napoleon, of Hitler, of the Red Army in Eastern Europe. If John was seeing this today he might describe it as an American or Chinese general riding into battle on a tank.

The second seal (6:3–4)

Following close behind the armed aggression of the first rider comes the violence of the second. This rider comes to take peace from the earth and let men get on with slaughtering one another. Appropriately, his horse is 'fiery red', so often the colour of war. His sword is 'large', as if to symbolize the scale of the killing which will take place. The red horse's rider brings the vicious civil conflicts of Sudan and Syria, the terrors of 9/11 and the suicide bombings in the Middle East.

The third seal (6:5–6)

The third seal is opened and the third rider emerges. A black horse stands for the darkness of famine. Unexpectedly, the rider holds a pair of scales—not the scales of justice, but for weighing out the daily rations. This time there is another voice. Probably it is John's reverent way of saying that the voice comes from the throne of God itself, decreeing the famine prices. 'A day's wages' translates the word 'denarius'—a sort of first-century minimum wage. If that is all you have, you can either buy decent food for yourself or poorer food for your whole family, but that is all. It is a picture of bare survival. 'Oil' is *olive* oil, and oil and wine were staple foods in a time when water was not often safe to drink. These are not luxuries, as some suggest (this was not the age of wine bars!); the call to preserve them is simply a limitation of suffering. So this vision is of severe shortages, but not yet of mass starvation.

The fourth seal (6:7–8)

Finally, the fourth seal is opened. A 'pale' horse appears—literally it is *yellowish-green*, a very unhealthy colour for a horse, but this one carries Death itself, accompanied by Hades, the world of the dead. The rider on the pale horse comes, as it were, to swallow up the victims of what has gone before: death in war, death too now from starvation, death by disease and death by wild animals, all accounting for a quarter of mankind.

God is in control

In symbolic form, then, conquest, war, famine and death ride out onto the earth. We need not suppose these are one-off historical events; rather, these four seals unlock themes that unroll throughout history. They are here all the time. And they are part of God's plan; these are the words of the scroll acted out, the scroll that has come from the hand of the Almighty on his throne. The riders ride out at *his* command and under *his* control. The first rider is 'given' a crown—given by God; similarly for the other three. How can this be? In one sense, these verses tell us nothing that we don't already know. We are well aware that there is violence, war, famine and disease in the world. What we struggle with is the idea that they are called down by heaven's throne.

From this passage emerge two clear pointers which will help us understand, at least in part. The first is that these evils go right back to the beginning of the human story. They are effectively working through *the effects of the Fall*. When God holds Adam and Eve to account for their actions that day (Genesis 3), he tells them that because they have sinned the whole world has changed. He tells them that in place of the perfect, peaceful world they had before, from now on there will be conflict, producing sufficient food will be a struggle and, for the first time, human beings will die. So already, on the very day of the Fall, the four horsemen are looming in the background. There is a curse on nature, and this is probably why it is the four living creatures who summon the four horsemen, because the living creatures represent the created world which has been sabotaged by human sin. The riders represent the inevitable penalty of that sin. Throughout human history, the crazy, self-defeating stupidity of sin, where we wave our fists in the face of our Creator, has been working itself out. That is the message of this chapter—that ever since the bitter tragedy of that first day of sin, which between us we have multiplied a billion times over, the whole race is living with the effect of the curse. As long as this world lasts there will be no respite, because man on earth is a rebel, an outlaw.

The second pointer is this. All that happens as the seals are opened is still *under God's authority, written in his plan.* The Bible doesn't answer all our questions 'Why …?', but it is crystal clear that God has all the power. Although we find it hard to grasp, these evils fall within his plans for the world. We look out at the world with our narrow perspective; we see the violence, and we conclude that God's power must be limited; his hand must be weak. But the Bible says otherwise: even these disasters are under his sway. In fact the descriptions show us that he curbs the extent of the evils. The famine described is not total devastation. Death is not awarded full sway over the world. Though many suffering people would protest that they see little sign of a limit to their pain, yet there *are* limits, and wherever evil and pain are limited, there is the mercy of God.

Beyond our understanding, God uses even the horrors of the world for his own purposes. It is not that he *does* any evil; God is faithful to all his promises and ever true to his character. Is God to blame for the Rwandan genocide or the Ethiopian famines or the miserably familiar violence of terrorism? No. God is good, all the time. Part of his purpose in these evil events is to warn us, just as Jesus said to his disciples when they asked him how they could know when he was about to return and bring the end of the world as we know it (Matthew 24:4–8). When you see wars and famines and disasters, Jesus says, it does not mean the end has come. But it does mean that we should be warned. He is coming back and the end *will* come. Meanwhile, he is in control.

We know there is a lot of evil in the world. Would we really prefer a God who is unable to do anything about it, so that we have no idea whether good or evil will finally triumph, whether wrongs will ever be put right? Isn't it far better to have a God whose plans we may only be able to glimpse, but who shows us that he has ultimate control of every event on earth—every sparrow that falls—as Jesus said? But of course the question is a stupid one. It makes no difference which kind of God we *prefer*. The Bible tells us very clearly what the *real* God is like: the God who is seated majestic on the throne, whose wisdom is so deep and whose power is so all-embracing that he is even able to include the evil acts of humanity within his purposes. This is our God, in whose presence we bow down in worship.

The end is now—Seals 5 and 6 (6:9–17)

These disasters, pictured by four horsemen, are dramatic, but they are not the end of the world. They warn of far worse to come. The warnings do not go on for ever; otherwise they would be empty. As the seals continue to be opened, the focus shifts back to heaven, before returning to earth and a sight of utter devastation.

The fifth seal (6:9–11)

The fifth seal concerns a cry for justice. It may be a surprise to find an altar pictured in heaven. But this is not an altar where sacrifices are made; it is actually an incense altar, which appears several times in Revelation. It is a place where praises are offered to God and it stands in front of his throne, as we shall see when it next appears, in chapter 8. Here we find another of those images that is very hard for us to visualize, for beneath this altar John sees the souls of all the Christian martyrs—every man, woman and child who has died because they belonged to Christ.

In this vision they are crying to God for justice. 'How long?', they call out. 'How long until you put right all the injustice on earth and punish our killers?' They are not seeking personal vengeance, but the ultimate righting of wrongs which they know their God is going to conclude. They long to see it. They long to see 'the inhabitants of the earth' judged. That expression, which first appeared in 3:10, is used frequently in Revelation and it always means, not everyone who lives on earth, but those who persist in rebelling against God—everyone who feels at home in the world as it is now, holding out against God. As John watches, each of these martyrs is given a white robe and is told to wait, because the time is still not quite ready.

Very clearly, the church of Christ does not escape the world's troubles. Quite the opposite—down through history, thousands upon thousands of faithful servants of God have faced death because they stayed true to him. It is still happening today and it will go on happening until the end comes. Most of them are not famous and never make it onto the television news. They are unknowns, like the evangelist killed in Nigeria one day, the group beheaded in Indonesia the next, the pastor murdered in Karnataka State in India the day after that, or the nameless prisoners being beaten to death in the prison camps of North Korea—nameless to us but known to God—and many thousands of others, tortured, shot, beheaded, starved, bombed, in Iran, Sudan, Indonesia, China, Mexico and too many other countries to name. They are the martyr church, a great stream of faithful witnesses.

On earth, they are helpless victims on the losing side, hated and despised by their killers. On earth, they are unknown. But how different it looks in heaven! Their place is nearest the throne, wearing the white robes of victory. They are the heroes of heaven, and they are our brothers and sisters if we are believers. If one day *we* are called to share their fate—and it may happen soon, even in the West—to shed our blood for the name of Christ, it will not spell defeat, but glory.

The martyrs under the altar cry out for justice. They are

right to do so. A billion times a day someone has good cause to protest, 'That's not fair!' The four horsemen have left massive injustice in their wake. The greatest injustice of all is when earth's inhabitants take the lives of God's own people, just as they took the life of Christ himself. In heaven they stand and plead for the day when all will be set to rights, when human rebellion will be properly punished and justice will at last be done.

The sixth seal (6:12–14)

They do not have to wait for ever, because now the sixth seal is opened, and with it the Great Day has come at last. Finally, events unfold which not even the most comfortable, not the most cynical, will be able to ignore. This is news that no one can switch off.

We must first stand back and look at the picture, which some might write off as the wild imaginings of a crazy visionary. But, whatever else this is, it is not John's imagination. In fact this is one of the least original parts of his whole book. This is the culmination of a track of prophecy that runs back for centuries, starting at least 800 years before John was writing. The prophets of the Old Testament looked forward to what they described as the Day of the Lord, a day when God would finally intervene to deal with evil, to destroy whatever stands against him and to reward the people who have been true to him. This is exactly what the martyrs are crying out for.

The most similar passages about the Day of the Lord include Isaiah 13:9–11; 34:4 and Joel 2:30–32. All this has been predicted for centuries. Finally, the Lord Jesus himself talks of it in Matthew 24:29–30 (with its parallels in Mark and Luke).[5] John was there in person to hear him say that. He sat with Jesus a couple of days before his death, there on the Mount of Olives looking across the valley to the temple, as Christ foretold the day when he would come back. John heard Jesus say it and now he sees it played out, as the same Lord Jesus, now glorified, rolls out God's plans and prepares to return to the earth which executed him. What the Old Testament calls the Day of the Lord arrives, signalled by unmistakable signs in the skies, awesome and terrifying sights that people will clearly see.

But what exactly is described in these verses? Again we must remember that these are *signs*: John is describing how the scene appears and, as we have already noticed, he struggles to find adequate words. It would therefore be wrong to press his words too literally and complain, for instance, that stars cannot actually fall onto the earth because they are light years away and they are much bigger than the earth anyway, or to say that the sky cannot roll up because it is not a solid sheet. John is saying that this is how it *looked*. He sees the stars falling like windfall apples, as we might describe it. The Bible constantly tells us that when God intervenes to bring history to an end, when Christ returns, there will be colossal upheavals both on the earth and in the cosmos. Christ's return is not some obscure back-page story; it will have an impact that the whole universe will feel. On that day, people everywhere will look up and see what has never been seen before. The sun, moon and stars will change for ever. The sky will roll up to make way for the new heaven and new earth which is promised. The earth itself will be shaken, so that mountains and islands are shifted from their places. Above all, everything that we think of as fixed and permanent will move.

The reaction of the earth's inhabitants (6:15–17)

This passage does not visualize Christ's actual return, but it makes it clear that the moment has come and it shows us starkly how the earth's inhabitants will react. They look up and realize to their horror that the world they have known and loved, the world that has been so good to them, is no more. With awful certainty it dawns on them that the day of reckoning, which they always hoped would never come, yet secretly feared, is here at last. No one is exempt. Every class and rank of people is included, with the ones who have held the greatest power on earth given priority in the list of terror. The fear by which they have ruled is replaced by their own. Finally, order gives way to chaos. Panic reigns, as from every town and city there is a mass exodus of people hunting for a hiding place. Running to the hills, they try to escape from the judgement by going underground. They long for death, because suddenly death seems more appealing than facing the fury of the God they have defied. The mountains are falling—but they would rather be buried in a landslide than face up to God.

It is stupid, of course (but then sin always is) to think you can hide from your Creator in the middle of his creation! It is foolish to think that death will allow you an escape from the one who holds the keys of death! But there is another kind of stupidity as well. There are some who think that Jesus is a softer, gentler face of God—not stern and angry, but all love, all-forgiving. These last verses tell a different story. The fury that people on earth will flee is the fury of 'the Lamb', Jesus Christ, just as much as it is his Father's. There is no soft picture of Christ here. We must not miss what these verses are saying, however hard the pictures may be to grasp. God's wrath, his anger against sin, is real. The Bible is clear on this. God's reaction to evil is very personal and very strong: it is pure, constant, unbending fury. This last picture shows how people on earth will respond when they finally see it coming.

Where will we be found on that day? If we belong to the Lamb, this is not written to terrify us. Quite the opposite—we are not in this picture of terror, this desperation to escape from the face of God. We are safe from this. Our place is in heaven, in company with the martyrs under the altar, suffering now, not when Christ returns. The next chapter will show us the great vision of the church around the throne of God. We escape this picture because the wrath of God towards us has been taken by Christ on the cross, the Lamb who was slain. This book tells us that, even if it seems as though the world is out of control, it is not. Even if we feel we are going to be swept away, we are not. Even as the four riders pace the earth, the one on the throne and the Lamb are reigning. Christ is coming back as Judge of the earth, but because of the cross we are utterly safe.

But for anyone who is not trusting in Christ, this scene should be terrifying. If you do not know Christ, then you *are* in this final picture, as the sky goes dark, the mountains collapse and the final minutes of human history tick away, and then Christ himself comes through the clouds. Like everyone else on the planet, you will have to face a God who is angry with your sin and give your account to him. Sin has to be dealt with: either on the cross, where Jesus Christ died to pay for the sins of the world, or else in hell, permanently. There is no third option. These words are written as a warning at a time when there is still a chance. Jesus Christ in his love went to the cross to take the wrath instead of us, so that we could be pulled out of this picture and made safe. History is moving on; the clock is ticking; Jesus is returning. Where will you be?

To discuss or think about

1. Understanding how evil can exist while God is all-powerful and loving is difficult for us. How has the chapter helped you to think about this? Do you think there is any alternative view that fits what the Bible teaches?
2. Even in heaven, there are cries for God to bring about justice. What does that tell us about the importance of justice, and how should that affect our own attitudes?
3. How do you respond to the Bible's descriptions of the end of the world? Does your response challenge you to change in any way?

From every nation one voice

Please read Revelation 7:1–8:1

As I write, the 2014 FIFA World Cup is well under way in Brazil. Huge sporting events like this generate a mass of memorable moments and some of the greatest of human gatherings. The stadiums where the matches are played teem with colour and excitement; the streets are full of music and impromptu multi-racial parties; and for those who cannot get tickets for the live action, there are the ever-popular 'fan zones' on beaches and in city squares. Even for those who have no interest in sport, it's impressive and exciting. But Revelation 7 shows us something even better. In terms of human gatherings, a World Cup is about as stirring as it can be—all that emotion, all that passion and excitement. But for Christians, it gets better. Revelation 7 is a vision of a vast *heavenly* assembly, where we are crowded, not around huge open-air stages, but around the throne of God; where the music is not about everything and nothing, but about the one great theme we shall all want to celebrate; and where the gathering doesn't finish in a few exciting hours, because it will last for ever. A single vast crowd unites every people and every race in a unified song of praise. This vision shows us that, whatever we are experiencing, whatever we may face, if we belong to Jesus we are 100% safe—with no questions, no caveats, no reservations. Our future is as good as it could possibly be; it is brighter than we could possibly imagine.

The command to the four angels (7:1–3)

Chapter 7 falls between the opening of the sixth and seventh seals, and it reads very differently from the end of chapter 6. We finish chapter 6 with the world coming to a terrible and dramatic end, with the planet left in ruins and its unrepentant citizens burying themselves under the falling mountains to escape from the fury of God. Now we find an angel calling out: 'Wait! Don't harm the land or the sea or the trees.' But you cannot harm a world that already stands destroyed. Either this angel has lost track of time—which is unlikely!—or else the film has been wound back to a point before all the destruction has started. We must remember how to read Revelation. This is not a single story where all the events portrayed follow one another in a linear sequence. It is a series of *visions*: John sees the same scenes from different angles, and frequently the scene cuts from heaven to earth and back again. Here we have a flashback. The last verse of chapter 6 raises the question: with the world demolished and the wicked swept up in the wrath of God, who can possibly survive?

We must also remember why this book was written—not to provide theologians with a collection of absorbing puzzles, but to help ordinary Christians to cope with a hostile world. It is about surviving when the world is against you. So there is the question: if all this trouble and disaster is coming on the earth, and if it is going to culminate in utter devastation, where does that leave us? This vision tells us the answer. We begin with four angels holding back four destroying winds which are threatening to sweep through the earth. Powerful winds are a very effective symbol of destruction. I experienced the 1987 hurricane in south-east England and I know! But there is more to it. Again, we should remember that the key to understanding Revelation is not a PhD, but a sound knowledge of the rest of Scripture. That is what fills John's mind as he sees these visions.

Look back once more to the opening verses of Zechariah 6, where we read about four horses, all different colours. Zechariah asks the angel who is standing there, 'What are these?' The angel explains that these are the four spirits of heaven, going out from God in different directions throughout the world.[1] 'Four spirits' can equally well be translated 'four winds'—the same Hebrew word, *ruach*, is used for both. The horses and the winds are two different pictures of God's agents at work in the world. That strongly suggests that the four destroying winds of Revelation 7 are none other than the four horsemen of chapter 6. The tape has wound back to the beginning again, and John is now viewing the scene before they are permitted to begin their destructive mission on the earth.

Now the angel calls out: 'Wait! We have to mark out the servants of our God before the destruction starts.' This is one of the rare occasions when we are able to eavesdrop on a conversation between the angels! God's people are to be protected in some way from the terrors which are about to be unleashed.

Identifying the two crowds (7:4–10)

It is at this point that we find one of the most controversial passages in Revelation. In this chapter, two crowds are described: the 144,000 in verse 4, and the great multitude in verse 9. Who are they, and are they the same? It is more than an abstract theological puzzle, because we need to know if *we* are in these crowds.

On first reading, it seems that the crowds could be different. One crowd is numbered, while the other one cannot be (7:9). One crowd is on earth; the other is in heaven. One seems to be made up of Jews from the twelve tribes of Israel; the other is from every nation. They certainly sound different. But, given that John is often shown the same scene from different angles, we should consider whether these crowds could be the same too. The church is very often described in the New Testament as the true Israel. In Romans 4 and Galatians 3, for instance, we read that all who believe are children of Abraham, whether they happen to be born Jews or not. In Galatians 6:16 the church is referred to as 'the Israel of God'. In various places it is Christians who are said to be the 'true circumcision'—that is, the real Israel (Romans 2:28–29; Philippians 3:3; Colossians 3:11; in Revelation, see also the letters to Smyrna and Philadelphia). Perhaps the differences between these two crowds are not so obvious after all. Certainly when the 144,000 reappear in chapter 14:1–5 there is no suggestion that they are Jewish.[2]

Maybe, though, the number 144,000 should clinch the argument? Not necessarily. We have already come across symbolic numbers in Revelation, and there is something very odd about these precise numbers from each tribe. Every tribe produces exactly the same number, the big tribes and the small. In fact many of the tribes were completely lost after the exile, yet somehow they still produce a turnout of 12,000 each for this crowd.

There are really two kinds of numbers in the Bible. When we read that the disciples caught 153 fish, for example, that is a statistic. There were 153 actual fish and we are meant to understand that someone was there as an eyewitness and counted those fish. We are meant to think: 'That's a lot of fish!'

But then there are numbers which are not statistics but symbols, and surely this is one of those.[3] Now 144 is twelve times twelve, and twelve is the symbolic number for Israel, the people of God. This number is telling us simply that the total of those who are sealed for protection is the complete number of God's people. Most commentators think the 'thousand' part is also a symbolic number. They could be right, but personally I think 'a thousand' just means 'a big number' as it often does in Scripture.

So here are two views of the same crowd: first they appear on earth; then they appear in heaven. I hope it is clear that all we have done to reach this conclusion is to study the passage in the light of the rest of Scripture; any of us can do that. The message is simply that all those who are sealed on the earth make it to heaven. You can give them a number, a meaning, but you can't count them. They are the true Israel, and yet they are from *every* nation. The same crowd who are preserved, kept safe on earth, are then glorified in heaven, and we are among them.

There are people who take the number 144,000 literally, notably the Jehovah's Witnesses. According to them, the 144,000 are not literally Jews, but they are the elite group who will actually make it to heaven. Recruitment for this group began in the nineteenth century and no more candidates need apply, especially if they were born after 1935. The list of 144,000 names is full, and all who belong to this number are members of the sect. All the other Jehovah's Witnesses will live on a renewed earth. They are the 'great multitude'. The strangest part of this interpretation is that in the vision itself the 144,000 are on the earth, while the great multitude is in heaven—exactly the other way round!

The other people who read this 144,000 as a literal number are Christians who believe that, in the last years before Christ's return, there will be 144,000 Jewish evangelists who will go out to make one last push for the gospel before the final end of the age. This view is very popular with those who understand Revelation in a 'futurist' sense, especially dispensationalists, like the writers of the *Left Behind* books. Once more, we have to say that this view ties in neither with the rest of Scripture nor with the flow of Revelation. It depends on seeing all the visions of Revelation as a consecutive history, ignoring the clear pattern of repetition from one scene to the next.[4] These 144,000 clearly do not suddenly pop up at the end of time.

With these points out of the way, we will now turn to what this wonderful vision says to God's people today.

Today is secure (7:1–8)

Look again at verse 3. The 'seal' here is a mark of ownership. Animals such as sheep would be marked to show whose property they were, just as today if you go walking in the hills in Britain you will find sheep with different coloured markings on their fleeces to show which farmer owns them. In Revelation, everyone is eventually pictured as being sealed with one of these marks—either the mark of the beast (chapter 13) or the mark of Christ. The message throughout the book is that you belong to one or the other; you cannot belong to no one. Many people think you can, as the poet Henley put it:

> It matters not how strait the gate,
> How charged with punishments the scroll,
> I am the master of my fate:
> I am the captain of my soul.

That is real pride: 'I am the captain of my soul.' But the truth is that we all belong to someone, and our destiny is determined by that ownership. The people who are marked with the seal of the living God are preserved through all the disasters of chapter 6, through all the hurricanes that blow through Revelation. But the people without that mark will have to face his wrath.

For anyone who bears the mark of Christ, the message is

this: you are utterly secure. Now we know perfectly well that Christians do not escape the troubles of this world. But look at the difference between the believer who is in Christ and the person who is not. They both face the same kind of disasters. In many ways, especially in some places, the believer actually has a harder time than the unbeliever. But for the unbeliever, this world is all he has and there is nothing else. When disaster strikes, that's it. However successful he may be, however wonderful her family or career, however long she may live, the time comes when it all ends and it has all gone. Nothing is safe; nothing is permanent; nothing is secure.

But if you are in Christ, no disaster can touch you. Psalm 91 says:

> A thousand may fall at your side,
> ten thousand at your right hand,
> but it will not come near *you* (Psalm 91:7, emphasis added).

It does not mean that you will never die: you will, unless the Lord comes back first. But it means that you are secure. You bear the mark of the living God; stamped on your forehead is the name of Jesus, and he will never let you go. What is more, he is working out his good purposes in your life, even through the apparent disasters. God can turn even our losses and our suffering upside down.

This is what C. H. Spurgeon wrote in his commentary on Psalm 91: 'It is impossible that any ill should happen to the man who is beloved of the Lord. Ill to him is no ill, but only good in a mysterious form. Losses enrich him, sickness is his medicine, reproach is his honour, death is his gain.' I don't think I would have dared to write that. I know how much I complain when life seems to be hard. But it is true. So the 144,000 endure the disasters of war and terrorism, famine, suffering and death that we read of in chapter 6; and some will still be there to see the earth shaken to pieces as the Lord comes through the torn-open skies—and can stand firm. As the four winds blow and bring suffering and pain to the earth, as the four horsemen advance and do their work, we can stand. As Toplady's great hymn puts it: 'More happy, but not more secure, the glorified spirits in heaven.' We are just as secure here as we shall be then, if we know him.

Tomorrow is glorious (7:9–17)

In verses 9–10 the scene shifts once more from earth, where the people of God are marked and protected, back to the throne-room of heaven, and here is the great crowd again. Every one of those sealed is here; every one who has been chosen and called is in this great scene. This is our destiny, after all that the world has thrown at us—to stand before God's throne as members of this crowd. So what will we see as we look around?

It is an international crowd (7:9)

People 'from every nation, tribe, people and language'[5] are here. There is no more need for interpreters. The curse of Babel, when the world's languages were confused, has been reversed. Humanity again has a single language, and the work of missionaries and evangelists down through the centuries has been rewarded. Those who have poured out their lives to take the gospel to earth's furthest corners will see the results and rejoice. Every people group is represented. There are no more unreached peoples now. They are here from the remotest parts of Central Asia, from Tibet, from the last hidden valleys of Papua New Guinea, from every tribe of Africa, from every island. If all this is a reward for the work of missionaries, how much more is it a reward for the Lamb of God himself! This is what his suffering has brought into being. This crowd from every nation is his prize.

It is a triumphant crowd (7:9)

The 'palm branches' are a symbol of triumph and joy. All in this great throng have made it—but more than that, they share the triumph of the Lamb who bought them at the cost of his own blood.

It is a praising crowd (7:10–12)

On earth, crowds get excited. We may get excited about a football match, but that kind of excitement flares up and dies away. Grand speeches are made about the brotherhood of humankind, or the glory of sport, but that is just a passing illusion. Here the praise is real and does not die away. We shall never tire of praising the Lamb and the God who has saved us. From every nation comes one voice of praise.

In verses 11–12 the angels join in. Revelation is full of angels, running errands, delivering messages, executing judgement on the earth, but what they seem to want to do more than anything is to gather round the throne and around the glorified church and celebrate what God has done in saving us. God never had mercy on the fallen angels. Christ never died for them. But he died for us.

It is a rescued crowd (7:13–14)

We should perhaps be grateful when we are occasionally given a direct explanation of these scenes! This great crowd has come from the 'great tribulation'. Some Christians think that refers to some special, brief period of a few years right at the end. But the 'great tribulation' simply means 'big trouble'. That is in progress in the world of today. It would be difficult to tell a Christian in Somalia, Iraq or North Korea today that the tribulation has not yet started! As Jesus told his disciples in John 16:33, 'In this world you will have trouble'—or *tribulation*, for it is the same word.[6] Sometimes the trouble is greater; sometimes it is less. It will get worse as the end approaches, but it is all the 'tribulation', and the faithful believers, marked with the seal, come out of it to stand in that great crowd around the throne.

It is a justified crowd (7:13–14)

Here the saints are pictured wearing robes washed white in the blood of the Lamb. We must catch the power of the symbolism here—white for purity, real whiteness being very difficult to achieve at the time this was written, just as crystal clear glass was almost impossible to produce. These shining white robes represent the righteousness of Christ which covers us, which allows us to appear in this crowd. There is no other way to come near the throne unless he declares us righteous, accepted by God, justified.

It is a worshipping crowd (7:15)

Before the throne, our business will be to serve God in every part of our lives, just as it is today—only then we shall do it far better! Verse 15 mentions God's 'temple' and his 'tent'. In effect the whole of heaven is a temple; the temple, like the tent, simply stands for the presence of God, which will be everywhere. When we reach the eternal state—the new heavens and the new earth—this will be all the more evident (see 21:22).

It is a protected crowd (7:16–17)

These verses are taken from Isaiah 49:10, where they describe how God would restore his own people, leading them home and providing for them, shielding them from every threat on the way. But now the identity of the Guide is at last revealed—the Lord Jesus himself, the Lamb who is also our Shepherd.

It is a comforted crowd (7:17)

This is one of the most treasured verses in the whole Bible and will be reiterated in 21:4. Yes, we may arrive in heaven with tears in our eyes: tears for the pain we have suffered in this life and even in death itself; tears of regret at what we have lost in this life; tears over our own failures—the tears that we know now in a world where we ourselves sin and where death reigns and disaster stalks. We may arrive there after a life that seems to have been nothing but heartache. But once we are there, there will be no more tears. God himself wipes every tear away. The lost years, the lost opportunities we shall mourn no longer. Pain will have left us, and our losses on earth will fade away as we stand before the throne and look into the eyes of our Lord. As God's people we have security today, but tomorrow is unimaginably glorious.

To discuss or think about

1. How comforting is it that Christians we are 'sealed' for protection, even though we may face terrible suffering and even violent death? Do you believe that you are really secure in Christ?
2. Are you satisfied with the explanation that the two crowds in chapter 7 are the same?
3. What features of the worshipping crowd do you find the most enticing, and why? What will it feel like to be part of that crowd?

7

Prayer and the purposes of God

Please read Revelation 8:1–5

In the 1980s the word 'Beirut' was synonymous with anarchy, violence and terror. A frequent tactic of the various armed factions was to capture Western hostages, often not in order to ransom them, but simply to generate publicity and to demonstrate their power. Terry Waite went to Beirut to negotiate the release of one of these hostages. A skilled diplomat, he was the Archbishop of Canterbury's special envoy and he already had a track record of successfully negotiating prisoner releases. He was known as something of a larger than life character—large both figuratively and literally. But in spite of all his skill and experience, this time events did not go according to plan and Terry Waite himself became a hostage. He was held there for five long years and for four of those years he was held in solitary confinement, hearing only such snippets of news as his captors chose to pass on. During those years, all over the world, people were following the story, eagerly waiting for news, and thousands of them tried to send him encouraging wishes.

Thousands sent their messages, but none got through—except for one solitary postcard, sent by a lady in Bedford named Joy Brodier, of whom Waite had never even heard. Now what chance did that card have of getting through? It was one chance in thousands, obviously. Somehow on that one day events conspired to get the card through. The strange address was taken seriously. Someone knew someone else who was able to pass the card on, and they passed it on down the line. So, because everything worked out right, that chance in a thousand came off, and the message got through.

Now ask yourself, 'What chance do you honestly think your *prayers* have of getting through?' When you pray, when you send your message to God, do you seriously expect it will get to him? Isn't it far more likely that somewhere along the way, it will be lost or turned back, like all those letters to Terry Waite? I am convinced that we all struggle with thoughts like these. Prayer is difficult! That great Christian you look up to—yes, he or she finds prayer a struggle too. We sit down to pray, as we know we should. But deep down we think: 'Unless I am feeling particularly spiritual, or I'm having a really good day, my prayer won't get through. If the Lord is in any way displeased with me, or I've had a family row, or I can't concentrate because I had a bad night—I will simply hit a blank wall.'

The beginning of Revelation 8 meets exactly that problem. These five verses assure us, not only that the Lord hears our prayers, but also that he even uses our prayers to advance his purposes in the world. We begin as the seventh and last seal on the scroll is finally opened (8:1). To our surprise, the opening of the seventh seal brings no new judgements, no new calamities, just silence. This tells us that that part of the story is over. The sixth seal told the story of God's judgement and the end of the world that we know, and there certainly is something to follow it—a new world, in fact a new heaven and earth—but that will come later. Meanwhile, from John's point of view, half an hour of silence is a chance to reflect on the devastating and awesome visions he has seen. John is probably very glad of that silence—all the more so because he is about to see a fresh vision, the vision of the seven trumpets (8:2). And then, as we wait for the trumpets to blow, there is this amazing, timeless cameo. If ever we feel small and insignificant, that our voice goes lost and unheard, then we should hear this: heaven waits while we pray! We are all too familiar with what prayer feels like from our perspective and how hard it can be. But this is what prayer looks like from heaven's point of view, and it is tremendously encouraging.

God hears our prayers (8:3–4)

The churches John was writing to in the first century had reason to ask whether God was listening when they prayed. They had to face persecution from the Roman authorities—remember that's why John was on Patmos in the first place, instead of at home with his church in Ephesus—and life was very tough. Already in 6:10 we have seen the picture of the martyr church beneath the altar in heaven crying out for justice. 'How long, O Lord, how long?' they call—the cry of the suffering church down through the centuries. Even in heaven, where they stand before God, they call for justice to be done, and on earth the question is: 'Does God see? Does he hear our prayers?'

For many of us in the twenty-first century West, the problem is a little different. Life is not too tough, but too *comfortable*, and maybe we are not bothering to pray at all. After all, if we are not sure that God hears us, what is the point? But in this vision we see that right in front of God's throne the prayers of the saints are rising up. The altar and the incense represent more Old Testament imagery, for this is how offerings were made to God in those times. There was a special altar in the temple where incense was burned (1 Chronicles 6:49), and the fragrant smoke rising up represented the worship and service of God's people rising up to him as an acceptable offering. Now another angel comes up to the altar (as John Milton pointed out, there are always plenty of angels on hand!), and he mixes incense with the prayers of the saints—their imperfections removed, as it were, by the fragrant smell of the incense—and offers them up to God. The prayers get through!

We may still feel that this seems a little remote. 'Saints' are generally thought to be people with haloes—people whom the pope has canonized because they were regarded as such great heroes of the faith, because they were so spiritual, because they could even work miracles. So we have Saint Peter, Saint Paul, and—as of April 2014—Pope John Paul II is a saint as well! But in the Bible a saint[1] is simply a believer, someone God has chosen and called to himself. Time and again in Paul's letters we find 'Greet all the *saints*', 'pray for all the *saints*', and so on, and he just means believers, the people of the church. Now zoom in on one vital word in verse 3: the word 'all'. Whose prayers are there with God? The people whose stories are in the Bible? Yes, but not only theirs. The heroes of the last 2,000 years? Yes, but that's not all. Your pastor's? Yes, but not just his. There are yours and mine as well: 'the prayers of all the saints'. God hears our prayers.

Do we feel that the Lord must be too busy to hear us—that in the midst of directing all the events of our history and while keeping billions of stars shining out in space, he could not possibly find the time? Look at this verse. Yes, even in the midst of all of that, he has time to hear from you, you saint! Does prayer seem like a lonely struggle, just you and the four walls around you? Turn to this verse, and see your prayers joined with millions of others as they go up before God.

One of the reasons we struggle with prayer is that we cannot see anything happening—our words are spoken, thought or sung, and they are gone. In Tibet, which I visited a few years ago, one of the most striking features of the landscape is that on every hilltop, in fact on nearly every housetop, there are clusters of little flags flying. Sometimes they are actually festooned across the hillsides. These brightly coloured squares of cloth are not some bizarre form of decoration; they are *prayer* flags. Every one has a prayer written on it; the idea is that it stays there, blowing in the wind, and as it flaps in the wind the prayer is wafted up to the gods. You go to the hilltops because that is closer to the gods. In the Buddhist monasteries, meanwhile, you find line upon line of prayer wheels which you are supposed to spin as you walk past, so that the prayers inscribed on the wheels will keep on being automatically recited as the wheels spin on after you have gone. People like that kind of idea because they can see something happening.

But we don't believe we can leave our prayers to be churned out on automatic! That makes it harder, because when Christians pray, there is nothing to see. We have to use our minds and our imagination to pray, not just hang up some bunting to flutter in the breeze. That is why it is so hard to persuade people to come to prayer meetings. You work hard to pray for an hour, but when you go home you don't feel sure that anything has really happened. It is much easier to sit around chatting. Even Bible study is a lot easier than prayer, because there is something to show for it. But Revelation 8 shows us what prayer looks like from heaven's perspective. This vision shows us clearly that our prayers *do* go up before God—not because they are wafted by Himalayan winds or spun by monks, not because we are super-spiritual, but because of the one who is there to receive them. We may wonder why the prayers are being processed by an angel. The angel is not a mediator, someone who stands between us and God; he is simply a servant, an agent. He is just there to stoke the fire.

A friend told me about the very first prayer she prayed. It was the middle of the night; she was in a hospital bed, and she prayed to a God who was completely unknown to her. She began her prayer: 'God, you don't know me, but you know my friend Jane.' Somehow she knew she needed a mediator. She was right about that, though actually the mediator is not called Jane; he is called Jesus! It is solely because of the Lord Jesus that sinners like us can approach a holy God and have him hear our prayers. That is why only the prayers of the *saints*, of Christian believers, are heard here—not anyone in the world who thinks they are praying, in a mosque or on a Tibetan hilltop. Those prayers do not come up before the throne. To see Jesus' place in this picture of prayer, look back at the end of chapter 7. The Lamb is there at the centre of the throne and he is interceding for the saints. God hears your prayers because you are in a love relationship with him. Terry Waite had never heard of Joy Brodier, who sent that postcard, but God has heard of you. Because of Jesus, you know *him*, and he hears your prayers.

God answers our prayers (8:5)

The NIV's translation 'hurled' in this verse is a little too strong—this is the ordinary word for throwing. But the picture is clear: the same angel who has placed our prayers in the fire on the incense altar and offered them up to God now comes and fills his censer with that fire and throws it down from heaven to earth, with dramatic results.

Now step back and look at these phenomena in verse 5: 'thunder, rumblings ... lightning ... earthquake'. We have met these already in 4:5. As John gets his first glimpse of the heavenly throne and the one who is seated there, he becomes aware that the scene is accompanied by these signs of God's majestic presence, the signs of theophany—for that is what they are. This is how God appeared at Sinai, in thunder and lightning, along with trumpet blasts so powerful that the earth shook. God's glory and majesty are presented in terms of the most dramatic and violent phenomena of nature. We meet them again here in chapter 8 and they appear twice more, in 11:19, at the end of the sequence of seven trumpets, and in 16:18, at the end of the seven bowls of God's wrath. In each of those cases they are to do with God establishing his final rule and majestic authority over the earth. The earthquakes and the hailstorms add to the picture when the action is taking place on earth; it would hardly be appropriate to visualize earthquakes and hailstorms in heaven! Taken together, they convey a sense of the devastating, holy majesty of the Godhead. Here in chapter 8, the same impression is being conveyed as a sort of prelude to the sounding of the seven trumpets. These awesome manifestations represent the power, majesty and glory of Almighty God being brought down from his throne to be displayed on the earth where we live. And it is the prayers of believers that bring that about.

This is extremely difficult for us to understand—not because the passage is unclear, but because the Bible never answers all our questions about prayer. The way God works through our prayers is a mystery, and always will be. But we can say for sure that through prayer God is involving us closely in his plans for the world. He could of course do everything without us. More than that, he knows exactly what he plans to do, and his plans always succeed. So he does not depend on our praying, or doing anything else. Yet in these verses we see our prayers bringing about God's work on the earth—his work of judgement, yes, but also his work of mercy. The seven trumpets are about both, as we shall see shortly.

God wants his people to pray so that we can play our full part in his plans, taking our places as his co-workers here on earth, seeing people saved, building his kingdom. The Lord told us to pray: 'Your will be done, on earth as it is in heaven.' This verse certainly brings the Lord's Prayer to life! If we do not pray, we miss out on that privilege. We remain mere spectators in the drama that is unfolding in our world, instead of taking our part as actors. In the last ten days, as I write this, I have twice been to the theatre and thoroughly enjoyed the shows I have watched. But I have only been a spectator; I certainly haven't been on the stage. I have done nothing whatever to influence the drama or to move the action forward. But in the kingdom of God, prayer does just that. In the kingdom, I don't want to be a spectator; I want to be part of God's action.

The Bible often urges us to pray. No doubt we have heard plenty of sermons and perhaps read many books about the vital importance of prayer to the Christian. Sometimes all that does is to induce guilt. But nowhere in the Bible are the cosmic consequences of our prayers seen as clearly as they are here. Our prayers don't disappear into the ether somewhere; they are offered on the heavenly altar and they rise up before God. Next time we struggle with our words, or prayer feels empty, think of this picture of how prayer is seen from heaven as our distant fumbling words are conveyed into God's very presence.

What is more, this vision should surely encourage us to pray *big* prayers. We are taking part in a cosmic drama which involves the eternal destiny of billions of people. Our prayers are being handled by mighty angels, being mixed with the fire of God and set ablaze.

Finally, it should encourage us to pray for the *world*. It has been well said that Revelation paints its picture of human history with a very large brush, but it also invites us to join in with the artist by praying for peoples and nations, and while the seven trumpets sound we shall help to shape their destinies as we pray the fire of God down into our world.

To discuss or think about

1. Do you sometimes struggle to believe that your prayers actually get through? Why do you think that might be? How does this vision help us here?
2. How can your prayer life reflect the truth we've looked at here: that our prayers are instrumental in taking God's purposes forward in the world?
3. Reflect on what this vision shows us about God's love for us as his people—his saints!

Part V
Seven trumpets: warning
(8:6–11:19)

Warnings that go unheard

Please read Revelation 8:6–9:21

In the early days of British television—a world that now seems very far away—if you turned on the television at any time of night and through a large part of the day, instead of seeing endless daytime soaps or repeats of makeover programmes, you used to see something called the test card. For younger readers, I should explain that the purpose of the test card was to enable you to make sure that your TV set was behaving itself properly. Back then, we didn't have automatic tuners, let alone remotes; we had to tune our televisions by twiddling little black buttons on the back. Watching TV was hard work in those days! Frequently the picture would be doing something strange: it would flicker, or race up and down, or sideways, or assume the appearance of a snowstorm.

But if you had the test card, you could make sure that you were properly tuned in. You could twist those buttons, adjust that aerial or—the one that always worked best for me—give the box a sharp bang on the side, until the colour on the card was perfect, the lines were straight and the lettering was legible. Then you would know that when the programmes eventually came on and your TV brought pictures of the outside world into your home, you would be receiving an accurate image, sharp and clear.

The point of the book of Revelation is just this. It gives us a test card to make sure that we are accurately tuned in—to see the world as God sees it. This is not a view that we see naturally. When we look out on the world, the view we usually see is distorted by interference from our sinful culture. It is discoloured by the lies that this world constantly feeds us and it is limited by our very human perspective. So it bears little resemblance to God's own perfect outlook. No wonder, then, that we find it so hard to grasp God's true attitude to this world: his reaction of holy wrath against sin, the love that sent Jesus down into the midst of it, the mercy that he has poured out on us and his passion for his own people. But Revelation gives us the true heavenly perspective—God's perspective—so that we can tune in and see our world and watch its story as he sees it. Revelation gives us this unique view of God's outlook, which, as faithful believers, we need to share. We can see how that works as we pause for a moment to look back over the earlier parts of the book.

A review of Revelation so far

Chapter 1—the prologue—is all about the man at the centre of history. The people who crucified him didn't think he was; the authorities who persecute the church today don't think so; most of our friends and acquaintances don't think so either; but God's perspective tells us that Jesus is just that. He is the one who stands at the centre and focus of this earth's story.

Then chapters 4 and 5 showed us the vision of heaven—a vision completely unseen by anyone who is tuned in to this world's TV channel. In this vision we see a throne at the centre, with one enthroned and surrounded by rank upon rank of creatures who know of no higher goal, no finer activity than to praise and worship him ceaselessly. Then we see the Lamb, the Lord Jesus Christ, opening the seven seals on that scroll that tells the story of the human race. He has the first word *and* the final word. All the way through that story in chapter 6 we see God's perspective, his take on our history. Then chapter 7, set among the opening of the seven seals, answers the question: 'Who are the most important people on earth?' We know who the world tells us they are: the most significant people are the great leaders, the political figures, the celebrities and the stars who are idolized. But that's not what God can see on his 'TV set'. No, because to God the most important people are *his* people, the church. That is why at the start of chapter 7 believers are shown being marked, protected against the dangers and the horrors of this world. Then at the end of chapter 7 we are shown as we shall be, gathered as one from every race and language around the throne to praise him for ever and ever with a single voice. Are we tuned in to that great vision?

When we come to the beginning of chapter 8, we see that in fact we are so important to God that all heaven waits while we pray. The seven angels are standing ready to blow the trumpets, and yet the action pauses while the Lord listens to, and answers, our prayers. Does the world see us like that? Of course not, but God does. In scene after scene through this book the Holy Spirit gently shows us: 'Never mind how the world looks to your human eyes, never mind how the rest of humanity sees you, this is how I see it; and this is how I want you to see it too.' Here is the test card. Let's get tuned in!

The vision of the seven trumpets

That brings us to the seven trumpets. There is a connection

with the prayers of the saints in 8:1–5, but it is not simply that believers are praying down judgement or wrath on the earth (remember how Jesus rebuked James and John for the suggestion of calling down heavenly fire on a village which rejected him—Luke 9:51–56). Nor, on the other hand, can we say that the saints are praying for wrath to be averted. The trumpets, as we shall see, combine judgement and grace. The prayers of 8:1–5 can best be understood as a pleading for God to intervene on the earth and act according to his majestic and perfect will.

Once again, as with the seals, there are six trumpets, then a long pause, while John is shown other visions, before the final trumpet is sounded. The language of these two chapters is among the most vivid even in Revelation, including locusts with women's hair, 200 million multi-coloured, fire-breathing horsemen, burning mountains, falling stars and a hail of blood. Reactions to this passage have tended to be extreme. Many Christians read one of these descriptions and think: 'I don't really understand this but it sounds a bit like ... That's what it must mean.' For instance, the locusts attacking people at the start of chapter 9 sound rather like aircraft—bombers, perhaps. The cavalry at the end of chapter 9 must be tanks with flame-throwers. It doesn't really fit, but it is the closest we can get. A classic example of this approach to Revelation came after the Chernobyl nuclear accident in 1986, when the word flew around the world that Chernobyl was the Ukrainian word for 'wormwood' and so the prophecy of the third trumpet had been fulfilled. It became a sort of Christian urban myth, in spite of the fact that '*chernobyl*' doesn't quite mean 'wormwood'[1] and the Chernobyl accident doesn't match up in any way—either in scale or in character—to the description here in 8:11.

As you probably know, there have been plenty of books, and preachers too, who have taken this kind of line. The best known in recent years is undoubtedly Hal Lindsey, who in 1970 published the book *The Late Great Planet Earth*, as well as others such as *The Apocalypse Code*—a title which makes his approach fairly obvious. So for Lindsey, the horses prepared for battle in chapter 9 are heavily armed attack helicopters. The crowns on the locusts are the helmets worn by helicopter pilots and, best of all, the red, blue and yellow of the riders' breastplates represent the Chinese national flag—which in fact has no blue in it at all!

Unless you are willing to suspend your critical faculties entirely, it quickly becomes obvious that trying to decode Revelation in this wooden kind of way simply doesn't work. And if you think that views like that don't matter, or can merely be laughed off, consider the fact that Lindsey was a personal adviser to President Ronald Reagan. Such a view of eschatology has had a significant influence on American foreign policy over the last few decades and it continues to do so. But the truth is that Hal Lindsey and others like him are asking the wrong questions of passages like this. We have already seen that reading Revelation like that makes it 100% irrelevant to 2,000 years of Christian history, because if Lindsey is right, no one who lived before the middle of the twentieth century would have had a clue as to what any of it meant. We don't need an 'apocalypse code' to make these images comprehensible in earthly terms. Revelation is not a code to be cracked. No, most of these apocalyptic visions tell us about events we are all too familiar with. We already know what they look like from the standpoint of earth. What the visions show us is how these events appear from heaven's perspective—on God's TV set, so to speak—and what they *mean*. If we persist in searching for earthly events which appear like the descriptions in this passage, we shall never get the point at all.

So what is happening in this vision? In chapter 6, the scroll was opened, stage by stage as the seals were broken, and the judgements of history unrolled on the earth. Those judgements can best be seen as the inevitable outworking of human sin, beginning with the Fall in Genesis 3, which left the ground cursed and disrupted the peaceful harmony of human relationships. That is at the root of all aggression, war, famine and death. Now, as we saw in chapter 7, the film of history has been rewound to the beginning, and with the trumpets we are going to view the same story all over again, but this time seen from a different angle. That is the way Revelation works. It shows repeats, but not like the channels on our televisions where we sit through the identical programme over and over again. In Revelation it is more like listening to a piece of music, a symphony, where the orchestra plays a theme and then a little later it recurs with fresh variations and additions. That may be a helpful way to think of it. So when we hear the trumpets blown, the underlying tune is the same as before, but new and different notes are now audible.

The distinctive note that the trumpets sound is *warning*. Throughout human history, through all the disasters and calamities that fall upon the earth, God is calling out a warning to the people who live here. But for the most part, the warnings go unheard; they are not heeded.

The text is full of clues which confirm that the seven trumpets represent warnings. First, trumpets in the Bible don't play in orchestras; they make announcements with a specific message (Numbers 10:1–7; 1 Corinthians 14:8). Second, this time, unlike with the seals, there is a distinction made between people who belong to God and those who do not. The difference is that those who belong to him don't need a warning, because our lives have already been given to him. Third, embedded in the story of the seven trumpets there are two very clear additional warnings about what is to follow. Finally, the end of chapter 9 makes it clear that the unbelieving world did not make the response to the trumpets' message that God was looking for. All this confirms that the seven trumpets are sounding warning notes.

The curse on creation (8:7–12)

Let us look at trumpets one to four, beginning in verse 7. It should be clear by now that we are not looking for some visual phenomenon that corresponds to hail, fire and blood raining down from heaven, any more than in chapter 6 there was a literal troop of four coloured horses. Even some of the best commentaries fall into this trap, but they are missing the point, which is to understand who is doing this and what the outcome is.

These first four trumpets, just like the four horsemen of chapter 6, come as a group. The first trumpet blast strikes the land and destroys the vegetation (8:7). The second one strikes the sea in a similar way (8:8–9). The third one strikes the fresh water, 'wormwood' being a kind of bitter-tasting plant (8:10–11). The use of the word here is not a forecast of the Chernobyl accident, but most probably an allusion to a pair of references in Jeremiah (Jeremiah 9:15; 23:15). The last of the four blots out the light (8:12). In each case the effects are partial: one third of the earth's natural resources, on which human life relies, is lost.

So what is going on here? Remember that the story has been wound back to the beginning. We have set out once more with a perfect earth, a pristine creation. Now, in this vision of the trumpets, one part at a time, the world's natural resources—its means of supporting life—are ruined. Humanity has done that. We started at the Fall, where creation was thrown out of joint by our sin, and ever since, not content with that, we have burned, polluted, poisoned and generally destroyed the world which the Lord commanded us to look after. So now we have a world where large areas are desert, and the deserts are spreading, the vegetation shrivelling. The sea is a place of storms and conflict, polluted and overfished. The wonderful creatures which God made to live there are dying out. Meanwhile our drinking water becomes undrinkable. Cities are darkened by smog. All of these scenes are killing people—less so in the pampered West, more so in other parts of the world. It is significant that, out of these four, it is the third trumpet that brings human deaths, because it is the loss of clean water that is the most certainly lethal. All these are getting worse. We probably haven't yet seen the full extent of these judgements, especially the fourth one, but they are becoming increasingly evident. With every passing year this earth becomes less able to sustain life.

Yet these verses are not an environmentalist's tract. The main point is not that we need to do a better job of looking after the world God gave us—though of course we do—but that God intends these environmental catastrophes to be warning signs to sinful humanity of much worse that is to follow. One third of the earth is affected: it is not complete loss, not annihilation. Most people's lives can still carry on as normal. These things are warnings that 33% can very easily rise to 100% if people do not turn back to God. Yes, we have brought these disasters on ourselves. They have been caused by rampant human sin. Exactly so. We have written out judgements for ourselves and God has responded by meting them out to us. They are sent down to our race as a *warning*. That is a measure of God's amazing grace: he is even willing to see his own perfect creation wrecked and ruined if it will wake people up to their rebellion against him, if it will get the message through that still more devastating judgement is following behind if they will not turn back to him. Is it a trivial matter that something so beautiful, so perfect, so intricate as this earth should be fouled and despoiled, and that the Creator should *allow* us to do it? From heaven's viewpoint, it is shocking. Read Psalm 104, with its lyrical, poetic descriptions of the Lord's delight in his world—its land, its waters, its living creatures—and then ask what horrible reason could possibly have led to his declaring a curse on it all. The answer is human sin.

It is a fourfold warning—warnings that stand written in the ashes of the Amazon forest, in the lifeless seas, in the rivers and wells poisoned by chemicals and in our polluted skies. Creation is cursed. The trumpets are sounding, stronger and stronger. Is the world listening?

Torment for the rebels

Trumpets five and six occupy most of chapter 9, but first look at 8:13. It is at this point that there is a decisive change. So far the warning judgements have had an impact on everyone equally. But from here on, it becomes personal. The eagle's bleak, triple message of 'woe' is for 'the inhabitants of the earth'. In Revelation, remember, that phrase has a very specific meaning. The 'inhabitants of the earth' are the people who feel at home here. This world is their home, and the last three trumpet blasts will strike those people, and those people only—and it is going to get worse.

If the descriptions in chapter 9 seem even more bizarre than those in chapter 8—and they undoubtedly do—there is a simple explanation. Chapter 8 described visions of the *natural* world, but now trumpets 5 and 6 relate to *spiritual* realities, which are that much harder to express in ordinary words.

Trumpet five: the locusts (9:1–11)

First, we have the locusts from the Abyss. A gigantic swarm of locusts rises from the depths, the pit unlocked for them by a fallen star. In the Bible the 'Abyss' is where the demons live. The fallen star, it seems clear, refers to Satan, the angel whose fall from the heavens to the pit is alluded to in Isaiah 14:12–15 (though the immediate reference is to the fall of Babylon).[2] He is permitted—strictly under God's sovereign control—to open the Abyss and release the unimaginable swarm of his demons onto the earth.

The reason they are pictured as locusts is very simple, I think.

Locusts are destroyers; what is more, there is nothing like locusts for making people's lives utterly miserable. Locusts sweep through and destroy everything in their path. If you rely on the land for your living, as nearly everyone did when John was writing, you would be ruined. In the book of Joel a real locust invasion is used to warn people of God's judgement on the land of Israel. Joel too spoke of locusts which had 'lions' teeth' (9:8) and were like horses going into battle (Joel 1:6; 2:4), but here God's judgement on the wicked is represented as a swarm of *demonic* locusts, strange, mutated and, as we read on to verse 10, far more terrible than mere insects. And their 'king' (9:11) is Satan again, now named as 'Abaddon', or 'Apollyon', the destroyer (the names are derived respectively from the Hebrew and Greek verbs meaning 'to destroy')—an appropriate name for the lord of the locusts. The duration of their activity, 'five months' (9:10), is just as symbolic as their appearance. It approximates to the length of a growing season and presumably represents a limited but devastating time span.

Yet there is something very strange about these locusts' behaviour. They are not to eat any of the vegetation, but only to sting human beings (9:4), to hurt them so that their lives become total misery. Even then they have to be selective. It is now that the mark that was placed on God's own people, back at the start of chapter 7, finally comes into play. God's people are wonderfully immune from the sting of the locusts.

All right, we ask, when does this terrible event take place? Are we going to see a vast smoking pit open up somewhere and hordes of flying creatures emerge? Again, no we are not. This is not what it will look like from the standpoint of earth; this is the view from *heaven*. This has already happened. With human eyes we cannot perceive them, but from his vantage point in heaven John sees the skies full of them. Satan's hordes are at work across the earth now, today, destroying people's lives, inciting them to commit appalling crimes against one another, making life utterly miserable for millions, holding them captive in false religions. In this fallen world Satan is being allowed to have his fling, and meanwhile the Lord's people are protected. This does not mean that we are protected against every evil—we know that—but we are protected from Satan's direct assault.

Just as the Lord did for Job, so he does for us. He says to Satan, 'This far and no further.' Job had more than his share of suffering, but the Lord brought him through to praise him at the end of it all (Job 42:1–6). He does that for us who have been sealed with his mark. He doesn't do it for the unbelieving world. To them, their suffering is aimless, endless, pointless, miserable. Yet, in God's merciful purposes, it gives them one more warning. They still have the chance to respond. As C. S. Lewis so memorably put it, 'God whispers to us in our pleasures, speaks in our conscience, but shouts in our pains: it is his megaphone to rouse a deaf world.'[3] For so many suffering people, the agonizing sting of torment in their lives has been God's megaphone to end their rebellion and turn their hearts to him.

Trumpet six: the horses and their riders (9:13–19)

Trumpet six brings cavalry from the east (9:13–16). Again we see that these are no ordinary horses (9:17–19); again they are led by fallen angelic beings (we know they are fallen because they are described as 'bound'). Yet they are fully subject to the Lord's sovereignty: it is the voice from the altar that commands their release. The number of horsemen is vast: the total of 200 million is not one of those symbolic numbers; it is simply so huge that it dwarfs any human army in history.

There are two key differences from the locusts which have preceded them. First, these cavalry can kill. Second, in this case a specific point of time is in view—notice the strong emphasis in verse 15. It is a specific time; we just don't know when it is. But, unlike the other warning trumpets which sound all through history, this sixth one must therefore refer to a single event at the end of days. The same happened with the sixth seal—that brought in the Judgement Day. And the same happens in close parallel when the sixth of the bowls is poured out in chapter 16: the river Euphrates is dried up and the battle of Armageddon is launched.

Revelation pictures the great climactic events of the close of history from different camera angles, and from this angle, even the onset of the last battle is seen as one final warning to the peoples of the world. There may be only minutes to go—the last battle won't last long; it will be too one-sided for that—but in God's grace even those few last, hectic moments will give a final chance to repent and turn to him. Even as the battle begins to rage, even as God's enemies are swallowed up, the torment is an opportunity for the rebels to repent—one final warning.

Warnings that go unheeded (9:20–21)

Yet, tragically, the warnings by and large go unheeded. The people do not repent; they do not give up their false religions; they do not give up on their sin. In verses 20–21 you can count off at least five of the Ten Commandments, though the foundational commandment that they break is not mentioned directly: 'You shall have no other gods before me.' They refuse to acknowledge him. After thousands of years of warnings, after chance after chance to turn to our loving Lord, still they will not hear his gracious voice. They close their ears to the warnings.

The challenges to us

As we reach the end of this chapter, we must hear the challenges it poses.

The first is for non-Christians. Will you hear the warnings and turn to Christ, or still persist in refusing him? Throughout your life, you have heard warning after warning. All that is happening in the world, with all the very real suffering and pain in your own life, should scream at you that something is wrong, that there is a God you must deal with—a God who is longing for you to come to your senses, stop your futile struggle against him and embrace his love. If the trumpets frighten you into turning to Christ, they will have done their job.

The second is for Christians. Can you see what is really happening in the world? Have you got your TV set properly tuned? The Bible shows us what the news bulletins do not. It shows us what our mere human eyes could never see. We live in a world that is dominated by evil forces that hurt people. We have an implacable enemy who wants nothing more than to ruin people's lives—and that is exactly what he is doing.

We need to understand what this world is like for us. John writes this book, not to the unbelieving world, but for the persecuted church. We should not expect to be accepted or understood—these closing verses prove to us that many, many people will never accept us or our message. When persecution comes we should not be surprised: it is normal. The Lord has sealed us with his mark so that we can survive and serve him in this world—until the day when he takes us to stand before his throne.

But although this world is hostile, although it hates our God and will often hate us, this passage reminds us yet again who is really in charge. It is not the random forces of nature; it is our God. It is not Satan and his demonic locust hordes or his all-conquering cavalry, but the one who lent him the key, the one whose awesome voice calls, 'Release them!' It is the Lord who, in his incredible grace, is sounding the warnings to the peoples of the earth. Our Lord, who reached out to save us, will bring all his people safely through. We shall not feel the sting of Satan and his demons; the powers of the Abyss cannot touch us. Even death has lost its sting for us! The 200 million will not sweep us away. Our God is still in charge, and he will keep us.

To discuss or think about

1. How can we avoid simply seeing our world through the eyes of the media? How can we see it more as the Lord does?
2. If you have been used to reading Revelation in the way that looks for visible and literal fulfilment of these visions, has this chapter helped you to see it from a different point of view? Whatever your own background, do you think the approach set out in this book is fair to Scripture?
3. Are you willing to face rejection and hostility from people who refuse God's warnings to the world?

9

The Word of God—sweet and sour

Please read Revelation 10

On 16 October 1987, southern England was hit by a hurricane. It was only a little one—in fact, officially it was not a hurricane at all—but it blew in, as it were, out of nowhere, with hardly any warning. It was terrifying enough, if you were living in Kent or Sussex, as I was at the time. Friends of ours there seriously thought the world was coming to an end. There, in the wild darkness of that early Friday morning, they thought that this was the beginning of the Lord's return.

But what will it really take to bring the end of the world? Hurricanes and tsunamis are terrible if you are caught in the middle of them, and yet they are not the end of the world. There are all kinds of events, natural and man-made, that people around the world live in fear of. Will it be nuclear war that finally spells the end? Or will it be environmental catastrophe, brought about by human selfishness? Is human history one day going to fizzle out as a result of runaway global warming? All of those things may happen, but according to the Bible they are not what will determine the end. As believers, we know that it is God who will declare when the end comes. But when will he bring it, and what has to happen first? Is it something the angels have to do? There seem to be a lot of angels in this book, after all. No, it is not that either. The answer is a surprising one. Revelation 10 tells us that the world will be brought to an end by you and me and a little book—a little book called the Word of God. When its work is done—its sweet and sour work—the end will come.

Chapters 8 and 9 brought us through the warnings of the trumpets—trumpets one to six, because number seven is still to come. Just as there was a gap between numbers six and seven when the seals were being opened in chapter 7, so now we have an interlude between *trumpets* six and seven. In the midst of all the disasters that followed the unsealing and opening of the scroll, we saw the church being kept safe for glory. That was the message in chapter 7. Now in chapters 10 and 11 we have another interlude, and it fits in the same way. In the midst of all the disasters that follow the seven trumpets, what is going on with the church? The answer is that the church is not just sitting around watching. Yes, we are secure. Yes, we have a glorious future. But we are not just waiting for glory. We have a job to do. In fact, we have the task of bringing the world to an end!

The vision of the angel (10:1–4)

As we launch into the vision of chapter 10, John seems to be looking from the vantage point of earth. He sees the awesome sight of a gigantic angel (10:1). If you read the description of this angel and compare it with the rest of Revelation, especially 1:15–16, you will realize that his appearance is very similar to the way that Christ himself is described. A few commentators have even thought that this vision *is* of Christ, but that seems very unlikely because he cannot be described as an angel, however powerful. Rather, the angel's awesome appearance expresses the fact that he is Christ's representative, sharing something of his dazzling glory, the fiery brightness and the majestic voice of authority, along with the rainbow of God's faithfulness and the cloud of his majesty. To emphasize his might and stature, he has one foot planted in the sea and another squarely on the land. In fact, the splendour of this angel serves to show how great *God* is. Here is this figure of staggering power and might, and yet he is not even named. He is simply 'another mighty angel'. Apparently, our God has plenty more of those at his beck and call! If this is the messenger boy, what must the one who sent him be like?

Along with many of the other angels we see in Revelation, this one has the task of introducing a new phase of God's plan (10:3–4). This seems very strange. What are the seven thunders? What do they say? And why are we not allowed to know? Thunder in Scripture often represents the voice of God and his authority (Job 40:9). So the seven thunders presumably represent another cycle, another camera angle on history unfolding, like the seals and the trumpets. Beyond that, there is not much that we can say, but that is just the point. God knows everything that is going to happen; we don't. We can know exactly as much about God and his plans as he chooses to reveal to us. If he does not tell us, then no amount of speculation will get us anywhere.

In fact there is a pointed message here for people who are too keen on figuring out the details of the end times—because here we see that God has deliberately not given us some of the vital clues! We don't know how long it will be before the end; we don't know exactly when Christ will return. 'Do not write it down', John is told. It is a reminder to us: don't try to be too clever.

The completion of God's plans (10:5–7)

But the angel is not here only to provoke the mysterious thunders to speak. There is something in his hand. Presumably it will be something matching his powerful appearance—a few lightning bolts, perhaps, to go with the thunder, or an atom bomb or two. But no. Instead this glorious figure is 'holding a little scroll' (10:2). It is a booklet! Unlike the scroll in chapter 5, this one is opened up for anyone to read. It doesn't sound at all significant, but apparently it is. If the thunders spoke what will remain secret until the end, this little scroll speaks God's words openly and clearly for all to read, for all to hear. The angel has brought it with him for a very good reason. It turns out that the contents of this little scroll, this booklet, are closely tied up with the timing of the end (10:5–7).

The oath is as solemn as it can be, in the name of the living God (another demonstration that the angel cannot be identified with Christ). The one who created the heavens and the earth has every right to choose when to finish it. As Creator, he knows exactly what he is doing. Now the angel says, 'There will be no more delay!' God is bringing everything to its conclusion: this world will not carry on in its present form for ever. When the seventh angel has sounded his trumpet, it will signal the end.

Just by the way, the Authorized (or King James) Version translates verse 6: '... that there should be *time* no longer' (emphasis added). From this some Christians have the strange idea that heaven will be timeless, which is not what the Bible says and would not make sense at this point anyway. The closing chapters of Revelation are quite clear that, although the heavenly city will be a place of permanent bliss and perfection, there will also be events and actions there. For there to be a succession of events, there must necessarily be the passage of time. In this world, time inevitably brings decay: order degenerates into chaos. Physicists call this the Second Law of

Thermodynamics. But in the perfect age to come, there will be no such thing as decay. The angel in this vision is saying, 'No more *delay*; the end is coming.'

The end is described like this: 'The mystery of God will be accomplished, just as he announced to his servants the prophets.' What does that mean? The word translated 'announced' is the same word that everywhere else means 'preached the gospel'. That tells us what the 'mystery' is. In the Bible, a 'mystery' is not a sort of Agatha Christie detective story where you have to try to puzzle out the ending. Rather, it is something previously hidden that has now been revealed. This 'mystery' is God's great plan of salvation, which was hidden until Christ came to earth and put it into action. The 'mystery', as Paul describes it in Ephesians 3:2–6 and in Romans 16:25–27, is that God is creating a new humanity in Christ—not just Jews, but men and women from *every* nation, united in Christ, with every dividing barrier broken down.

This is the mystery of God. It means that God has been following the *same* plan through the whole of history and all the way through Scripture. There is no 'Plan A' and 'Plan B' with God. He is still on Plan A, and it is right on track. The promises he gave to the very first prophets, to Adam, to Noah and to Abraham, have not been forgotten or changed. They are fulfilled in Christ. The end comes when the mystery is 'accomplished'—that is, when the full number of God's people have been brought in through Christ. That is what the angel now declares. To finish the story, to complete God's plan for mankind, the gospel has to be heard in every place, by every people. That is what the little scroll is—the Word of God, and specifically the gospel message, the good news of God's rescue plan through Jesus.[1]

That is where God's people come in! This is the part that the angels simply cannot do. Angels are very good at carrying God's messages. They are perfectly equipped for offering incense, blowing trumpets and making announcements. But they cannot go and tell their friends what Jesus has done for them; only we can do that. This is where spectating ends and taking part begins.

The command to John (10:8–11)

Imagine yourself at a great sporting event—perhaps the conclusion of an Ashes cricket series (apologies if you can't stand cricket—I love it!). You have been there all day in the crowd. You have been gripped by the action as the runs have been scored and the wickets have tumbled. Now at last, victory is in sight. Already you can see that victory parade in your mind's eye. Suddenly, the England captain walks towards the crowd. In fact he is coming right towards the section of the stands where you are sitting. He has the ball in his hand, and as the crowd falls silent he points directly at you and calls you out. 'Here, I need you to come on and bowl a few overs. We've got to get these last two Australian wickets. We've got to close out this victory.' In a daze you step out onto the playing surface. You take the ball from the captain; and all the time the thought is running through your mind: 'What can *I* possibly do to win this match? If those other guys can't finish off, what can I do?'

Now that is exactly how John is feeling here. So far he has been a spectator. Yes, he has been moved to tears (5:4) and has exchanged a few words with one of the minor players (7:13–14), but he has been a spectator. At most he has been like a reporter taking notes on what he is seeing and hearing: amazing scenes played out by angels, visions of the throne room of heaven and even of the Lamb of God himself. It has been wonderful, awe-inspiring, gripping and, yes, it has been a message of hope and comfort to take back to a church under tremendous pressure. Most recently he has just heard this solemn declaration that the end is coming. The victory procession is ready to set off with no further delay.

But now, suddenly, at the height of the action, a voice from heaven speaks to him (10:8). 'John, yes you, John, you see that little book that the angel is holding? Go and take that scroll. John, it's up to you now.' 'What, me? Can't these mighty angels finish it off? If they can't bring it to an end, what can I possibly do? Can't they do it?' 'No, they can't. Angels may be powerful, but they are not part of the salvation story. You are! They cannot preach the gospel. But you can! They cannot teach your church. They cannot talk to your friends about Jesus like you can. It is up to you and that little book.'

So John steps out of the stands and onto the playing surface. 'Take it and eat it. It will turn your stomach sour, but in your mouth it will be as sweet as honey' (10:9). So he does, his mind no doubt turning over God's very similar command to another exiled prophet about 680 years before (Ezekiel 2:9–3:3). He goes to the great angel, takes the little scroll and eats it—a picture of digesting and absorbing God's Word and its message, internalizing it, as we would say (10:10–11). It turns out just as he has been told. The message of salvation tastes wonderful; it tastes sweet. It is good news for everyone who knows it. But the gospel is not just for us to believe; it is for us to *tell*. And proclaiming the message, telling it out, is not so easy, not so sweet. The gospel has some very bad news before we get to the good news. The gospel can have a very bitter taste, a very sour taste, when it is rejected, when people hate you for mentioning it. But John ingests it, both the sweet and the sour, and now he is ready to play his part.

This is the climax of the vision—not the mighty angel, so vast that he straddles land and sea, but the booklet he holds in his hand. It is more powerful than the angel is! Not the seven thunders with their concealed message, but that John must speak the Word of God while there is still time—*that* is the point of the vision, and *that* is what will bring the world to an end. In the whole book of Revelation this is the one thing that John is told to go home and *do*. Apart from that, he just has to record what he sees. But here, at this one point, he is told not to remain a spectator, not to stay in the stands: 'When these visions are finally over, John, your task is not to go and sit back and enjoy the memory, nor even just to celebrate the glorious truth that God is in charge and we are on the winning side. No, your job is to play your part. Your job is to join the match and actually to win the victory.'

John is not exactly in the first flush of youth. In all probability he is at least ninety years old. He must be tempted to think he has had his day, his task is done. Hasn't he been a faithful church leader all these years? Didn't he write a Gospel and hasn't he endured exile? He has been preaching God's Word all his life, which is why he has been sent to Patmos in the first place. To cap it all, here he is scribbling down all these visions for later publication! He is the last apostle left. Hasn't he done enough?

No, John, you have not finished yet. Before the story ends, before Christ can return, you and many people like you have to take the message that was in the scroll and proclaim it across the world: 'You must prophesy again about many peoples [and] nations'; in fact it can equally well be translated 'against' those peoples and nations. The message will not go down very well much of the time—that is part of the sour taste that the gospel has. But they must all hear it—'peoples, nations, languages and kings'.

We don't know when Jesus is coming back. But the clearest clue Scripture gives us is just this, in Jesus' own words: 'And this gospel of the kingdom will be preached in the whole world as a testimony to all nations, and then the end will come' (Matthew 24:14). So here is the message for tired preachers, children's workers, youth leaders: 'Keep going! Keep up your confidence in the Word of God, whether today it tastes sweet to you or sour.' This is what it means to be a faithful servant of Jesus. This is what he asks you to do. The one thing you can do to finish off the victory is to preach the Word, in season and out of season, so that the gospel is heard by everyone.

You know, we can get through life at church, or in a university Christian Union, as spectators. We can stay in the stands and enjoy watching the action. But that is not what we are called to. The stands are the comfort zone. That is not where the Lord wants you. Here is the message for every believer, old or young. John was around ninety. Personally I praise God for the example of my own parents, who as I write are in their late nineties and still active in ministry, as I pray that I will be if I reach that age. The church is not a retirement home!

The victory is secure. It is not a tantalizing struggle that will remain on a knife-edge until the very end. Jesus has won the victory already—but it is up to us as believers to finish it off. We are not here to congratulate ourselves on being part of the elect, simply to look forward to heaven, or to be spectators looking on from the stands. We are called to take this little book in our hands, digest its message and tell it out—until he returns. And when we have finished, he will.

To discuss or think about

1. Have you ever thought about the connection between us proclaiming the gospel and the end of the world? What part do you have to play in telling out the message in the little scroll?
2. How do you look forward to your own later life? Do you think growing old as a Christian should involve retirement from active ministry?

10

The Word of God—unstoppable

Please read Revelation 11

I am sure many of us have had the experience that I call 'spare-part syndrome'. You have bought your new self-assembly piece of furniture, or your new lawnmower, or whatever it might be, and you take it home and eagerly start putting it together. Obviously, if you are male, you won't have done anything so foolish as to read the instructions at this stage! Finally, you get to the end of the process and you call people in to admire. Then someone says, 'Hang on! What's that bit there?' Sure enough, there is a part left over. It is still lying on the floor. It is typically small, metallic, with a hole in one end and a sort of flange at the other—and you don't have a clue what it is for! So what are you going to do with the spare part? Perhaps there is a little gap you can push it into. Or if you bend it into a different shape, it might just go where you need it. What job is it supposed to do anyway? And if you do just quietly drop it into the bin and forget about it, will you ever actually miss it?

That is the parable of the spare part. And in my parable, the spare part represents the church. This world does not know what to do with the church. It exists, but it is like a spare part that simply will not fit in. It is here, but what is it for? If we got rid of it, would we miss it? The rulers and authorities in this world try to make the church into all sorts of things that it is not. They either try to squeeze it into a convenient gap, or they want to bend it into a different shape for their own convenience, or else they want to get rid of it altogether. Look at the story of the UK, for instance. In the 1980s the Thatcher government wanted the church to prop up society by being a strong moral voice and keeping the masses in line. The church then was told off for being too soft on the poor. New Labour, which followed, said the church was nice and lined it up with the other 'faith communities' that all have the same wonderful, universal values to teach us—as long as you don't claim there is anything unique about your message. The recent Coalition government has urged the re-assertion of Britain's Christian character, while increasingly denying Christians the right to live out their faith publicly. In America, the church finds herself invited to dinner with presidents of both parties. The picture is similar in many African countries. Meanwhile in many other places, the church is hounded to death. The spare part can be dropped quietly in the bin and forgotten. We don't need the church.

But what does the Bible say? The Bible tells us that the church is not here for the government to use to enforce its policies. It is not here tamely to teach people universal morals alongside other religions, or to reinforce American values. In fact no government has the right to tell the church to do anything at all. Revelation 11 shows us why the church is here—to be a faithful witness to our Saviour, on *his* terms, whatever the cost, and to preach the unstoppable word of God.

In chapter 11 we are still in the interlude between the sixth and seventh trumpets, the trumpets blown by angels which represent God's warning blasts of judgement on the earth. This chapter expands and explains the instruction at the end of chapter 10 to proclaim the gospel of Christ around the world. I have to admit that it is among the hardest chapters of Revelation to understand. Not surprisingly, then, it has generated probably the widest-ranging and most far-fetched interpretations of the whole book. Who on earth are these two witnesses who are also trees and lampstands, with built-in flame-throwers besides? What is this mysterious city that seems to be Sodom, Egypt and Jerusalem at the same time? However, we *can* understand it. Once again, the key to understanding Revelation is not a theology doctorate but simply a sound knowledge of the rest of Scripture, especially the Old Testament.

Difficult questions

We shall start by trying to tackle some of these more tricky questions.

1. What is meant by the temple?

First, what is this 'temple' that John is told to measure? (11:1). Is it the temple in Jerusalem, or something else? It can hardly be the physical Jerusalem temple, since that had been thoroughly demolished about twenty-five years before John is writing. There are no worshippers to count, and there is little point in putting the tape measure over a pile of rubble. The New Testament never says that the temple will be rebuilt. The temple's days ended with the ministry of Jesus, when at the moment of his death the curtain was torn in two. That means this temple must be symbolic.

2. What are the two cities?

In the same way, the 'holy city' in verse 2 is not Jerusalem, which lost its claim to be the holy city when it rejected Christ.[1] No, in this vision we have a picture, where the Jerusalem temple is used to represent God's people, the church. The 'holy city' in Revelation is the *new* Jerusalem (see 21:2,10), and God no longer lives in a temple but in his people's hearts. In the old temple, the outer court was where the Gentiles were permitted to come. But after the coming of Christ the great divide is not between Jews and Gentiles, but between the church and the world, between Christians and everyone else. So here, once more, that language of 'Jews versus Gentiles' is used to stand for 'church versus world', just as the New Testament sometimes does elsewhere (see Galatians 6:16 and also the letters to Smyrna and Philadelphia in chapters 2 and 3). So the temple stands for the church, and the holy city for the new Jerusalem; then in verse 8 we come across a second city, 'the great city'. As we go on from this point in Revelation, we shall see that these two cities are the two rival centres of all humanity. Everyone lives in one of these two cities, the 'holy city' or the 'great city'.

3. What do the numbers mean?

In this chapter we have periods of forty-two months, 1,260 days and three and a half days. To understand these we need to look at Daniel 12:5–7, which comes right at the end of a series of very baffling visions. Daniel himself was certainly baffled! But notice that the 'man clothed in linen' sounds very similar to the mighty angel we met in Revelation 10. For a detailed description, look at Daniel 10:5–6, where you will see that the two tally very closely. Again, he reaches up to heaven and swears in the name of the one who lives for ever in a strikingly similar gesture to the one we read of here. But in Daniel the angel is looking ahead through the period of time before prophecy is finally fulfilled, and that period is described symbolically as 'time, times and half a time'—in other words, three and a half *years*. That also works out as forty-two months, and forty-two months of thirty days make a total of 1,260 days (a period we shall find mentioned several more times in succeeding chapters). What is it that happens at the end of that time? Look at Daniel 12:7: 'When the power of the holy people has finally been broken, all these things will be completed.' In other words, when God's people are defeated, we have arrived at the end. That fits right in with Revelation 11.

4. Who are the two witnesses?

This time the background is in Zechariah 4. Again it is a rather baffling vision; again there is a conversation with an angel and there are two olive trees and a lampstand. The oil that flows from the olive trees to the lampstand seems to represent the Holy Spirit at work and flowing through his people. Now John knows his Old Testament well and, as the Lord shows him these visions, all these pictures, with all that they stand for, will flood into his mind. Let us put it all together. From Daniel, we have a long period of time, symbolically labelled as 1,260 days, that runs up to the defeat of God's people. From Zechariah, we have two faithful servants of God, empowered by his Spirit—the olive trees and lampstands. Put that together with the meaning of the temple and the holy city, and it should become clear. Remember that this whole section of Revelation is about God, all through history, warning the world by means of the trumpets. So the witnesses stand for the faithfully witnessing church of Christ down through the years, all the way from Jesus' ascension on to his Second Coming. The 1,260 days represent the full extent of this 'gospel age'. The whole of verses 1–14 is about the church in the world—the church that the world treats as a spare part.

Now, having clarified these difficult issues, we can delve further into the text. Assuming that we will indeed get up out of the spectators' seats, eat the scroll and proclaim the Word, what happens when we do?

The church protected (11:1–2)

John is given a metre rule, or a yardstick if you prefer, and told to measure the temple and the worshippers. We are not given the results, not even in symbol form. The point is that the measurements are made; the count is taken. God knows how many people on earth belong to him. This is a reminder of what we saw at the beginning of chapter 7, where God's people on earth are sealed with a special mark to show that they are his. So, even while the unbelieving world, the 'Gentiles' of verse 2, are trampling on the city of God, even while they despise the church and attempt to tread us down into the dirt, God's own people are kept safe. He knows exactly how many of us are his, and he will not let go of a single one of us.

The church commissioned (11:3–4)

Those first two verses were a quick reminder of one of the key themes of Revelation: that the Lord is going to look after us, however deep the darkness may become. But the main point of this vision is about what we are called to *do*. Now there have been an astonishing range of suggestions for the identity of these two figures, all the way from Joshua and Caleb to Jesus and John the Baptist via most other pairs of biblical characters you care to mention. Others, like the books in the *Left Behind* series, suggest that they are literally two men who appear at the end of the age and stand at a particular location and speak. They also breathe fire. On the basis of that kind of literal interpretation, you might just as well say they are literally two trees.

All these ideas are misguided and they make the vision irrelevant for the great majority of history. No, these verses are simply a call to the whole church to speak God's Word.

Taking away the strange imagery for a moment, you see this is exactly the same as what John is told to do at the end of chapter 10: to prophesy to the whole earth—that is, to speak God's Word *faithfully*. Obviously John is not expected to do that all by himself. This vision shows him that he will not be alone. Probably another reason that he is shown *two* witnesses, rather than one or seven, or some other number, is that in the Jewish law two witnesses were required to prove a case. The evidence of one was not sufficient. The 'sackcloth' is there because the message is solemn and serious, and it calls for repentance. The gospel, as we saw in chapter 10, is sour as well as sweet.

So this is what the church is here for. It is not here for any of those purposes that world governments try to force upon it. It is here to be lampstands, shining the light of our pure and blameless lives into a dark world; to be olive trees, standing firm, with the oil of the Holy Spirit flowing through us; and to prophesy—to speak out God's Word faithfully, even when the world attacks us. This is our commission.

The church defended (11:5–6)

The two witnesses stand for the whole of the church and, just as we do not literally appear as trees or lampstands, these verses too need to be understood as part of the symbolic language. We should not see this passage as suggesting that the church is eager for retribution; in Scripture, vengeance is always left to the Lord (Romans 12:19, quoting Deuteronomy 32:35). In verse 5 we see the inevitable consequences of opposing the Word of God. So God says to Jeremiah, for example, 'I will make my words in your mouth a fire and these people the wood it consumes' (Jeremiah 5:14). God's Word is unstoppable; ultimately, anyone who refuses it is writing and signing his own death warrant. Suddenly the church doesn't seem quite so 'nice' after all. In the Bible the church is anything but 'nice'.

In verse 6, the rain and the plagues clearly allude to the ministry of Elijah and Moses, who *literally* brought drought and a plague of blood. The point is to show that, just as those calamities were used by God then to shock the world and save his people, so he will use all sorts of events now to *warn* the world and *protect* his people. God is well able to send or divert storms in answer to prayer; sometimes he does. He has a whole range of weapons in his armoury; and those who set out to refuse his Word and to crush the true church are asking for trouble.

You can see this working out in history when you look at some of the great persecutions. One less familiar example is Louis XIV of France, the so-called Sun King, one of the most arrogant and terrible persecutors that Europe has ever seen. In France the Protestant church, the Huguenots, were protected by the Edict of Nantes, which guaranteed them religious freedom for ever. But in 1685 Louis XIV revoked the Edict of Nantes. At least 200,000 Protestants were scattered across Europe; many of them came to Britain. Many thousands more (including a couple of my own ancestors) were massacred in the most barbaric ways. In most parts of France the Protestant church was wiped off the map. But Louis spent the rest of his life in futile wars. He died, bitter and exhausted, in 1715. Later in that same century France collapsed in the bloodbath of the revolution, in which the French monarchy effectively disappeared, while in England God gave us Wesley and Whitefield, two faithful witnesses if ever there were.

Kings touch the church at their peril. What happened to the twentieth century's greatest persecutors, Stalin and Mao? Obviously, both are long dead, but what has happened to their memory? Stalin is reviled and Mao's legacy is fast receding, while the Chinese church grows towards a hundred million strong. So while individual believers suffer and die—and they still do suffer in great numbers in the former Soviet Union and in China—the church is defended. God's Word is not silenced; it is unstoppable.

The church overwhelmed (11:7–10)

All through history there have been great attacks on the church. Sometimes we hear people say, 'What we need is a bit of persecution.' Can I suggest that we *don't* say that until we know what it feels like? It is not something we should ever look for. There have been times, as with France in the seventeenth century, when persecution succeeded all too well. It happened right across north Africa when Islam swept through in the seventh century and many of the great early centres of Christianity were simply obliterated. That is part of the pattern of history, but these verses describe a single terrible event at the end of time, when the church falls under unprecedented attack and to all appearances is killed off completely.

This is a shock after all that we have read about God protecting and caring for his people. The onslaught is led by the beast from the Abyss whom we will meet further on in the book. But see how people react. That familiar phrase, 'the inhabitants of the earth' (11:10), is an important one in Revelation. It means everyone who is at home in the 'great city' (11:8). This is the city which stands against the City of God, the great city which contains every power and impulse that opposes him: the spirit of Sodom, notorious for its sexual licence (Genesis 19), but equally for its injustice to the poor (Ezekiel 16:49); the spirit of Egypt, where God's people were captives; and also the spirit of Jerusalem, which rejected and crucified the Lord.

So now in the main street of this city lie the corpses of God's faithful witnesses. The inhabitants throw a party, delighted that the church has gone. Men and women 'from every people, tribe, language and nation' are celebrating. It is a sort of *anti*-church mimicking the every-nation breadth of the real church. At last the world has found something it can agree about. Do you think the church is meant to be popular? Not at all. From Islamist militants right through to Western liberals writing in their newspaper columns, people all over the world today would be thrilled if we disappeared. The true church, the *faithful* church, has always 'tormented' the world (11:10). The church that refuses to be twisted or petted, that will not retreat to its private ghetto or stick to talking about 'values', that truly preaches Christ, has always been hated by the world, and it always will be.

The church resurrected (11:11–14)

But now see what happens. Three and a half days pass—just a short time, compared with the three and a half *years* that represent the full span of the church's ministry. The world's triumph does not last long. Before their terror-struck eyes, the witnesses are restored to life and summoned from earth up to heaven (11:12). We have not lost after all. The gates of hell do not prevail. The church will go down for a while, but God's purposes and his Word never fail. The world that gloated over the church's death now recognizes that its punishment is approaching. The earthquake underlines the moment that normal history has come to its end.[2] The earth is shaken, with people running in all directions in panic (cf. 6:12–17). The survivors glorify God—finally! But this is no mass conversion, no scene of joy. It is too late for that. The church has gone; her witness is taken away; the final warning blast has faded off into the sound of chaos. This is described as a 'woe' (11:14), because it is only with terror that the inhabitants of the earth now acknowledge the Lord, not as their Saviour, but as their Judge.

The seventh trumpet (11:15–19)

Now at last, after this long interlude, the seventh trumpet is sounded (11:15). This is the moment when the age-long prayer,

'Your kingdom come', is finally answered! In the light of the rest of the chapter, this verse is very pointed. The world that set itself up so proudly, so defiantly, against the Lord and against his church is gone in a flash. Instead, the kingdom that has grown slowly and quietly, suffered patiently and witnessed so faithfully to its King, is established for ever, and our King takes his rightful throne. In heaven, the elders fall down and worship; they praise God that, at long last, he has set everything to rights. There is a sense of relief that God is acting decisively for the final time and that his infinite power will now be seen for what it is, and this terrible discordance in the world, where evil has been permitted to have its day, is being terminated.

Then, in verse 18, the meaning of God's decisive act is spelled out, both the wonderful and the terrible aspects. In words which clearly recall the warnings of Psalm 2, the elders say, 'The nations were angry; and your wrath has come.' The oppressors are judged; God's people from every age ('prophets' and 'saints') are rewarded; those who 'destroy the earth' (all those who have added to the moral ruination of the Fall) are themselves destroyed. Now the unchallengeable reign of God begins.

Verse 19 brings this whole section to a close with a glimpse into God's very presence, no longer veiled by barriers and curtains, as the earthly temple was. The ark of the covenant stands first and foremost for God's faithful presence with his people, and that is just what chapter 11 has clearly demonstrated. However hard the days may seem, especially the days when the witnesses lie dead in the street, God is faithfully caring for his own, and in the end he will bring us safe home.

For the believer, this chapter has a threefold message. We must know and understand which city we belong to—not the 'great city' of this world and its inhabitants, but the 'holy city' of God. We must be ready for the suffering which is a normal part of Christian experience. If the church in our own land faces persecution, we must be prepared. If necessary, that will include defying the law. The church is not here to be 'nice'. Above all, we must be faithful witnesses, for that is our commission: to shine in the dark world like a lamp on its stand, depending on the Holy Spirit, until the day when we hear him say, 'Come up here.'

To discuss or think about

1. 'Everyone lives in one of these two cities, the "holy city" or the "great city"'. Do you feel sure of your own citizenship in the 'holy city'? What difference should that be making to your life right now?
2. How does the story of the church portrayed in this chapter encourage us, and how does it help to prepare us for challenges and trials ahead?
3. Are you committed to the worshipping and witnessing life of a local church, so that you can play your part in the story?

Part VI
Signs of cosmic conflict
(12:1–14:20)

11

The ultimate battle

Please read Revelation 12

The space race makes a fascinating story—the tale of how the two superpowers, the USA and the Soviet Union, competed throughout the 1950s and 60s for supremacy in space, leading up to the first moon landings in 1969. Somewhat embarrassingly for the Americans, the father of the American space programme also happened to be the father of Nazi Germany's missile programme in World War II, Werner von Braun. Von Braun's greatest achievement in the war was the V2 rocket. After many years of research and testing, the V2 was finally ready for action in September 1944. It weighed around twelve tons and could carry a ton of explosives to a target 500 miles away. It was a fearsome weapon, far more advanced than any of its predecessors. During the next six months over a thousand V2s successfully reached Britain, killing and destroying many, especially in London, until at last its launch sites were overrun by the Allied armies in the spring of 1945.

But the V2 was a weapon of desperation. By the time it was

ready for use, it was already too late for Hitler. The war was effectively lost. The V2s killed or injured thousands, but they had no impact whatsoever on the outcome of the war. In London and Washington, they knew the war was won. But they also knew that they were in a fight with a powerful adversary who still had fearful weapons at his disposal. There was still pain and struggle to come for a little while longer. The enemy was beaten; his time was running out, but he was not giving up. Now look at Revelation 12:12:

> Woe to the earth and the sea,
> because the devil has gone down to you!
> He is filled with fury,
> because he knows that his time is short.

This is the situation *we* face. The message of this chapter is that believers are in a fight with a powerful adversary who has fearful weapons at his disposal. But he is a beaten enemy. These two vital themes run through the chapter: the enemy is still there, and yet he is beaten.

As we concluded chapter 11, we heard the seventh trumpet blowing and the inauguration of the eternal kingdom of God and of Christ. Earth has had its final warning; judgement has come; the story ends. But that is not the end of the book. As we have seen already, the pattern of Revelation is that it keeps panning through history time after time, showing us the same drama from one angle after another. Even within each of those sections, we have seen interludes where the film runs back to the start again to show us what is happening to the church—repeat after repeat, one new view after another. Now we begin yet another of these different angles. The next three chapters form a section we shall call 'Signs of cosmic conflict'. There is no book in Scripture which paints a bigger picture, and paints it with a bigger brush, than this book of Revelation, and within

Revelation there is no more visually dramatic and vivid scene than this chapter provides. For the first time in the book, we now see the hellish spiritual opposition which confronts us as God's people.

The characters in this vision

In chapter 11 some of the characters were hard to identify, but that is not the case here. The picture may seem very strange, but John makes it abundantly clear who is who.

In verses 1–2, we meet *the woman*. She gives birth to a child and is then repeatedly harassed and threatened by the dragon, along with the rest of her children. She is a 'sign', which tells us clearly that she stands for something else. Once more, we need to think back to the Old Testament where we recall that in Genesis 37 Joseph had a dream about the sun, the moon and eleven stars—a dream about his family, the founding family of Israel, the nation called out by God. Joseph himself would make a twelfth star. As we read through this chapter it becomes very clear that the woman indeed represents Israel, but not just Israel, because at the end of the chapter, Israel has become the church. So the woman is a sign for the people of God right through to the present day. She is robed with the sun, and has the moon under her feet, with a crown of stars on her head. This is a picture of cosmic beauty and majesty—a picture of the one God loves, foreshadowing the even more beautiful picture of the perfected bride in chapter 21.

Then in verse 5, we meet *her son*. Again, there is no chance of mistaking his identity. Those words are taken directly from Psalm 2, a Messianic psalm which the New Testament frequently applies to Christ. Israel provides the human ancestry of Jesus, the one who is born to be King.

The final main character is *the dragon* (12:3). With apologies to all Welsh readers (and the Welsh love their flag!), in this vision the red dragon is a picture of all that is evil. 'Red' is the colour of war, as with the second of the four horses in chapter 6. The dragon's identity is made crystal clear in verse 9: '... that ancient serpent called the devil, or Satan, who leads the whole world astray'. 'Ancient' here means not 'old and decrepit', but 'the original one', the senior of all the angelic beings.

Now folklore and fiction have given us all sorts of ideas about dragons. Apart from the Welsh flag, they appear in all kinds of myths and legends from many different countries. These days you can find dragons in children's books and on TV, where they are likely to be friendly and harmless, even comic. Dragons can be found in the pages of Harry Potter, where they are fierce and dangerous, but quite easy to bamboozle and control if you know the right tricks. This dragon is not like any of those. If anything, he is more like the dragons in the works of Tolkien, who knew better than most how to portray terrifying monsters, such as Smaug in *The Hobbit*. This dragon is greedy, voracious, cruel and utterly cynical. He is almost indestructible, the ancient prince of hell. He is our enemy, Satan, and that very word should send a shiver down our spine.

The characters, then, are clear enough. If there is scope for confusion in this chapter, it is about timing. At first sight, the times here seem rather mixed up, until you remember the way Revelation works. Once again we have a repeat within the one vision. So verses 1–6 tell a story; then verses 7–17 tell it again from a different viewpoint and with fuller detail. There are three scenes in this vision.

Scene I: The dragon thwarted on earth (12:1–6)

John sees this majestic picture of the woman 'in heaven'—or possibly 'in the sky' would be a better translation: Greek used the same word for both. The woman, Israel, is about to give birth. The moment is approaching; the pains are increasing.

At this point John sees another sign. The dragon appears and is poised waiting for the child to appear, so that he can immediately devour it. This is what he has been waiting for these thousands of years, ever since that day in Eden when God cursed him and warned that the day would come when Eve's distant offspring would crush him (Genesis 3:15). There in Eden he appeared as a snake, as verse 9 reminds us. Now he appears as a dragon, depicted with horns and with seven crowned heads, emphasizing his power and the authority that he holds, and with a tail that sweeps a third of the stars from the sky. Some think that this is a reference to the fallen angels who have followed him in rebellion; others point to Daniel 8:10 where the context is the persecution of the faithful people of God and think these stars represent persecuted saints. Either way, this is another expression of Satan's awesome power. This enemy is terrifyingly powerful. In chapter 10 we saw a mighty angel who straddled land and sea, but Satan is mightier far than that.

The child is born and Satan sees his chance. In fact, as we know from the Gospel accounts, he makes many moves to devour the child. Under his inspiration, Herod massacres the babies of Bethlehem—but Jesus is already gone. Later on, Satan personally confronts Jesus in the desert after his baptism; he tries everything to entice him away from his mission—to devour him. He urges him to take a short cut, to misuse his power, or to accept Satan's assistance. Finally, in the garden, hours away from the cross, Satan tempts him to find an easier way out, to call down the angels to help him, or to start a revolt. But it doesn't work. Jesus goes to the cross; his mission is completed, and he is taken up to heaven, right to the throne of God. Now in this vision, most of that is unsaid. Instead it simply shows us the moment when the Son of God comes within range of the dragon's claws and the moment when he escapes them for ever (12:5). The focus is on one key fact: Jesus, the woman's male child, escapes from the dragon utterly unscathed. Satan's chance is gone.

Meanwhile, the woman makes her escape (12:6). Again we refer back to the Old Testament, and here especially to Exodus. The Bible views Egypt as a symbol of evil, of rebellion against God. At one point the Egyptian Pharaoh is actually pictured as a dragon, or something similar (Ezekiel 29:3). The thought here is of escape from Egypt into the safety of the desert, a place where God will look after his people, feeding and housing them until the time comes for them to move into the promised land. The desert is the place of refuge for God's people. We notice how long they are there. Once more it is 1,260 days, the time of the witnesses in chapter 11, the time of the whole church age from Jesus' ministry through to his Second Coming. The church is out in the desert, living in a temporary camp, waiting for the promised land.

Scene II: The dragon thrown out of heaven (12:7–9)

In the second scene the film winds back and the story starts again. Satan's rebellion happened a very long time ago. He has been in outright revolt against God since before our race was born and there has been conflict ever since. We must realize that, when it comes to battles between angels, there is only so much that we can understand. We are like soldiers from the Battle of Hastings in 1066 trying to understand how a helicopter works. But Michael is the name of the guardian angel or archangel of God's people (Daniel 12:1), and this scene describes the moment when Michael and his angels are finally able to take the dragon and his forces and expel them from the realm of heaven. That moment arrived when Jesus won the victory on the cross. The battle could not be finally resolved until Jesus completed his mission and then returned to heaven in triumph. Satan's whole agenda was to destroy God's plan of salvation. Ever since the Garden of Eden his one aim has been to prevent the Fall being reversed, to forestall the coming of the Saviour.

But now Satan has been thwarted on earth. Any chance that he ever stood of sabotaging our salvation is gone. The cross spells decisive victory over Satan's power, and it is that victory that finally breaks him, as Paul explains in Colossians 2:9–15. The victory of the cross has cosmic consequences, consequences that echo through heaven as well as across the earth. Until that moment, Satan still, as it were, had his foot in the door of heaven. He still held a stake in the story of humanity. But now, as Christ returns to glory, Satan and his hordes are thrown out of heaven and down to the earth. Verse 9 recites his notorious titles: the 'ancient serpent' who deceived our first parents; 'the devil', the slanderer, telling lies about God to us and about us to God; 'Satan', which means the accuser, who will take every opportunity to show believers in a bad light. He 'leads the whole world astray'. As 2 Corinthians 4:4 puts it, 'The god of this age has blinded the minds of unbelievers, so that they cannot see the light of the gospel of the glory of Christ.' But now his final defeat is confirmed.

Scene III: The dragon's final onslaught (12:13–17)

Now for the final scene. Expelled from heaven and thrown down to earth, Satan still refuses to give up. He goes after the woman, the church, pursuing her. Now this repeat view has caught up with verse 6, as the woman is pictured being given eagle's wings to fly to her desert refuge, just as Israel's escape from Egypt is described in Exodus 19:4. Once more, the time period is the same: 'time, times and half a time'—that is, three and a half years, or 1,260 days—and still he attacks both the woman and her offspring. Verse 15 shows him spewing out a torrent of water in an attempt to sweep the woman away. The flood comes from his mouth, which suggests that his deceptive words are his most destructive weapon. But still the church is safe, even if she is none too comfortable!

Yet still the dragon will not give up. The end of scene three is left open: it leads on into chapter 13, which tells us more about the unpleasant methods Satan has devised to make war against the faithful people of the church. He is enraged, but not because he thinks he can win. Satan is throwing everything at the church, not because he is triumphant, but because he is beaten. He knows that. All his onslaught has no more effect on the outcome of the ultimate battle than the V2s did in Hitler's war.

The song of heaven (12:10–12)

The dragon is thwarted on earth; he is thrown out of heaven; he makes his final onslaught—and in the middle of it all, we hear the song of heaven. Verses 10–12 are a loud hymn of triumph. Satan the accuser has been thrown down. The plague of God's people has been banished. The victory has been won: salvation is secure; the kingdom of God has been launched; Christ is reigning. There is much to rejoice about, yet down here on earth, we are warned, we are still in for a rough time (12:12). The fight is on; our adversary still has fearsome weapons and we are in the firing line.

But the song of heaven also tells us how we can overcome our great enemy and win the battle (12:11). The battle was decisively won at the cross. We do not defeat Satan by some new wonder weapon, but by 'the blood of the Lamb' and 'the word of [our] testimony'. Satan is 'the accuser', as verse 10 reminds us. He accuses us time and again of being worthless, of being failures, of being hopeless.

The first answer is 'the blood of the Lamb'—that was the price that was paid for us. Here is the answer to Satan's accusations.

We are not *worthless*: we have only to look at what the Son of God gave for us. We should realize that we are worth more than the angels, for there was no salvation plan for them. Yes, we are often *failures*, every day of our lives, but when we fall down, Jesus picks us up again. And we cannot be *hopeless* when his blood has bought us a new destiny, eternal life.

The second answer is 'the word of [our] testimony'. Satan wants us to keep silent. But the picture of the church in these last two chapters is a church that speaks. Satan would like his defeat to be kept as quiet as possible. He does not want Christians telling their friends about Jesus, and he has ways of making it very tough when we do. Sometimes, as we have seen, the cost may be very high. 'They did not love their lives so much as to shrink from death' (12:11). That is the bottom line of discipleship, the ultimate cost of taking on the dragon.

The meaning of the vision for us

The vision in this chapter, this vision of the ultimate battle, makes the connection between what happened on the cross, what has happened in heaven and what happens in our own lives. There are three vital lessons for us here.

1. Remember the big picture

The postmodern worldview that is widely embraced in the West tells us that there is no big picture; there is no great overarching story which makes sense of my obscure little life. To use the technical word, there is no 'metanarrative'—just a lot of little personal stories and a lot of chaos, but all of it going precisely nowhere. The Bible tells us that there *is* a big picture, and nowhere does it do so more clearly than in this chapter. In seventeen verses we run through a story that covers thousands of years of time, the lives of millions of people, the healing of heaven, a vast battle involving angels, demons and the Son of God, as well as all humanity, in one single overarching story.

That is what gives the significance to our lives, even if many deny it. Satan would love to deny it too, because if people remember the big picture, they will remember that, beyond the struggle of my little life today, Satan is defeated. In the big picture, there is the Last Judgement; heaven is singing praises to King Jesus, and we are going there to join in. In the big picture, believers are kept safe and sound until the King returns.

What we do in the meantime does have significance. Satan will be very happy if we keep our heads down, focus on our own busy little lives and forget the rest. But we know better. The struggle with sin and temptation every day is not just about us; it is part of a cosmic struggle between good and evil, a tiny part of a huge battle that has raged on for century after century and which is going to come to a conclusion. We are part of the big story.

2. Know our enemy

In war, it is necessary to know your enemy. Most people today don't believe in a personal devil. Even many Christians apparently don't believe Satan exists. Naturally, he is quite happy about that; it is one of the biggest lies of all. We are faced with an enemy who hates us personally, who has an individual dossier on every believer. He has had thousands of years of practice to hone his cynical methods. Like Paul, we must be able to say, 'We are not unaware of his schemes' (2 Corinthians 2:11).

3. We are on the winning side

The battle has been won. All that is left are the mopping-up operations. The futility of Satan's position is like someone trying to bail out the sinking *Titanic* with a teaspoon—or a sieve. He is furious, but he is doomed to failure. No matter what he fires at us, he has lost and we have won. However we may feel, if we belong to Jesus we are on the winning side. We have won because of the blood of Jesus, our hero and champion, and we have a big story to tell.

To discuss or think about

1. How clearly have you grasped the 'big picture' of salvation and judgement—Satan's defeat and the victory of Christ—that we see in Revelation 12?
2. Do you believe that Satan is defeated but still dangerous? What part do you think you have in his final downfall?
3. Can you identify with the triumph of the saints in verses 11 and 12?

12

The beast and his number

Please read Revelation 13

Since about the turn of the millennium, a new name has grown horribly familiar. It is a name we associate with ruthlessness, suffering and death, a name that we dread hearing on the news because it generally means some fresh atrocity has been carried out. The name is Al Qaeda. Growing from its obscure origins in the camps of Afghanistan, Al Qaeda has gradually spread its influence to every part of the world. Since 1999 it has been responsible for bombings and attacks in countries around the world that are too numerous to list. It has used aircraft; it has bombed trains, ships, embassies, banks, night clubs and offices. Its tentacles are everywhere. Around the world, governments and intelligence services are at their wits' end trying to get on top of it. An attack may be thwarted today, but they will try again tomorrow.

Al Qaeda is an organization that aims for nothing less than worldwide domination, where everyone will have one of two choices: to submit to it, or to be destroyed by it. It is driven by an ideology that does not hesitate to kill on a grand scale and without any warning. Every time it seems to be defeated in one place, it pops up in another with a different name. It is a monstrous organization, deadly evil, a deadly enemy. Now what would the Bible have to say about a group like that? The Bible would say that Al Qaeda is one small example of what Revelation 13 calls 'the beast', a monster in the service of Satan. This chapter unmasks Satan's top agent for destroying the church of Christ.

The previous chapter left us with the picture of Satan, the red dragon, setting out to create mayhem among God's people for the limited time he has left. Once again in this chapter we shall come across the symbolic time period labelled forty-two months, or 1,260 days (13:5). In each of chapters 11 to 13, we find this time span that stands for the whole church age, the time from Jesus' death and resurrection through to his Second Coming: forty-two months for the church to witness (chapter 11); forty-two months for God to protect his church while the dragon rages on earth (chapter 12); and now forty-two months for the beast to be given authority over mankind. It is clear by now that we are not looking at a few brief events that will happen at the end of time—although it certainly gets worse at the end. We are looking at what happens in our *own* time, right through until Jesus comes again.

So as we arrive at chapter 13, there is the dragon, standing on the shore, where the sea meets the land, intent on his schemes for striking at the church and doing as much damage as he possibly can before his time is up. He summons, not one beast, but two, one from the sea and one from the land—two beasts to serve him, working in tandem to enslave the world and to crush the church. There are two beasts: the tyrant and the liar. The layout of the chapter is very simple: in each case John introduces the beast, tells us what he does and then tells us what *we* need to do about it.

The tyrant (13:1–10)

The portrait of the beast (13:1–3)

Look at the description in verses 1–2. It is not a very attractive one. Yet again, as so frequently throughout this book, we are taken back to the Old Testament, in this case to Daniel 7, one of a series of spectacular visions the prophet was shown by God. From the opening verses of the chapter, it is easy to see that the beast in Revelation 13 is a sort of hideous composite of the four beasts that Daniel saw. One looks like a lion, one like a bear, one like a leopard, and there are all the body parts incorporated in Revelation. The fourth, the most terrifying of all, has ten horns. All four beasts emerge from the sea, which for the Israelites had none of the alluring connotations it does for us. The sea was a symbol of chaos; they feared it.

Further on in Daniel 7 we find even more of the background to the beast of Revelation. Verse 17 explains what the four beasts are, and verse 24 that the ten horns represent ten kings. To make matters more complicated, another horn has appeared in verse 8, and in verse 25 it is heard insulting God and his people for a period described as 'time, times and half a time'. The natural way to understand this is as three and a half years, or forty-two months. Now, 650 years later, John is given a vision of a hideous beast which combines all the nastiest features of Daniel's beasts, reigns for forty-two months, blasphemes the Most High God and attacks the saints. Daniel's beasts represent four specific kingdoms or empires.[1] Revelation puts them all together into one, and its identity is clear—not a single individual, but the beastly power of earthly empires throughout the age. Like the dragon, the beast has seven heads, just to remind us who its master really is. This is tyranny in the service of Satan.

Pause here for a moment! Doesn't Paul say in Romans 13 that government is a gift of God and that Christians should obey their rulers and recognize that they are God's servants with an important job to do? It is sometimes suggested that Romans 13 and Revelation 13 contradict one another. How can the Roman Empire, for instance, both be good—God's gift—*and* a hideous, ravening beast? The answer is that government *is* a gift of God. No Christian should ever be an anarchist. We accept the Bible's testimony that all men are fallen and sinful, and therefore we need governments to restrain evil and keep order. We should be grateful for good, peaceful government. If you want to know what happens when government is taken away, look at the recent history of Somalia, which spent twenty years without one, and ask if you would rather be living there or in a Western democracy. But, like many of God's other good gifts, government can be seized by Satan and used for evil, and that is what we see here. The beast doesn't stand for *all* governments: he stands for tyranny, government perverted into an instrument of Satan to enslave the whole world. This passage shows us what it looks like.

It seems to have had a fatal wound (13:3), but it has been healed. The beast seems invincible. Like Al Qaeda, it can be knocked down in one place but it just pops up in another. Every time a Berlin Wall comes down in one capital, an ayatollah or a Mugabe takes power in another. You think the beast is defeated, but somehow he never is. Tyranny marches on.

The popularity of the beast (13:4)

Verse 4 shows us that the beast is popular. That might surprise us, but the story of any great tyrant shows that the great mass of the population are perfectly willing to follow such men, either gladly or in fear. Hitler, Mussolini, Franco—for long periods they were almost literally worshipped by millions. They were national saviours and strong leaders; their people were proud of them. So it is not surprising that the tyrant takes the place of God (13:5–6). The tyrant sets himself up as an alternative God, a replacement God. This beast even has blasphemies inscribed on his heads! Frequently, dictators create their own personal mythology, or have others do it for them. Most of all, they demand people's unquestioning and unconditional submission—something that only God himself has the right to do.

The purpose of the beast (13:7–8)

That leads neatly on to Satan's key objective. The beast is Satan's tool to attack the saints, to make war against the church of Jesus. Down through the years it has been the greatest tyrants who have unleashed the fiercest persecution. After all, the whole point of being a tyrant is that everyone should serve you, not some god. So, whether it was Roman emperors, the Habsburgs during the Reformation years, Louis XIV, Stalin or Idi Amin—wherever there has been a faithful church which refuses to worship the beast, the beast makes war on them. We know that God is building his church from every language and nation. But here we see again that Satan is building a people as well—an anti-church from every language and nation. Everyone who does not belong to Jesus, who does not have his name written in the Lamb's book of life, is a member of the beast's anti-church.

In fact, a closer look at the first beast reveals him to be a mocking parody of the Lamb. His multiple crowns are a claim to the kingship that belongs to Jesus Christ. His recovery from a fatal wound parallels the resurrection of Christ. The cry 'Who is like the beast?' echoes Exodus 15:11 in mockery. And this four-fold description of the humanity over which the beast wields his authority echoes the description of the crowd around the Lamb in 7:9. He claims the worship that rightly belongs to Jesus alone. His relationship to the dragon is similar to the relationship of the Son to God the Father. In all these ways, the beast is set up as an alternative to the Lord Jesus Christ.

The beast's followers are described four times in this chapter with that now-familiar expression, the 'inhabitants of the earth'—the people who are at home here on earth, who know no other world. The Lamb's people know they are *not* inhabitants of the earth. The next chapter shows us the final outcome of this great divide, but the solemn truth is that you are either with the Lord Jesus or you are with the beast.

A call to faithfulness (13:9–10)

'He who has an ear', says John, 'let him hear' (13:9). This message is for Christians; it is a warning of what we can expect, at any time. John's first readers were in the middle of such trials, as are many believers in the world today. We in the West are not, so far, but there is undoubtedly suffering on our horizon. So how do we guard ourselves against such times? Is democracy the best defence against the beast? Hardly. We should never forget that it was a democratic election that produced Hitler. It was democracy that brought Robert Mugabe to power. We don't put our faith in democracy any more than in any other human system. Even in Britain, democratic governments are beginning to turn the screws on the church! No, for believers the answer is quite different.

Verse 10 warns us that suffering will come. We are not told to look for it, but neither are we told to run away from it. When we find ourselves under the beast, believers are told simply to endure and stay faithful. That has not always happened. Hitler didn't have to persecute the churches very much. Most of them were compromised and simply rolled over. Only a few showed this patient endurance and faithfulness.[2] They were faithful to Jesus, and the beast persecuted them. There are times when the one place where a believer can be faithful to the Lord will be the execution cell, when all the church can do is to suffer and wait.

The liar (13:11–18)

The second half of the chapter tells us how the first beast achieves his results so successfully. The dragon, as it were, faces the sea to summon the first beast from there, and now turns to call forth the second beast from the earth (13:11–12), probably representing his direct opposition to heaven. His appearance 'in sheep's clothing' should remind us of Jesus' warning in Matthew 7 of false prophets, but any doubts about the second beast's identity are resolved in 19:20, where he is directly named as 'the false prophet'. He it is who serves the first beast and enables him to do his dirty work. Indeed, having noticed the parallel between the dragon and the first beast and the Father and the Son, we are now meeting the third member of the 'unholy Trinity'. The second beast relates to the first somewhat in the same way that the Spirit relates to the Son.

The beast and his methods (13:13–17)

Every tyrant needs a lie to keep him in power. The bigger the lie, the better it works. Four methods are picked out here. He puts on *a great show*—verses 13 and 14 reveal him doing all kinds of dramatic and spectacular signs to deceive people, inducing them to worship the first beast. He goes on to create *a personality cult*, making people set up an image of the first beast. Meanwhile the dragon, Satan himself, cleverly stays well in the background all through this process. People are mostly not so stupid, nor so depraved, as to worship Satan directly and knowingly. But they love his servants. Then the second beast enforces *a reign of terror* (13:15). All these methods fit together very neatly: follow the lie, join the personality cult, or else ... But people might still escape, so there is one final method—*economic control* (13:16–17). Everyone is made to wear a mark to prove they belong to the beast—that is, the *first* beast. If they refuse, they will starve.

So what is the second beast? He is, simply, *every ideology that has ever been set up to support godless tyranny*. He is the

Communism of the Soviet Union, with its spectacular parades through Red Square, its cult of Lenin and Stalin, its party card for the privileged. That was one lie. He is Nazism, with its Nuremberg rallies and its Hitler Youth—Nazism, which marked its supporters with the swastika and its victims with coloured stars. That was another lie. He is the state-led tribalism of Rwanda, which swept people up into genocide and forced them to take part, until close on a million lay dead in the fields; the statues of Saddam which infested Iraq; the wall posters of Chairman Mao. All were signs of the second beast, the liar, at work.

But the second beast is not just those great ideologies of the twentieth century. Even more than that, and working still more closely hand-in-hand with the first beast, he is the liar of *false religion*. That is where the miracles and signs really come in. The second beast is the false prophet, the great deceiver. Even some believers are deceived, because sometimes the second beast can disguise himself as a church. This is something else that Jesus warned us about in that famous passage in Matthew: 'At that time if anyone says to you, "Look, here is the Christ!" or, "There he is!" do not believe it. For false Christs and false prophets will appear and perform great signs and miracles to deceive even the elect—if that were possible. See, I have told you ahead of time' (Matthew 24:23–25).

When the Roman emperors began to think of themselves as gods, trouble arose for the church. Revelation was written during the reign of Domitian, whose chosen title for himself was *dominus et deus*—'lord and god'. No wonder he exiled people like John. Today, most of the toughest places for the church are where false religions hold their sway, and worst of all where those religions walk hand-in-hand with governments and the two beasts grin at one another as they persecute the church of Christ. The false prophet supplies the backing for the tyrant to continue his work. To be an Arab, they say, is to be a Muslim. To be a true Indian, you must be a Hindu. If you are a Christian, you are obviously a traitor. You are not wearing the right mark. Let's have a look at your identity card. There are even places today where you cannot buy or sell unless you belong to the beast. On the day I am writing this, there are examples in two different prayer diaries I am using. One was from a village in India where a crowd of Hindu extremists had attacked a church and later called for a boycott against the Christians, to prevent them from using the village well or buying food in the markets. The other case was from West Africa, where a young man had converted to Christ from Islam and could not find work in his home village because of his Christian faith. He didn't have the right mark.

It is not politically correct today to describe anything as a 'false religion', but even so it is true that Islam, Hinduism, Buddhism—as well as aggressive secularism and atheism—and many others are false religions, offering false Christs and deceiving the inhabitants of the earth. People who are following these religions are following the beast; they are believing the great liar. Our task is to help them escape, to be free.

The number of the beast (13:18)

What, then, is the believer's response to the liar? At first sight, John seems to be suggesting that we should solve a mathematical puzzle, a sort of cosmic Sudoku—verse 18 being one of the best-known of the whole book! What are we to do with this mysterious number? A popular answer starts from the fact that in many ancient languages, such as Hebrew and Greek, the letters of the alphabet were used to stand for numbers. So any name can be turned into numbers and the numbers added together to give a total which stands for that person. Some say that 666 was a code for the Emperor Nero. But that only works if you call him 'Nero Caesar', take the Greek spelling, transliterate it into Hebrew (which hardly any of John's readers would have understood) and then spell it wrong! It seems that this theory about Nero arose only in the nineteenth century. Other people have worked out schemes to make 666 fit a whole host of other candidates, including Domitian (the emperor in John's own day), Mohammed, Cromwell, Martin Luther and Napoleon. More recently still, people have found the number 666 in computer-readable bar codes or in credit cards. But all of this is misguided, springing from the false idea that Revelation is a kind of cosmic puzzle book where, with the right skills, or the right teacher, the codes can be cracked and the puzzle understood.

The truth, I am confident, is far simpler. The number of perfection, the number of completeness, seen over and over again in this book, is seven. Six is one short of seven. The ideal symbolic number for someone who repeatedly attempts to imitate that perfection, who pretends to be all that God is and yet ultimately fails, time after time after time, would surely be 666—the number of the beast, of fallen man, of empty failure. If I can put it like this, it is the Bible's way of thumbing its nose at the beast. The text does not say, 'This calls for a maths degree.' It says, 'This calls for wisdom'—the word used in verse 18 for 'insight' is actually *nous*—spiritual discernment, which is what the Bible means by 'wisdom'. It is nothing to do with intelligence or education. The message is that with a spiritual mind and understanding you will be able to recognize the beast for what he really is—a counterfeit, a falsehood.

Tackling the beast

This, then, is how the two beasts serve their master, Satan. Some of us might think this has little to do with us. Yes, it sounds terrible—tyranny, the grip of false religions; how grateful we should be that it is not like that where we live! But this picture is entirely normal. Not only are many Christian believers persecuted today, but that is what we should expect. If we live in the West, we can be very grateful for the freedoms we enjoy, but we shouldn't be too shocked when they are closed down. Our spiritual ancestors fought long and hard against the beast, and for the last few hundred years he has been kept more or less quiet, as far as the UK and many other Western countries are concerned. But what our ancestors fought for is now being pulled down, and the beast is on his way back again. Our freedom may first be cut down by the very polite false prophet of political correctness, the false prophet who says the only truth is that there is no such thing as final truth.

1. *We must recognize the beast*

Our first response must be to recognize the beast. We have got his number; we know who he is and what he is up to. Believers in the safe West should support their brothers and sisters who are under far greater pressure. We should pray often for the persecuted church and for support groups who boldly speak the truth about false religions and care for the persecuted. Recognizing the beast also means watching out for what he is doing in our own nations. Recent changes in the law in the UK and elsewhere, and plans to introduce more far-reaching legislation, are a faint indication of what is to come. We must understand what is going on. We need the insight to calculate the number of the beast.

2. *We must declare, against the beast, that Jesus is Lord*

That was the great cry of the early church when they were called on to say that 'Caesar is Lord' and thereby to escape death. We insist that *Jesus* is Lord—not just '*my* Lord', inside my own head or my own private space, but far more: 'He is *Lord*'. It is an absolute statement. The beast cannot stand that. Satan knows it is true, but he cannot bear the thought of it. With that determination in our hearts, we endure patiently and faithfully.

The beast has limited time; his days are numbered. But we have for ever!

3. We must remember that our names are in the book of life

We are not the inhabitants of the earth, content to be led astray by the false prophet and worship the beast. No. There is a list in heaven, and if we have confessed Jesus as Lord then our names are on it, in permanent ink that no power can remove.

To discuss or think about

1. How does this chapter help us to understand what is going on in our world and the apparent success of evil leaders and false religions?
2. What is the basis of the 'patient endurance and faithfulness' we are urged to display in v.10?
3. How can we best support Christians who today are facing the worst onslaught of the two beasts?

13

The fatal division

Please read Revelation 14

No one really expected it to happen. After all, Mount St Helens had been quiet for well over a hundred years. It was a peaceful haunt for hiking, camping and exploring. No one seriously thought the volcano would actually come to life again. So it was a major surprise when, in the spring of 1980, worrying signals began to emerge from the mountain. There was a series of earth tremors and avalanches. Then a column of ash and steam emerged from the summit. Scientists discovered that the northern side of the mountain was developing a huge bulge which was growing at the astonishing rate of several feet per day. The warnings were now very stark. Mount St Helens was not going to remain peaceful for much longer.

There was a man called Harry Truman—a real old curmudgeon, the sort the media loves. Fifty years previously he had built his own lodge by the beautiful Spirit Lake, just below the mountain. There he had entertained a string of famous names; now, at eighty-three years old, he had no intention of moving away. The warnings were coming thick and fast; others were taking heed and evacuating; his lodge was one of the nearest habitations to the mountain and he was urged repeatedly to get out. But Truman was well known for his defiance of both nature and government. He had survived by staying put up to now; there was no way he would leave. Was he brave, or was he very, very stupid?

On Sunday, 18 May 1980, just after 8.32 in the morning, Mount St Helens blew. A vast flow of superheated rock and ash gushed down the mountain, devastating 200 square miles of forest. The lodge by Spirit Lake was buried deep. Harry Truman would not have had long to contemplate his approaching death; the flowing cloud from the mountain came on at around 300 mph. One scientist remarked that he would just have had time to turn his head and see it.

When Mount St Helens erupted, the wise had already left. The stubborn remained to be burned, suffocated by volcanic ash or buried alive. There was a fatal division between those who heeded the warnings, and lived, and those who refused, and perished—a division based on their decision about a dangerous volcano. Revelation 14 shows us a divide just as permanent, just as irreversible, just as fatal as that—in fact even deeper. And the most important decision that anyone has to make in their life is on which side of that division they are going to stand.

This chapter brings to a close the section we have called 'Scenes of cosmic conflict'. It contains three distinct visions, much as the NIV splits the chapter into three blocks. They are not intended to be in precise chronological order; if we try to force them to fit in that order we shall confuse ourselves. Rather, they are different ways of viewing the reality of the final days of this world. Together they point us to the awesome solemnity of the chasm between God's people and the world's people.

The church perfected (14:1–5)

The previous chapter showed us the beast and the people he is gathering for Satan. But now look at this wonderful contrast. Already the divide is made stunningly clear. In place of the hideous beast, combining all the most unpleasant features of the world's dictatorships, the great slave-master of history, we see the Lamb of God, the Lord Jesus who became a servant of all and laid down his own life for his people. In place of a people enslaved in the worship of the beast, here is a crowd redeemed from across the earth and joyfully, wonderfully *free*. Instead of the mark of the beast and his number 666, the number of failure, stamped on their faces, these people bear the name of the Lord Jesus and his Father. In fact we are back with the crowd of 144,000 we first met in chapter 7—God's people, both before and after the time of Christ, the whole church throughout history. They are standing with him 'on Mount Zion'.

Now Mount Zion, literally, is the hill on which the original city of Jerusalem was built. But if you look on to v.3, it is clear that the scene is actually set in heaven, not on earth. The Zion referred to anticipates the *new* city, the city that stands for the people of God, the new Jerusalem that will form the centrepiece of the renewed earth.[1] Yet again we find here an Old Testament prophecy being picked up, this time from Zephaniah 3, which looks forward to a day when God's chosen people will be serving him in purity and faithfulness. The setting is Jerusalem, and the promise is that God's people, gathered out of the nations, will at last serve him with pure devotion. They will do no wrong, tell no lie, and the Lord will rejoice over them and be with them for ever (Zephaniah 3:13,17). In Revelation 14 that wonderful vision is seen fulfilled. Every believer is here, from Adam and Eve down to you and me. At the end of time, God has gathered his people, the church, together.

1. It is a church that can sing! (14:2–3)
What a description this is! The sound of the music is as loud as thunder, but it is also melodious and beautiful. Musicians will enjoy that, but in heaven we shall *all* be able to sing! You may be a byword for tone-deafness now, but then you will sing better than the world's greatest singers of today! It is a new song that only the redeemed can sing. The angels cannot sing it because they don't know what it is to be bought back from the rule of the beast. In chapter 5 heaven bursts into song when the Lamb is revealed, and here again it is what the Lamb has done for us that will inspire us to sing.

2. It is a church that is committed (14:4)
What did you think when you read this verse? The Greek text actually says, 'They are virgins.' The expression, 'did not defile themselves with women', seems very odd, given that 50% of the church is female. Is this evidence of some biblical anti-sex agenda? No, it is about the church's commitment to Christ. Here is what Paul says in 2 Corinthians 11:2: 'I promised you to one husband, to Christ, so that I might present you as a pure virgin to him.' Revelation also pictures the church as the bride of Christ, especially in chapter 21 and, like so many images in this book, this one has deep roots in the Old Testament. The prophecy of Hosea is the most obvious example. This verse is speaking of the church's purity and loyalty to her Lord. God's people don't get into bed with this world and its seductive appeals; this will become all the more pointed when we reach the vision of the great harlot in chapter 17. They are saving themselves for Christ. They follow him wherever he goes, wherever he calls them to go.

3. It is a church that has been bought (14:4)
It has been 'purchased from among men', at the cost of the lifeblood of the Lamb. In chapter 7, 144,000 were marked out

and sealed on earth. Here, in chapter 14, we see how many of those have made it to heaven: every single one. Not one is missing.

4. It is a church that is blameless (14:5)

This is a people whose mouths do not lie. The inspired dreams of the prophets like Zephaniah are fulfilled at last, as this world's time draws to a close and God gathers the last of his people together from earth to heaven. It is not the church as we know her here, struggling, weak, imperfect and sinful; it is not the church that people here can see, which this world either mocks or abuses. But it is the church as she will be in heaven, massed around the throne and in the company of the elders and living creatures. This is where we are going.

5. In a sense it is also the church here and now

Even now, we are the people bought by Christ and loved by God. Even now, while the beast rages in the world and while we still live in it, we know that our King Jesus is living among us, giving us power to stand against the beast and all his works. Even now, he is teaching us to praise him, and his Spirit is at work to mould our lives into his shape. This is the church as Christ is making us, the church that we want to be; and one day soon we *shall be* the church perfected.

The destinations presented (14:6–13)

In these verses, the scene changes and we encounter a team of three angels flying through the skies and announcing the judgement that is to come. These angels do not actually make anything happen; they are more like heavenly newsreaders highlighting the key events of the day. They are publishing God's decrees. This vision moves us swiftly on towards the end.

A final call to repentance (14:6–7)

Angel number one is carrying the gospel. Now angels do not

actually preach; they don't tell people the gospel—that is up to us to do. This angel is announcing, for one last time, that the gospel is still on offer. It is the final, late edition. Just before the end, as judgement is announced, the gospel is still available to everyone—'Last call: respond!' 'Fear God and give him glory.' Worship your Creator. One final call to repentance: 'Your time is almost up; judgement is coming.'

***The destination of those who reject Christ* (14:8–11)**

Angels numbers two and three declare what that judgement will mean. Both of these look ahead.

In verse 8, Babylon has fallen. 'Babylon' is very closely associated with the beast; its fall is described in great detail in chapters 17 and 18. For now we hear only a brief cry of triumph: Babylon, which stands for human rebellion against God down through the ages, will fall at last.

But the third angel brings a very personal warning (14:9–11). Remember, there are only two camps we can be in. We can be in the loving grip of Christ, or we can be in the enslaving grasp of Satan and the beast. Simply being part of this world, going along with the beast, has always been so easy. It certainly makes life much more straightforward. But now the terrible price of rejecting Christ and his gospel, the price of being on the wrong side of the divide, is made crystal clear. The choices made here on earth will have their consequences in eternity, in heaven or in hell. This is the first description of hell in Revelation, but it will not be the last. If sin is not dealt with by Christ on the cross, its consequences must be borne by the sinner, eternally.

The warning speaks of having to drink the cup of God's wrath—the relentless fury of God against sin, which burns with a ferocity we cannot imagine because we simply do not realize how evil sin is and how pure our God is. That is the cup that Jesus accepted and drank in his suffering on the cross. It speaks of being tormented with burning pain—the penalty of sin which

Christians no longer have to pay, thanks to Jesus. It speaks of torment in the presence ... of the Lamb'. Hell is sometimes described as the *absence* of God, but that's not right. Hell is the presence of God in judgement rather than blessing. Specifically, in this passage, it is the Lamb, Christ himself, who is seen to be the overseer of hell. Grimmest of all, it speaks of eternity—'for ever and ever'—and of no respite, at any time, for those who have rejected Christ and accepted the badge of the beast. These verses make it clear, in language we cannot possibly escape, that the punishment of the wicked will be *conscious*, and it will be *eternal*. There is no hint of simple annihilation, let alone a state of limbo. It is a subject we may find hard, even impossible, to contemplate, but it is a truth we have to face. Our God is just, and he punishes all evil. The cross is there for us; the offer of the gospel is still open—now, but not for ever. For those who reject it, the destination is terrible.

A call to perseverance (14:12)

At this stage in Revelation, however, that is still a warning, not yet an actual event. The angel is looking ahead to the judgement and describing what will follow. And meanwhile, what is the church to do? We are to wait patiently (cf. 13:10). One day, God will intervene and justice will be done. Until then, the beast is still active; the church still suffers, and the saints are called to wait patiently and leave God to be in charge.

The destination of the church (14:13)

But verse 13 reminds us that there is something else that we do not have to wait for. This is a promise for every believer, right now. All those people who have rejected Christ find no rest. But for Christ's own people, there is eternal rest. The good that we have done on earth will follow us into heaven—not the good works vainly done in a pointless effort to satisfy God, but the good deeds of the believer, done in grateful service to our Lord.

Since we are safe in Christ, death for us is not a terror; it is a blessing.

What a contrast between the two destinations set out here! For God's enemies, there is a place of unceasing pain and torment without respite. But for his own people, there is a place of rest and reward—not because we are any better, but because our Saviour has bought us, rescued us and given us a place with him.

The judgement executed (14:14–20)

Now we come to the point where the pathways finally divide for ever. These verses at first sight seem a bit repetitive. There are four characters: one is described as 'like a son of man' and the other three are angels. Apart from the angels, the imagery here is totally different from everything we have met so far in the book and, while *we* may not be in the habit of wielding sickles and reaping the fields, for John's readers these pictures of harvest time would have been just as familiar as a trip to the supermarket is for us. Jesus in his parables several times uses the picture of the harvest at the end of days.

Harvest is a very final sort of picture! Once you have picked a fruit, or cut down a field of wheat, you cannot very well take what you have cut and stick it back in the ground, or back on the tree, and hope that it will carry on living, or do better second time round. Once it has been harvested, that's it.

There are in fact two separate descriptions of harvest here: first, the harvest of the people of God, the righteous, and second, the harvest of his enemies, the sinners.

The harvest of the righteous (14:14–16)

The first one involves the 'son of man' and an angel. There is little doubt that this 'son of man' represents Christ (a few commentators think it is another angel, because he receives instructions, but it is most likely that the instruction in verse 15 originates, like many in Revelation, from the throne itself and that the angel merely passes it on). Again there is a reference back to Daniel 7, the chapter which lies behind much of the 'beast' imagery of chapter 13. In Daniel 7:13 it is the appearance of the 'son of man' that brings the reign of the beast-kingdoms to an end. So it is here. The appearance of Christ will spell the end of the age-long cosmic conflict. Just as in Daniel, he appears with a cloud; in the Old Testament that is generally associated with theophanies, appearances of God. He is crowned to prove his authority, and he is equipped for his task with a sickle, or a scythe, the standard instrument for reaping grain. The angel emerges from the presence of God and calls on him to begin the harvest, and the Lord goes out to gather his people together from the four corners of the earth and bring them safely home. It is a comforting image, a happy tale of harvest home; all is safely gathered in.

The harvest of judgement (14:17–20)

The second view of the harvest, however, is very different and it follows straight on in verses 17–20. This time there is a pair of angels: one to convey the message and one to go out and reap. Now it is portrayed as a grape harvest (14:19). Once again, people who knew the Old Testament would remember that there were prophecies along these very lines: they come in Isaiah 63:1–6, and especially in Joel 3:12–13. But Revelation takes the picture even further. I find this one of the most haunting, terrifying portrayals of judgement in the whole of Scripture. As the grapes are trodden down, crushed in the winepress—again, a very familiar picture in the world of John's day—what do we see flowing out? (14:20). Instead of the expected red grape juice flowing out to make the wine, an overflowing river of blood gushes forth and runs away for mile upon mile.

The measurement given is '1,600 stadia'. Given all the Old Testament references in this vision, this dimension—about 180 miles—could refer to the physical size of the biblical land of Israel, measured from north to south. The idea then would be that the entire land is flooded with blood. But whether it stands for that or whether, as some believe, it is a purely symbolic number, the scale is simply staggering. It is a vision of the blood of a billion people draining away. It is picture language, but that does not make it less real. The picture shows us that God will vent his fury on everyone who has rebelled against him, all who have refused to bow to him, all who have rejected his salvation in Christ. In eternity, they will suffer for it, and it is God who will punish them. This is not something we want to think about, but it is here and it is not in doubt. People who do not know Jesus Christ will face the wrath of God through eternity. The only question is what we are going to do about it, because—as we believe Scripture—we know it is true.

We have to be clear that nothing is more important than knowing that we are on the right side of the divide. In comparison with that, *nothing else matters*—just as, on that day on Mount St Helens, nothing else mattered for Harry Truman. All that mattered was that he had ignored the warnings, time after time, and now the moment of reckoning had finally arrived. So are *you* on the right side of this fatal division? God's anger is not random and impersonal like an erupting volcano, but steady, unwavering, heartfelt opposition to sin—and you will face it if Jesus has not saved you from it. Are you safe with Christ?

If we *are* on the right side, what does this vision mean to us? We can sometimes go for days or months without thinking of what is waiting for people who are outside Christ. It is desperately hard to think about, but it is the reality. Meanwhile, we have the good news to offer. We know Jesus and what he has done for us; we know which side we stand. Surely if this vision means anything to us, it means we have to get the good news to the people who need to hear it.

Finally, looking from the right side of the divide, can we see what we are in the view of heaven? For us Jesus faced that crushing, burning wrath, took our place at the focal point of God's anger, took our punishment, suffered our hell, proving how much we are worth in his eyes. Now we are learning his song, the song of the redeemed. Doesn't this vision of the perfect church make us want to be like that now—pure, committed, obedient, willing to follow the Lord Jesus wherever he leads?

To discuss or think about

1. Does this chapter change your own thinking about hell? In what way?
2. Should the reality of hell be our main motivation for evangelism, or are there other more important motives?
3. How does the vision of the redeemed at the start of this chapter encourage you to walk faithfully with Christ?

Part VII

Seven bowls: God's wrath

(15:1–16:21)

14

The song of the winners

Please read Revelation 15

I love it when England scores a sporting victory. We have been consistently hopeless at football in my adult lifetime, but we won the Rugby World Cup in 2003 and cricket has seen some glorious victories too: notably the great Ashes triumphs since 2005 (alternating, though, with some very dismal defeats!).

I love remembering those days when Trafalgar Square was jammed solid with fans and the heart of London resounded with the songs of victory. At last we were winners!

In sport, we know what victory means: glory for the winners, a thrill for the followers. It means a few weeks on the sports pages of the newspapers, a few days maybe on the front pages as well, basking in the adulation of the public, open-top bus parades with the crowds chanting their names, winning coveted awards from the BBC or others—that's what victory means.

Here in Revelation 15 we come across another winning team who are here to celebrate victory. This team are not standing on a sports field, or gathered round an award in a television studio;

they are standing in heaven. And they are singing songs of victory, but not 'Swing low, sweet chariot', or even 'Land of my fathers'; they are singing 'the song of Moses the servant of God and the song of the Lamb'. They are singing because they are the winners in the age-long cosmic conflict between God and his enemies—the battle that has now been won. It is a winning team that includes everyone who belongs to Jesus, everyone called and chosen by God the Father, and strikingly, their songs are not about themselves, or the heroic exploits they accomplished on earth—their songs are about *him*.

The scene has shifted once again. One more time, the tape is rewound and played from the beginning as we come to this next section of the book. There is one more series of seven to come: the seven bowls of God's wrath, the same events played out in history, but this time not primarily as suffering (as with the seals), nor as warnings to repent (as with the trumpets), but as the wrath of God poured out in judgement. From here on, though we are still looking at events in human history, the emphasis falls more and more heavily on judgement. There is finality: notice how chapter 15 starts and ends with the word 'completed', or 'finished'. The reference to God's wrath being 'completed' applies only to judgement on earth, not to eternity. But for every individual, no matter when they have lived, the time eventually comes when warnings have finished and judgement sweeps them away. In the end, it will be too late for everyone who is outside Christ.

The song (15:1–4)

Chapter 15 describes an interlude before the seven bowls are poured out. Just as there was an interlude before the seals on the scroll were opened and another before the seven trumpets were blown, so here, as the seven angels appear, there is this song before they pour out their bowls. Clearly, we are supposed to relate the song they sing to what these seven angels are just about to do. So John looks, and in front of him again is the 'sea of glass' which he described in chapter 4, the sea of glass that surrounds God's throne—clear as crystal, beautiful, costly, reflecting his purity and holiness. But this time there is a difference: now the glass sea is shot through with flame, the glass mixed with fire to reflect the burning judgement that is about to take place.

A song of victory

Standing in a great crowd next to the sea are the winners. Here they are, with instruments ready to play (15:2). When we are in heaven, not only shall we all be able to sing, we shall all be able to make music as well! These people have been 'victorious over the beast and his image and over the number of his name'. So the tyrant who has done his utmost to destroy them has been defeated instead, and now at last they stand where he can reach them no longer. Satan and all his allies have done their worst, but that is in the past now. For the winners it is no longer the time of struggle. It is the time of song.

The song of Moses and of the Lamb

And they sing 'the song of Moses the servant of God and ... of the Lamb' (15:3–4)—not two different songs, but one. To understand the 'song of Moses' we need to look at Exodus 15. Although many of the *words* used in Revelation 15 actually come from other parts of the Old Testament, such as Jeremiah 10:7, it is in Exodus that we find the parallel in *meaning*. Moses has just led the Israelites out of Egypt and Pharaoh has pursued them with his army. The people were trapped, but God has parted the Red Sea and they have walked through on dry ground. And *now* Moses sings this song: 'The LORD is my strength and my song; he has become my salvation' (Exodus 15:2).

The song is a celebration, but significantly it is mostly about what has happened to the Egyptians. The crossing of the Red Sea was not just salvation for Israel; it was equally disaster for Egypt. 'The horse and its rider he has hurled into the sea' (Exodus 15:1). The Exodus itself was not just about salvation for Israel; it was also judgement on Egypt, God's enemy, through the plagues. That is why Moses is singing.

It is also the 'song of the Lamb', because what God did for Israel in Egypt, where the blood of lambs spared them from the angel of death, is just a small foretaste of what he has done for his people through Jesus Christ. He is the true Lamb of God, who brings us out of slavery to sin, but also brings judgement on his enemies. The cross which spells salvation for God's own people also spells doom for those who oppose him. The cross shows more clearly than anything else could that God takes sin seriously—so seriously that only the death of his Son can deal with it. Only the death of his Son can turn away his fury at sin. The victory of Jesus on the cross, his victory over Satan, starts the countdown to the final reckoning. So the cross points to judgement as well as salvation.

Praise for God's marvellous deeds

Look at the song the winners sing: 'Great and marvellous are your deeds.' John has already used those words to describe the seven angels in verse 1. The 'great and marvellous' deeds are God's acts of *judgement*. In their song they praise him for his justice and truth (15:3).

They praise him for being King, for being in command. The English translations differ slightly in verse 3: where the NIV84 has 'King of the ages', other versions including the NIV11 have 'King of the *nations*'. This is one of those rare occasions where the Greek manuscript evidence is evenly divided between two variants. In fact, it matters little which option we choose here—in one case God is King of all time; in the other he is King of everywhere. Either way, he is in charge.

He is praised for his holiness and his 'righteous acts' (15:4). Again, this is a reference to his utter uprightness and perfection. God's righteous acts are the expression of his very nature. The winners are praising the Lord because he is utterly true, totally holy, completely intolerant of sin, and everyone will have to acknowledge it. 'All nations will come and worship before you'—some gladly, yes, but not all will do so voluntarily. For some it will be because they are forced to submit.

There are some aspects of God's character that we find it hard to praise him for. It is easy to praise him for creating us, for all that he gives us, and above all for saving us through the Lord Jesus. But here on earth it is very hard to praise him for his judgements. It is difficult to think, and still harder to talk, about the fact that this loving God will condemn millions to hell. It is not the topic of choice in evangelism. Yet in this vision, as judgement looms, God's people are not shuffling about feeling embarrassed, or trying to look the other way. No, as the final demonstration of God's wrath is prepared, as the angels step forward to do his bidding, his people are praising him, declaring his righteousness and his glory. When we are standing there with them, with no sin in our hearts, nothing to cloud the attitude of our minds, seeing at last with clear eyes, we too will praise our God that every evil is going to be punished, every wrong set right, and even that his enemies will be condemned. On that day we shall fully understand the horror of sin: we shall understand the desperate cost Jesus paid to save us, and what it means that our God is awesome and holy and that sin cannot endure in his presence. And we shall worship him.

The angels with the seven bowls (15:5–8)

So the outpouring of wrath begins. Out from the temple—that is, out from the presence of God—the angels appear (15:6). The 'tabernacle of the covenant law', it is called (15:5).[1] John could have said simply 'the temple' (as he does in a closely parallel statement in 11:19, also in a passage that concerns judgement), but this chapter is full of language that recalls the Exodus and the events that surrounded it, both the grace of God and his wrath. The 'covenant law' is the law God gave to Moses, which was inscribed on tablets of stone and placed in the ark of the covenant. It symbolized God's presence with his people; it laid down what his righteousness demanded of them, and it expressed his very character. Probably the meaning also includes the words of Jesus himself. So from the very place where God's requirements are laid down, the angels emerge to bring his wrath on those who have flouted them.

John in his vision sees these angels dressed in shining clothes with golden sashes—a little bizarre to us, perhaps, but the meaning is clear enough: their clothing represents purity, dignity and the authority of God which they carry. One of the four living creatures who surround God's throne—here probably symbolizing the created world which will be so closely involved with the events which follow—gives each angel a bowl to pour out on the earth (15:7).

The scene is set for God's wrath. As the angels stand ready, the temple fills with smoke (15:8). The scene recalls the account in Isaiah 6 of the day when the prophet went up to the temple in Jerusalem and experienced that devastating vision of the living God, enthroned and high. Then, as the seraphs cried out praises of his holiness, the whole edifice shook and the temple was filled with smoke. It recalls, too, the day when Solomon dedicated the temple and the building was so filled with the clouds of God's glory that the priests could not enter (1 Kings 8). And it recalls the events in the desert when God's glory settled on the tabernacle and Moses himself could not go in (Exodus 40). Thus the awesome God reveals himself. In the Old Testament God's people saw it and praised him with awe and wonder. On that day in heaven we shall see it and praise him once more. Here and now we are forcibly reminded what a God it is we serve—not a cosy, cuddly figure who will turn a blind eye to sin and eventually wave everyone through into heaven. Still less does he resemble the dying, decrepit figure of the Philip Pullman novels. No, this is our God: all-knowing, all-seeing, glorious and holy.

What this vision teaches us

There are two key messages from this vision, both already familiar from the earlier chapters of Revelation.

1. Victory is ours

The first is that we are the winners. In chapter 7 we first met the 144,000 servants who are sealed for the living God before the trouble begins, and we saw that they stand for the entire church throughout history. At that point they were on the earth. In 14:1 we meet them again, but this time they are in heaven. Once again, there are 144,000 of them; not a single one has been lost. Every single man, woman and child whom the Lord has called and chosen for himself and who has known Christ here on earth makes it to heaven. God brings us all home. And the winners here in chapter 15 are exactly the same people once again. In spite of all that the dragon and the beast can do, in spite of the fact that they sometimes seem to be getting on top, God's people are the winners.

But in the meantime, we are in the battle, whether we like it or not. The Bible knows nothing about Christians who put their feet up, or retire, or would rather not be too keen. This is still a war with pain and casualties. Anyone who is in the battle already knows that. Being on the winning side is not an easy ride; we are not gathered at God's throne just yet. These words were first written to a church under severe pressure. Real victory in the Christian life does not mean ducking every difficulty, escaping all trouble, taking the line of least resistance. It means facing the worst that evil can do and being faithful to the end. *Then* comes the victory parade. But the crowds will not be chanting *our* names; they will be singing the song of the Lamb, and so will we.

2. God is in charge

As we have seen before, there is no book like Revelation for showing us the big picture. One of the features of this book is the way that the scene constantly alternates, switching between the view of heaven and events on earth. If all we can see is the view on earth, there are times when we are liable to despair. On earth, the dragon rages, the beast rules his kingdom and the false prophet deludes millions. Horrors unfold through history; believers suffer and sometimes Satan seems to have won. But then the view changes and we see the scene in heaven. We see God on his throne. We see that he is sovereign over all that takes place. We see, at the centre of it all, the Lamb who was slain, the wounds for us still visible in heaven, declaring for eternity the extent of his love for us his people. And when we see that, we have no doubt that our God, and only he, is in charge, 'King of the ages'.

To discuss or think about

1. This passage shows us the crowd of victorious saints now at rest in heaven—'retired', we might say. How do you think about retirement here on earth? Should it be a time to relax and switch off spiritually, or do you believe that the Lord will always have work for you to do as long as your life on earth continues? Does your attitude need to change?
2. How does seeing the heavenly perspective on judgement help us with the difficulties we feel in thinking about it from our earthly point of view?
3. Are you confident that you will be a member of the victorious crowd?

15

The fate of the losers

Please read Revelation 16

In November 1949 a double murder was committed in London. The victims were a woman named Beryl and her daughter Geraldine, and their bodies were discovered at the family's address—an address which from that day on became notorious: 10, Rillington Place. Beryl's husband, Geraldine's father, was named Timothy Evans. It was Evans who first raised the alarm by going to the police and confessing that he had murdered his wife. But soon afterwards, when the two bodies were discovered, strangled, inside the wash-house in the garden, he accused his neighbour, John Christie, of carrying out the crime. By the time Evans was put on trial, he had changed his story twice more. He insisted throughout on his innocence and claimed that Christie was the real murderer. The jury, however, were not convinced. Evans was convicted of the murder of baby Geraldine and sentenced to death.

Three years later, however, a new tenant at 10, Rillington Place stumbled on a disused pantry containing the bodies of three women. Christie was tried and convicted of murdering his own wife, Ethel. He admitted the murder of Mrs Evans as well and later indications were that he had been the murderer of Geraldine too. Christie was hanged that July. He had actually murdered at least ten women and children over a period of ten years.

Timothy Evans was the victim of one of the most serious miscarriages of justice. When the mistake became obvious, there was a public outcry. In 1966 Evans was given a free pardon—but of course, it was too late by then. The case of Evans and Christie was one of the main reasons why Britain abandoned the death penalty for murder. If we still had it, there would have been many other unjust executions since that of Timothy Evans, notably the 'Birmingham Six' and the 'Guildford Four', who were convicted of terrorist attacks on faulty evidence. Of course this is also one reason why in the USA, where many states do have the death penalty, there is such controversy about it; in spite of every advance in technology and all the checks and balances that are supposed to prevent corruption of evidence, miscarriages of justice are unavoidable. There is no court system in the world, no human judge, that is infallible. We are reluctant use the death penalty in case we get it wrong. We simply cannot be sure.

But with God, we *can* be sure, because our God is utterly just and true. The best legal systems on this earth can at most aspire to be imitations of the justice of God, and they will always be fallible. But we can be sure that no evil goes unseen or unpunished with him.

Revelation chapters 15 and 16 form a pair. In chapter 15, we saw the seven angels poised ready to pour out their golden bowls full of the wrath of God. Round his throne in heaven are gathered his redeemed people, and they are singing the song of the winners. They are not embarrassed to see his judgements being carried out; rather, they *praise* him, his justice, holiness and perfection. That chapter focused on God's people, saved by the Lamb, the Lord Jesus Christ, the winners. But there are also *losers*. Today, of course, 'loser' is something that you are likely to be called if you are a Christian. It is a regular insult that is liable to be fired at anyone who is not 'one of us'. But in eternity, if you belong to Jesus Christ, you are a *winner*. The loser is the one who has rejected Christ; that is what we see in chapter 16. It is not yet hell that is pictured here. This chapter shows us how the wrath of God is poured out on rebels even in this life, here on earth. We need to come to God's Word with our imagination, trying to capture the vision that John saw. The imagery is used to create an impression in our minds. It would be wrong to try to press every detail, or to try to make each separate vision tally precisely with all the others. This kind of writing simply doesn't work that way; it is not intended for scientific analysis. But what it portrays is real, all the same.

The seven bowls and the seven last plagues

So, in this chapter, the seven bowls containing the seven last plagues are poured out by the angels. The voice of authority, which can only be the voice of God, gives the command in verse 1, and it begins. Once again the scene switches from heaven, a place of peace, sinless beauty and the never-ending worship of God, to the earth, where there is sin, where people hate God and Satan still stalks the land—the earth that we know.

Parallels with the seven trumpets

We have noted before how these seven bowls are parallel to the seven trumpets of chapters 8 and 9. If you compare them carefully, you will see the closeness of the match. The first trumpet is directed against *the land*; so is the first bowl. The second trumpet involves *the sea* being turned to blood; so does the second bowl. The third trumpet and bowl both relate to *water in the rivers and springs*. The fourth of each series relates to *the sun*. The fifth trumpet blows, and from the pit of the Abyss comes smoke and *darkness*; with the fifth bowl there is darkness on the throne of the beast. The beast, remember, is one of Satan's allies, the power of tyranny on earth. At the sixth trumpet the four angels at the river *Euphrates* are released, making way for an army; at the sixth bowl the Euphrates is dried up, making way for an army. The seventh trumpet brings the cry of heavenly voices that the kingdoms of this world have become the kingdom of Christ—*it is all over*. And the seventh bowl concludes: 'It is done!' Now some of these phenomena are hard to imagine, but the fact is that they are the same in both cases. That really proves that we are right to see the story of Revelation not as a single long line of events, but as a constant replaying of the same drama, for what is now the final time.

Judgements, not warnings

But there are some key differences too. This is not just a rerun of what has gone before, but a new angle on it. God is well able to make the same events serve his purposes in many different ways. The trumpets blew warnings to the peoples on earth, but now these are not warnings any more; these are *judgements*. In verse 2, for instance, instead of a general impact on the world at large, we see judgement directed personally at the enemies of God, at everyone who has been part of the beast's system and opposed to God's rule. Now they are made to suffer individually, directly, painfully. Verses 3–4 present a horrible picture of the earth's waters reduced to a cold, congealing mess. When the trumpets were blown, a fraction of the earth was affected. Now it is total. These are judgements, not warnings. If all the fresh water becomes undrinkable, everyone dies. Then, as the sun blazes out (16:8–9), people are scorched by the heat, but there is nothing to drink, and all the rebels can do is to curse.

Parallels with the plagues of Egypt

We have noted before that these chapters are full of references to the Exodus, that day when God brought his own people out of Egypt and when a nation was born—the day which the Israelites never forgot and which they celebrated every year in the Passover. Several of these plagues look like a scaled-up version of the plagues of Egypt: the blood, the boils or sores, and so on. The ruler of Egypt hardened his heart and in the end he was incapable of responding to God's warnings; now the same thing has happened to the rebels on earth. If you keep on refusing God, that is what happens. The use of the word 'plague' itself is a deliberate echo of those ancient events. The plagues of Egypt are now seen to be a foreshadowing in miniature of the way the Lord will deal with the whole world in the last days.

Once again, we see here a pattern that we have noticed before, with the seals on the scroll and with the trumpets: the first four bowls form a group, located in the natural world, but then at number five there is a change of gear. From events in the physical world we switch to the spiritual realities that stand behind them (16:10–11). Remember what happened to Egypt as the plagues neared their climax. Plague number nine was the plague of darkness—throughout the land of Egypt *except* where the Israelites were living. It was a targeted judgement, and so is this one. Just as Egypt oppressed God's people then and held them down, so the beast is the tyrant who grinds God's people down today. Now God says, 'I am going to plunge the beast's kingdom into darkness.' Just as his kingdom is not a visible, physical kingdom, so the darkness is not a visible, physical darkness. This is not some sort of electricity failure, a power cut. It means that God will throw the beast's kingdom—Satan's mockery of the church, *God's* new society—into chaos. Through the tyrants of this world—the Stalins, the Hitlers, the Mugabes, many Islamic states today—Satan builds his *anti*-church, a godless society founded on lies, a world that turns its back on the true God and on Christ.

But when the bowl is poured out, it all goes dark. Confusion reigns, and just as with ancient Egypt, the system is paralysed. In the end, Satan's kingdom simply falls apart. Every tyrant, every human empire, ultimately comes crashing down because, eventually, the fifth bowl is poured out on it. When we, God's people, see that happening, as when a Berlin Wall comes down, as when a proud nation descends into chaos, we should understand the times and keep on praying for *Christ's* kingdom to come on earth—which it assuredly will. Meanwhile, all that the losers do is to blame it on God, but like Pharaoh of old, they do not turn to him because their hearts are so hardened.

The final battle

Now from this point on, with bowls six and seven, we are no longer dealing with events that take place through history. Just as we saw with the trumpets, numbers six and seven refer to the end times, to the final battle. We see Satan stirring up the peoples of the earth and their leaders for one final onslaught against the people of God (16:16). Unfortunately, 'Armageddon' is one of those words which have jumped out of the context of Revelation and taken on a life of their own. 'Armageddon' has come to mean nuclear war, but Scripture scarcely supports that interpretation! Almost certainly, 'Armageddon' means 'Mountain of Megiddo'. Megiddo is a real place in northern Israel; it is mentioned several times in the Old Testament and was the site of some important battles. Some people therefore believe that the final battle will take place literally at this site.

However, there are good reasons to disagree with this view. First, there is this very odd expression: 'the place that in Hebrew is called Armageddon'. Now John's readers didn't speak Hebrew, so what is the point of saying that? If I want to tell you I am going to Wales, I don't say, 'I am going to the place that in Welsh is called Cymru.' I suggest that what John is doing is pointing us back to the Hebrew Old Testament references to this place and to what happened there.

Secondly, there is in fact *no* mountain of Megiddo. It is a flat plain. In fact it is a *gap* in a mountain range, which is why so many battles were fought there. In particular, there was the battle that spelled the end of the kingdom of Judah (2 Kings 23:29–30). Pharaoh Neco was on his way north to join the Assyrians at Carchemish; on his way he passed through Judah. Good king Josiah stupidly took his army out to meet him and they fought at Megiddo. In the battle, Josiah was killed and the last hope for Judah was gone.

Now put that history into the context of this chapter. Pharaoh Neco comes from Egypt; when he fights Josiah at Megiddo he is on his way to the 'Euphrates' to meet up with the 'kings from the East'. Remember that the Old Testament story is our key to understanding Revelation. So I suggest that if you are John, looking for a strong symbol for the final battle between God's enemies and his people, Armageddon is the name you might well choose. But the key point is that the battle takes place. *This* time, God's enemies, the losers, are swept away. Then bowl number seven is the end.

Lessons for believers from the seven bowls

We have not dealt with every detail of the seven bowls. But as we see the beginning of judgement, as we contemplate the fate of the losers, there are some important things for believers to see.

1. God's judgements are right

I was once talking to a Muslim friend and we got onto the subject of judgement. Muslims rightly believe that God has a record of everything that we do in this life; this record will be the basis for decision on the Day of Judgement. I explained to him that a just God has to punish sin and that no one has done what pleases God. Even my very best deeds are mixed up with sin. I never do anything without a mixed motive and I richly deserve to be judged and condemned. He replied, 'Well, God is merciful, and he may forgive.' Muslims are commanded to live between hope and fear. They are told that they cannot know whether God will choose to overlook their sins or not. But God is just. Sin cannot simply be ignored. I long for our friend to be able to say, 'Jesus died for me', because I know that that is the only way he will escape what this chapter describes, and worse.

Take verses 5–7, for instance. They form a kind of commentary that comes in after the third of the bowls. The 'angel [...] of the waters' (as the Greek actually has it) is either the angel with the third bowl or (less likely) an angel associated with that part of creation. In the previous chapter we heard the crowd of the redeemed praising God for his judgements; now this angel and the altar also join in. Think back to 6:9–10, where John sees under the altar in heaven the souls of the martyrs crying out for justice: 'How long, Sovereign Lord, holy and true, until you judge the inhabitants of the earth and avenge our blood?' They were told to wait a while, but now the waiting is over and the martyrs—in fact all God's people who have been hurt by the beast—are about to be vindicated. The Lord has responded to their plea. Everyone who does not belong to Christ, who bears the mark of the beast, will face this judgement. In heaven they are absolutely unanimous: God's judgements are right, true and just. In heaven there will be no need for public enquiries about false convictions. It may be hard for us to grasp because we are so used to dealing with (and being!) people who are fallible. But God has never made a mistake.

2. God's plans will triumph

In 16:13–14, we see Satan launching his counter-attack. 'The dragon'—that is Satan—'the beast' and 'the false prophet' constitute an unholy trinity to set against the real one. Out from their mouths come a miniature plague of frogs (another echo of the Egyptian plagues), but not the kind you find in your garden pond. They are evil spirits whose task is to gather all the armies of the world together for the final battle—Armageddon. Satan knows his time is running out, as we have seen before, but he thinks he will at least have his day and go down fighting. But see whose day it turns out to be: 'the battle on the great day of God Almighty'! Satan thinks this is his show, but it is not. He will find out at last that all along he has simply been serving the purposes of Almighty God.

So Armageddon is launched (16:16). And the result? The amazing fact is that this chapter doesn't even bother to tell us. That is the measure of Satan's utter futility. This vision simply passes on to the end. To see the final outcome, turn over to 19:19–20. And with the seventh bowl we simply have these words spoken, as the voice of God comes once more from his throne, declaring, 'It is done!' It has happened! The vision ends with a final, terrifying deluge of destruction on God's enemies: the lightning and thunder, the earthquake and a hailstorm such as the world has never seen— the seventh bowl followed by a worldwide version of the seventh plague of Egypt. All these are signs of God's majesty and power, emanating from his throne. The earthquake brings down the cities; the islands flee and the mountains collapse. And 'God remembered Babylon the Great and gave her the cup filled with the wine of the fury of his wrath' (16:19). The next two chapters will show us exactly what happens to Babylon. What a grim scene! What a bleak finish this is, as life for a world of rebellion is brought to a close!

God's plans have triumphed and Satan's have utterly failed. What we see in Revelation 16 is how that triumph and failure work out on the grand scale. At the end of this age, Satan will finally be nailed down. Satan is still very active today, but God's plans will triumph. This passage tells us that, yes, Satan still has his allies and, yes, he still has his little victories. But it gives us the assurance that Satan loses. Even the little successes that he has—the lives he destroys, the suffering that he brings—God can turn round, until the day of Satan turns out to be the day of God Almighty.

3. God's people must be prepared

Dramatically, just as John is watching the build-up of Satan's forces for Armageddon and the armies are gathering, there is this sudden intervention in verse 15. Unmistakably, it is the risen Christ whose voice now rings in John's ears with this picture of a thief, arriving when he is least expected and finding the homeowner unprepared, asleep and wearing pyjamas—or even less![1] It is a picture used by both Paul (1 Thessalonians 5:2) and Jesus himself (Matthew 24:43–44). Clearly, it is an encouragement to believers to be ready for Christ's return, a warning given as the end approaches, as the seventh and last bowl is ready to be poured out. 'Don't go to sleep on the job,' Jesus says. He is *not* saying that believers will be lost. They are safe in his hand and he will neither drop them nor allow them to jump out! But the New Testament is full of warnings to be ready, to stay awake, not to be caught out. The enemy will use every trick in the book to catch us out. Even miracles are not proof that someone is genuine. There are 'false Christs'—the beast—and 'false prophets', Jesus says. Christians must be careful about what is genuine and beware of picking up the latest popular fad.

We live in a time of trouble, a time of war. This chapter reminds us that judgement is already being poured out on the earth and the Jesus we love is coming back for us soon. Meanwhile, Satan and his allies are trying everything to drag us off course, to spoil our lives, to ruin our ministries, so that we shall not be ready when the Lord returns, so that we shall be caught with our trousers down—that is the image. We don't want to be ashamed when the day comes and he returns to bring us home.

To discuss or think about

1. Are you awake and ready for the return of the Lord Jesus?
2. Are you confident that God's judgements at the last day will be absolutely just and true, or do you think there is any possibility that his justice will make mistakes as human courts sometimes do?
3. How does the assurance of God's justice comfort and help us as we look at the many injustices in the world today?

Part VIII
The triumph of Almighty God
(17:1–20:15)

16

The ugliest woman in the world

Please read Revelation 17

These days we see all kinds of crazy and extreme programmes on the television. Some of it is good; some is rubbish, and some of it is frankly appalling. But there is one kind of show that seems to have gone out of fashion in recent years: the beauty contest. You might remember the 'Miss World' format. A large gang of suspiciously similar-looking girls would parade in national dress and then in reasonably modest bathing suits—which was probably the reason that most of the male audience watched—and then came the interviews, where deep and searching questions were used to elicit equally profound responses from the contestants! The contestant would be asked, 'What is your greatest wish?' and the reply would be: 'World peace, of course!' 'And your personal ambition?' Obviously, 'To travel the world and work with children.' It was both bland and predictable.

But if beauty contests have become controversial, how about an *ugliness* contest? What about a competition to find the ugliest woman in the world? I wonder how popular that would be. But in fact, we don't need to run the competition, because we already know the winner. I hasten to reassure you that it is not anyone who is reading this book! The ugliest woman in the world is actually the one we meet right here in Revelation 17. The strange thing is this: we can understand why so many men want to go out with beautiful models; it is obvious why there is such a long queue to be with them. But the longest queue of all is not for any of the beautiful women; the longest queue is for the *ugliest* woman, the prostitute of Revelation 17. And, as we work through this chapter, I want to pose two very blunt questions: 'Are we in bed with the prostitute? And if not, are we flirting with her?'

In the last chapter we looked at the scene of judgement, as the bowls of God's wrath are poured out on the world in rebellion against him—a fearsome scene as we saw how, even in *this* life, even in the world that we know, God is judging and punishing people who stand out against him. We saw how it all comes to a great and terrible conclusion as the armies marshalled by Satan are blown away by God and his forces, the world is shaken to its foundations by a gigantic earthquake and the history of this rebellious world is brought to its end.

Right in the middle of that description of the chaos of the end, we read this short, almost throwaway line in 16:19: 'God remembered Babylon the Great and gave her the cup filled with the wine of the fury of his wrath.' And the next two chapters, 17 and 18, take that short line and expand it into a grand drama of judgement. In the overall structure of Revelation, we are now moving towards the end. Until now we have been looking mostly at events that unfold in history, the times we know. We have seen these three series of sevens: the seals on the scroll, the trumpets and the bowls. But now we are coming on to look at the final triumph of Almighty God, and it's at the beginning of this new section that we meet the world's ugliest woman!

The introduction to the vision (17:1–2)

One of the seven angels from the scene we have just left is going to be John's guide (17:1). First he explains what John is going to see. She is a prostitute on a grand scale, because she has slept, not just with a few kings and rulers, but with huge numbers of the world's population as well.

There are a couple of extra points that we need to note at the outset. The NIV adopts the translation 'adultery' in these verses. The word used in the Greek is not quite as specific as that. It really means 'sexual immorality' in a more general sense, or 'fornication'. Adultery implies being married to someone else, but that is not implied here. This prostitute seduces everyone she can get her hands on.

Now note that expression 'the inhabitants of the earth', which is familiar from earlier chapters. As we have seen, in Revelation it means not everyone on the planet, but those who are at home here—not the Lord's people, not the church, but *everyone else*: those, in fact, who wear the mark of the beast.

The woman and the beast (17:3–7)

The woman described

So, after this dramatic introduction, John is whisked off in his vision into 'a desert' (17:3). The desert is the place where you go to see something clearly, a place where you are detached from the ordinary events of the world. There he sees her. It is an astonishing picture. John himself is 'astonished', and who can blame him? Some scholars even understand this to mean that he is rather taken with this impressive lady to begin with, and that is why the angel responds so indignantly! Indeed, this woman is really something. Her clothes are striking. In John's day the only way to produce clothes in these colours was with a dye extracted from thousands of tiny shellfish. That was why ordinary people wore brown or off-white, the natural colours of wool or yarn. Purple and scarlet were the colours of royalty. And she is covered with jewels, gilded with gold; she is rich—indeed, the picture is one of excessive ostentation, of gaudiness.

That, however, is as good as it gets. In her hand she holds a cup of gold, but its contents are disgusting. She is drinking deep of immorality and every kind of evil. Worse still, she is a murderer. She is drunk with the blood of believers, the people who love Jesus—with *our* blood. And stuck on her forehead is this title:

BABYLON THE GREAT
MOTHER OF PROSTITUTES
AND OF THE ABOMINATIONS OF THE EARTH.

This woman's identity is quite clear, and if there was ever any doubt it is dispelled in verse 18, where she is named as 'the great city that rules over the kings of the earth'. Down through the ages, all through the pages of Scripture, Babylon has stood against God and his people, right from Genesis until the days of Israel's exile there, and Babylon comes to be used as a symbol for the godless rebellion of humanity against our Creator.

Two women and two cities

We shall return to that great scriptural theme in the next chapter. Meanwhile, here she is—a woman who perhaps appears attractive at first glance, but in her true identity is hideous, disgusting, revolting. Of course, the fact that she is pictured as a prostitute doesn't mean that her sin is all about sex. The point about prostitution is that it is a mockery of marriage, the sexual relationship for which men and women are designed. In the Bible, marriage is used time and again as a picture of the Lord's relationship with his own people; that beautiful picture appears again at the close of Revelation. A relationship of love, of intimacy, of the deepest friendship, and an exclusive relationship at that—such is the relationship between the Lord Jesus and his bride, the church.

But, in mockery of that beautiful love, this vision shows us a prostitute having casual sex with whoever fancies her. Whereas prostitutes in our world are very often victims of others, this one is the great victimiser. Her whole life is about seducing people, drawing them in to her perverted ways, opposing God and assaulting his church. Her personal ambition is not travelling the world and working with children; it is *selling* the world and *destroying* its children. Scripture presents us, then, with two women: the bride of Christ and the prostitute, the ugliest woman in the world. They represent two cities: the new Jerusalem, our city; and Babylon the great, ruler of the inhabitants of the earth.

The beast she sits on

So where does this woman get her power? How is she able to lead so many people astray? The answer lies in what she is sitting on (17:3). We should recognize him well by now, this 'beast'. Back in chapter 13, and surfacing frequently ever since, he is Satan's leading ally. His description here is just the same as in chapter 13 with the addition of the colour 'scarlet', and since red is the dragon's colour, Satan's colour, it suggests an even closer connection between the beast and Satan himself. There he is, in all his satanic power, blaspheming God, as ugly as they come—and he is the vehicle, the engine, for the prostitute's work.

By the way, there is no suggestion in the original Greek that she is *riding* the beast, controlling it as you might ride a horse. For some of us, if we get on a horse, it is very much the horse that is in charge, and the horse knows it! We just happen to be on the top—for the time being. And that is the situation with this woman and the beast. The beast carries her along; she is not the one in control. Underlying the power of Babylon, blinding and leading astray the whole world, is the servant of Satan.

In the rest of this chapter, John's guiding angel gives him more explanations about the beast and his heads and horns. It is not the easiest part of the book to understand, and there is a lot of disagreement about how we should read it. We shall look at it briefly. But I must say again that we should not treat Revelation like a puzzle book. That word 'mystery' in verses 5 and 7 does not mean anything like a Hercule Poirot detective story. In the Bible, a 'mystery' is not something you can figure out for yourself. It is something that you either know or you don't know, and if you *do* know, it is only because God has graciously told you the secret.

Unfortunately, too many people, including some Christians who have sold a lot of popular books, look at a chapter like this as if it were a kind of Sudoku puzzle. In Sudoku, you get some of the numbers filled in, and you have to work out the rest. These people come to this chapter and think, 'Great! The angel has filled in some of the numbers for us; he has given us some explanations. Now we have to figure out the rest.' So verse 9 says, 'This calls for a mind with wisdom,' and they think, 'Aha! This sounds like an *expert* level Sudoku. I would probably need a PhD for this one!' But this is nothing to do with intelligence. It is *spiritual* insight that is needed here, not for cracking a code, but for recognizing what the beast is up to.

The meaning of the vision (17:8–14)

So the angel explains. He says that the 'seven heads' represent 'seven hills' and also 'seven kings', of which five have been and gone, number six is around now and the seventh is still to come. And the 'ten horns' are ten *more* kings, who are yet to come and will award their power to the beast to make war against the Lamb and his armies. Now commentators have had a field day with these verses. The commentaries are full of schemes involving lists of Roman emperors, world empires and so forth. And, on the wilder shores of interpretation, older readers may remember the suggestion back in the 1970s that the ten kings represent the European community, which at the time had only nine members. The idea was that when the tenth member joined, that would be a sign of the end. Not surprisingly, now that the EU has twenty-eight members, you don't hear that suggestion any more!

So what does it mean? Briefly, here is what I think. Just as the prostitute is a kind of false church, so the beast, the tyrant, is a mockery of Christ, our King, and of God. God is described as the one 'who is, and who was, and who is to come' (1:8). By contrast, the beast is the one who 'once was, now is not, and will come ...'—but only to be destroyed! (17:8). Whereas God is constant and true, with the beast it is a case of 'Now you see him, now you don't'. While the Lord is eternal, the beast will be destroyed. And, just as the Bible awards him the number of failure, 666, so here again the beast is shown up for what he really is. The seven heads and seven hills surely refer to Rome, famously built on seven hills. That would have been the obvious meaning for John's original readers, and we must never lose sight of them. And yet it is more than that. The beast is not just the power of the *Roman* Empire; he is the power behind *every* evil empire, every tyrant who raises his head against our God. That is why he is the eighth king who belongs to the seven.

What of the series of seven kings? Some of those schemes about the great world empires may even be right, but they are not the whole story. We must not read Revelation saying, 'Aha! *This* stands for *that*. Now I have solved it; now I can move on.' The message is that there are *always* great empires, one after another. At any time there is always some great power out there to terrify us and to crush God's people, but the end is coming.

The procession of evil powers will not last for ever; in fact we are nearing the end. And when the end comes, as we saw in the previous chapter, the beast and his friends will gather the world's rulers together for one final battle against God and his church. That is what chapter 16 describes as the battle of Armageddon, chapter 19 describes as the battle of the rider on the white horse and this chapter describes as ten kings giving authority to the beast and fighting a brief but utterly futile battle against the Lamb and his people (17:13–14). In other words, it is the final showdown, in which we win and they lose.

The destruction of the prostitute (17:15–18)

Now let's return to the ugly woman herself. The earthly Babylon stood by a broad river, the Euphrates. But this woman is seated above waters which represent the nations she rules over: 'peoples, multitudes, nations and languages'. Again we are reminded that Satan is building his *anti*-church from every nation, just as the Lord is building the *true* church from every nation and language.

But what happens next is a surprise. Surely the beast is very attached to the woman? Surely Satan is going to look after her? On the contrary, they 'will hate the prostitute. They will bring her to ruin and leave her naked...' We should never think that Satan cares about the people who belong to his kingdom. It is not a question of Jesus being on one side of the room, as it were, and Satan on the other side, both sincerely wanting what is best for us and lovingly calling us to join them. Jesus really does, of course, but Satan hates his own people just as much as he hates Christians. He doesn't want what is good for *anyone*.

This is what Jesus spoke of in Mark 3:24–26, referring to Satan's kingdom being divided. In that case, 'his end has come'. Exactly so. All through this age, Satan has been ruling a kingdom of his own through lies, deceit and terror. But at the time of the end, as his kingdom falls into pieces around him, Satan will turn on his own followers and tear them to pieces: 'They will eat her flesh and burn her with fire' (17:16). It will happen because God *drives* them to do so (17:17). While verse 13 speaks of *their* purpose, *their* united intention, verse 17 shows us that all along it is our God who is pulling the strings. As we saw in the previous chapter, the great day of Satan becomes in the end the great day of God Almighty. God's words are fulfilled and judgement is done.

It should be very clear to us who this ugly woman is—this prostitute, so seductive, who traps people into Satan's anti-Christ world and holds them there for ever, the woman who looks so appealing, seems to have so much to offer, but is unmasked here for what she really is. She is the ugliest of mistresses, deep in every kind of sin, delighting in every kind of abuse, and herself hating and abusing everyone who sleeps with her. Here she is shown up as the ultimate loser, because in the end Satan himself will turn on her.

Whose side are you on?

Let's return to the questions I asked at the beginning of the chapter. Are you in bed with the prostitute? If you don't belong to Jesus Christ, that is exactly where you are. You have joined up with someone who can give you thrills for a while. She can give you an exciting life, until the excitement wears off—and an easy life too. As long as you are with her, you will never have to take a stand for what you know to be right. Will you realize that you don't have to stay there, that there is a way for you to escape from her clutches, that you can join the winning side, where it is tough but in the end you are a winner, because there is someone who doesn't hate you, someone who gave his life to rescue you from her grip?

But what about the second question? You may not be in

bed with her, but are you *flirting* with her? This world and all that it offers are so attractive—irresistible, it may seem to you. The woman reaches out to you and whispers, 'I can offer you the world. Look at what I've got for you.' For each of us, the attraction is a little different. It may be the lure of the glittering prizes of success, making a pile of money, a great career. Ambition takes many forms and it is so easy to be drawn in. Motherhood itself becomes idolatry when being the best mother becomes your driving passion! Even our ministry can be our idol, when we want people's applause more than God's 'Well done'. 'Success, success, success,' whispers the woman on the beast.

What is it for you? Maybe it *is* related to sex. Perhaps it is internet pornography, the most secret, unseen of temptations, and so easily available; or else the age-old temptation to sleep around, like everyone else does—or so they tell you. Or it may be the soft comforts of an easy life, the safe dreams of a smart home with two cars in the garage. Whatever it is—and she has many, many voices—the woman may whisper in your ear, or she may shout aloud, 'I can offer you the world.' But look at who she is! Tattooed across her face are the words: 'World's biggest slut.' She is the original vampire—she wants to drink our blood! Do we really want to flirt with the ugliest woman in the world?

There is a wonderful alternative, of course. As if to remind us constantly who is really in control, who is the real King, he puts in an appearance in this chapter: 'The Lamb will overcome them because he is Lord of lords and King of kings—and with him will be his called, chosen and faithful followers' (17:14). At the end of the age the Lord Jesus Christ will sweep away all that remains of the woman, and the beast, and the rest of them. All this world's temptations, all those whispers that we listened to, will be shown up for the stupid, empty, pointless enticements that they really are. We cannot love the world and also love Christ.

It is simply impossible. The same Lord Jesus, who laid down his life to save us, the Lord Jesus we love, now calls us to be true to his name. He will overcome Satan's armies at the end of this age, and he will give us the power to overcome *now*. He has called us; he has chosen us. Now, are we willing to say, 'The world is not enough,' and be faithful to *him*?

To discuss or think about

1. John seems to have found the woman initially quite impressive. Where are you tempted to flirt with the prostitute's temptations? What might she be whispering in your ears?
2. What is the most effective response to the temptations you face? Where does your love for the Lord Jesus, the Lamb, feature in that response?
3. When we speak about sin, do we need to be more honest about the fact that sin is initially very often attractive and enjoyable?

17

The great escape

Please read Revelation 18

It has to be one of the best-known and most loved war films ever made. With an all-star cast headed by the young Steve McQueen, *The Great Escape* tells the story of a mass breakout by Allied prisoners of war towards the end of the Second World War. It is based on a true story—with the exception, that is, of the iconic scenes of McQueen on a motorcycle, which are pure Hollywood and which were added at his own request! There really *was* an escape from this camp. There really *was* a series of tunnels known as Tom, Dick and Harry. There were hundreds of forged documents to give those who managed to escape a chance of making it across occupied Europe to safety. There were tiny compasses made from broken gramophone records and tiny slivers of magnetized razor blade. And one night in March 1944, seventy-six men succeeded in escaping through the tunnel called Harry, all 336 feet of it, and getting away from the camp.

But in spite of all the ingenuity and preparation, the Great

Escape had a tragic and horrible aftermath. Only three prisoners made it to safety. The other seventy-three were all captured and, of those, fifty were shot by the SS, in groups at the side of the road.

What is less well known is that the story does not end there. After the war, special investigators were sent to the region to track down the perpetrators of the massacre. They found that some of them had died in fighting at the end of the war. But of the remainder, nearly all were found, put on trial and convicted. Thirteen of them were executed; justice was done.

Now in Revelation 18 our God is calling us to a great escape. This escape does not involve digging tunnels under prison-camp wire, or travelling across country with forged papers. But it is about breaking out of a city which God is going to destroy, a city where he is going to make sure that justice is executed. This chapter is a summons to us to understand exactly what we are up against as Christians. It is a call to see clearly the power of the system that Satan has set up against us and, above all, a call to make our escape from it, to get out quick. The city's name is Babylon. In chapter 17 we saw her as a *woman*, the great prostitute who aims to seduce us with her enticing temptations. In chapter 18, the picture changes from a woman to a *city*, and yet her identity is the same. As the end of chapter 17 tells us, 'The woman you saw is the great city that rules over the kings of the earth.'

What 'Babylon' stands for in Scripture

She is a city whose name resounds throughout Scripture. In fact, out of the sixty-six books in the Bible, Babylon is mentioned in no less than twenty of them—plus one more, Lamentations, which is all about what Babylon does but somehow manages not to mention her name. Babylon runs like a thread through the entire biblical narrative; she is found in every major division of the Bible and she loomed large all through Israel's story. Almost from the very beginning, she has been present as the beating heart of godless rebellion. The first mention of her is in Genesis 10:10, but her story really begins in Genesis 11 with the Tower of Babel (Babylon). The scheme of humanity is to build a tower that will reach up to heaven and be on a level with the gods, in the hope of making a name for themselves that will stand for ever. God looks down; he sees the terrible potential of godless mankind; and he passes judgement. The languages are divided and the people are scattered, and the half-built tower remains as their memorial.

After that not much is heard of Babylon for quite a while. But then during the period of the monarchy, Babylon emerges again, first as a distant threat and then as an imminent menace. In Judah, King Hezekiah hears of the new power that is rising in the east. Foolishly, he entertains visitors from there and shows them round, and Isaiah tells him that the time is coming when all the wealth of Jerusalem will be carried off to Babylon, along with his own descendants, and God's people will be exiled. And so it happens. They are led off across the desert and marched in through the great Ishtar Gate, which is covered with pictures of Babylon's gods, into the city that is dominated by the temple of Marduk, the city whose very name recalls the first time when it shook its fist in the face of God.

There in exile, God's people have to learn what it means to live for *him* in Babylon. A man named Daniel leads the way and shows that it is possible to serve God within the godless city, to rise to become a leader in Babylon while retaining his integrity.[1] It is Daniel who is there when God declares his judgement on the city at King Belshazzar's feast, where a mysterious hand appears, writing on the wall words that spell Babylon's doom. Daniel has the doubtful privilege of telling the king what the words mean. That very night, in one hour, the doom has arrived.

Back in Judah, even before the exile, the prophets Isaiah and Jeremiah are proclaiming that the godless city will be judged. You can read what they say in Isaiah 21:9 and Jeremiah 51:6–9. The words should sound familiar if you have read Revelation 18. These are prophecies of Babylon's destruction, written at a time when the city is still alive and well. There are countless other references in the prophets to Babylon's overthrow, and many of them, like these two, are echoed powerfully in Revelation 18. Jeremiah calls for a great escape, and in the end the escape comes. A remnant returns from exile and the nation is rebuilt.

But the restored Jewish nation retains such a powerful sense of what Babylon means that when Peter writes his first letter, 600 years later, he can write, 'She who is in Babylon ... sends you her greetings' (1 Peter 5:13), without any need to explain that he is referring to the church in Rome, the Babylon of his own day. The heart of godless rebellion has shifted from the city that stood on the River Euphrates to the one that stands on the Tiber, where the evil emperors Nero and Domitian have their throne.

This city in Revelation 18 is *not* the literal, earthly city of Babylon. That should be obvious. How could it be, when the earthly city had long been destroyed and all that was left was ruins and a poor village? That literal Babylon had stood hundreds of miles inland, so it would have been tricky, to say the least, for the ships and the sailors we read about here to trade directly with her! Nor is this Babylon just a code-word for Rome, as some have suggested—that doesn't fit either. Yes, the Rome of John's day is here, and so is the Babylon that Daniel knew. And she is also Sodom *and* Egypt, as chapter 11 told us. And in a sense she is also twenty-first century London or New York, for this Babylon is no one earthly city. She is *every* city and town that has stood in rebellion against our God. She is the *real* Babylon, of which the one whose ruins you can see today near Baghdad was no more than a pale copy. She is the Babylon who sits on the back of the beast, the realm of Satan. She is the world we have to live in.

This chapter is where her long story is finally brought to a conclusion. In this chapter we hear from three angels. The first one declares Babylon's doom (18:1–3). The second one describes the reactions to her downfall (18:4–20). The third gives us a dramatic demonstration of what her fall will mean (18:21–24).

Babylon's doom is announced (18:1–3)

The first angel, one we have not met before, though he echoes the words of 14:8, comes down from heaven with God-given authority to declare judgement. In words which are lifted almost directly from those Old Testament prophets, he loudly announces: 'Fallen! Fallen is Babylon the Great!' Six times that word 'great' is applied to Babylon in this chapter—the 'great city' first alluded to in chapter 11, where God's faithful witnesses spoke out and were martyred. But now it is declared that her greatness is over, that all that is left is a ruin. The city once full of every kind of evil is abandoned to become merely a haunt for homeless demons and for carrion birds picking over the bones. She is 'fallen'.

Reactions to Babylon's downfall (18:4–20)

Now the second angel speaks. He too begins by calling for judgement. She is so proud, this great city: 'I sit as queen; I am not a widow, and I will never mourn.' That is ironic, if you recall the previous chapter! 'I sit as queen'? She doesn't mention what she is sitting *on*, or maybe she would rather forget! But she is proud and she is secure, or so she thinks. But see verse 5: 'Her sins are piled up to heaven, and God has remembered her crimes.' What does that remind you of? Babylon the Great, Babel, whose aim was to raise a tower all the way up to heaven, so that even God would see how great she was! But at the end of the age, it is not her proud tower that reaches up to heaven; it is her heap of sins. Here is God's messenger proclaiming that they have all been remembered; every perpetrator has been tracked down and justice is going to be done. She is going to be repaid exactly as she has dealt out to others (18:6–7). As in Isaiah 40:2, 'double' here means an exact match. She has given herself 'glory', which means she has made herself the centre of her world, and she has given herself 'luxury', another word that appears several times here and conveys the idea of sensual delight, of huge self-indulgence. That is what it is to be godless: to put yourself in God's rightful place and to worship yourself. That is what God sees; those are her sins, right in his face.

There is simply no escape from the justice of God. Occasionally at night we have a police helicopter buzzing around over our house. I don't think it is us they are looking for! Sometimes it keeps us awake; sometimes we sleep through it. But when God looks down on the sins of this world, on the sins of Satan's realm, and brings judgement at last, no one will be able to sleep through it. It will be impossible to miss what is going on. And, just as when Cyrus marched into Babylon on the night of Belshazzar's feast, so the great city will be brought down quickly and unexpectedly. In a chapter that is full of repetitions we read again and again: 'In one hour your doom has come!' (18:10); 'In one hour she has been brought to ruin!' (18:19: cf. 18:17). The reference is probably not to a literal hour of sixty minutes, but it will be quick.

The angel gives us the reactions of three interested parties to Babylon's downfall. First there are the 'kings of the earth' (18:9–10); then there are the 'merchants' (18:11–17); then there are the captains and crews of the ships (18:17–19). It is striking that all three groups respond in the same way. They are all pictured standing at a distance, watching the smoke rising from the burning city—all very upset, but far too much afraid of her fate to attempt anything to help. They know that they too are implicated in her sins.

For the *kings* it was her *power* that impressed them (18:10). They were the elite of the earth who were only too glad to participate in her self-indulgence and sinful ways.

For the *merchants* it was her *beauty* that impressed them (18:15–17)—notice that verse 16 is carried over almost precisely from the description of the woman in the previous chapter! It is not surprising that the merchants are worried, because it was they who sold her all these costly items. Verses 12–13 give us a list, and it is an impressive one, covering every kind of valuable and expensive commodity from every part of the known world: incense from as far away as Arabia and Somalia, precious stones from India, pearls from the Red Sea and the Persian Gulf, gold from Spain, and so on. They are distressed because suddenly their markets have vanished and there is no one to buy all their cargoes any more.

But before we feel too sorry for these merchants, have a closer look at the last item in their cargo manifest: '... and bodies and souls of men' (18:13). These are no innocent traders, making an honest living from their buying and selling. They are slavers, quite happy to regard human lives as a commodity on just the same level as metals or wood or foodstuffs. Babylon just keeps on buying, callous and unjust as she is. 'Sweatshops in the Far East? What do you mean, "human rights"? It's just business. What do you mean, "fair trade"? It's just the free market, my friend!'

The last group are *the sea captains and their crews*. They are simply devastated at the loss of this great city, with all its opportunities for getting rich quick (18:18–19). Babylon has got everyone firmly caught in her net. Her system traps everyone. They are all so admiring and so dependent. They don't *love* her;

none of them tries to prevent her fall. But this is how Babylon works: everyone is involved; everyone is sucked in.

The finality of her downfall (18:21–24)

So, finally, the third angel puts in an appearance. But he doesn't just speak of the city's downfall; he acts it out (18:21). There is a very similar picture in Jeremiah 51:59–64, where a man heading for Babylon is told to take a scroll carrying words of judgement, read it out loud, then tie it to a stone and throw it into the Euphrates as a sign that Babylon will fall, never to rise again. But this angel goes one better. Instead of picking up some pebble lying by a riverbank, he grabs a boulder the size of a millstone—weighing hundreds of pounds—and hurls it not into a river, where it might be dredged up one day, but far out to sea.

As John sees this boulder disappear under the water and the last ripples dying away, he knows that the city it represents has gone for good. Item by item, the angel declares the end of the life of a bustling city. Music becomes silence for ever. The tools of every trade fall to the floor, never to be picked up. The production of food ceases for good. Every lamp is extinguished. Wedding bells will never ring here again. The closing epitaph, as God pulls the plug on Babylon for ever, is in verse 24. The greatest condemnation of all on Babylon is that she hated the church of Christ and persecuted his people. That is simply a measure of how much the Lord loves us, how much we are worth to him. We cost him the suffering and death of his Son, and God is angry when anyone lays a finger on us. So Babylon, the loser, disappears into final darkness and silence. Her story is ended, and she will never be heard of again.

The meaning of Babylon for today

Do we understand Babylon? When we saw her as the ugly prostitute seated on the beast, we could see that she was a mockery of the beautiful bride of Christ. Now when we see her as the godless city that enslaves the people of the earth, we realize that she is a mockery of the beautiful city of God, the new Jerusalem we shall meet in chapter 21. But just as the woman ended up being destroyed, so does the city. Babylon is not just ruined, but vanishes without leaving a trace in eternity, while *our* city lasts for ever.

Babylon is everything and everyone who opposes our God, who does not belong to our Lord Jesus. She is all that our God is not. Babylon is us putting ourselves in the place of God. She is the callousness and cynicism of this world, which does not care about justice and fairness as long as she can have whatever she wants, *now.* She is a rich country that is happy to steal from a poor one to make herself even richer. She is the self-indulgence of a society that demands to be entertained twenty-four hours a day, that demands that every whim be satisfied, that throws off every restraint in pursuit of her pleasure, that will laugh at God, mock his people and acknowledge no rule or law but her own. All that comes straight from Revelation 18. Now does it remind you of anything? Does it sound at all like the place where you live? When the Rastafarians say that we are living in Babylon, they are right, and this is where they got the idea.

Two commands to God's people

So what are we as believers to do? We are like Daniel, and like him we must learn to live faithfully in Babylon. We have no choice but to live there. In any case, how could we share our hope in Christ if we *could* all go off and shut ourselves away on some desert island?

The command to rejoice (18:20)

This chapter gives believers just two commands. One of them is in verse 20.[2] The angel calls on heaven and all God's people to be thoroughly glad that Babylon is being judged. It takes us back to chapter 15 and the song of the winners—the song that we shall be singing when we contemplate God's judgement of all evil.

When we see it from heaven, with our sight no longer clouded by sin, we shall rejoice at what he is doing. And we can start to rejoice *now* that none of the evil we see in our world is going to escape his notice. Be glad that the people who have exploited the poor, and lived in luxury while others suffered, will be held to account. Be glad that the authorities who persecute our brothers and sisters in North Korea, Iran and China are not going to get away with it. Be glad simply that the evil in the world is not to continue for ever. The day is coming when God will bring it all to an end. Evil does *not* go on multiplying for eternity and Satan's realm does *not* last for all time. That is good news. Only God's kingdom, only the heavenly city, is eternal. 'Rejoice,' because 'God has judged her.'

The command to come out of her (18:4)

The other command is the great escape. In words that echo through the centuries, first written for God's people when they faced captivity in a Babylon built out of stones, God calls us out of her. Clearly, this time it is not a call for us to escape an earthly city, as if we would find more godliness in some neighbouring town than we do in our own! But it is a call for us to flee from her *ways*, the ways which are bringing judgement on her, the sins which are piled up to heaven. When Paul writes to the Corinthians who were coming to Christ out of paganism and idol worship, he uses these words, again alluding to the prophets:

> Therefore come out from them
> and be separate,
> says the Lord.
> Touch no unclean thing,
> and I will receive you (2 Corinthians 6:17).

Babylon is guilty of many sins: pride, immorality, injustice, the lure of power. They all come from giving God's place to something else. Some of those we are good at pointing out; some of them we can see clearly. But there is one sin here that I think has infected us without our noticing, and that is Babylon's insatiable *greed*. Western society pursues comfort and luxury at any cost, and I fear that spirit has infected God's people too. Look at many Christians, listen to their conversation and, sadly, it is obvious what they really care about. Serving Christ is not their passion. We will put him somewhere on our list of priorities, but what fills our ambition is to get onto the housing ladder, to be materially secure and safe, to have a comfortable retirement, to be entertained.

We will be first in the queue at the sales, and we don't want to know what our purchases have cost in human suffering far away in some sweatshop factory or coffee plantation. When everything else is covered, *if* there is anything left over, God might just get a look-in—a few pounds to spare, an hour or two of service. We have a blind spot: we can't see how exactly our lives match those of people around us. It is not a popular message and it is hard to give, not least because I feel the drag of the same deadly sickness in my own heart and I have to fight it. That is why it is so refreshing to meet Christians who have not been infected with this virus of pursuing their own pleasure, who are passionate for Christ, longing to make him known, seeking a *heavenly* city, not the one down here.[3]

If you had to choose one picture to symbolize your Christian life right now, what would it be? The Bible only offers one. Jesus said, 'Take up your *cross* and follow me.' What is the symbol for your Christian life? Is it a cross, or something a little less threatening? Is it Christ at any cost, without compromise, or is it comfort and safety first? The heavenly voice calls us: 'Come out of her, my people.' Make the great escape because, whatever the world has to offer, whatever Babylon's charms, Christ is better.

To discuss or think about

1. Look back over the page you have just read. How far have you been infected by 'Babylon's insatiable greed'? What do you need to change?
2. Have you known Christians who are examples to you of living without this greed for pleasure? What can you learn from them?

18

Our hero

Please read Revelation 19

What makes a good fairy story? I don't mean the kind that Enid Blyton wrote, the sort that you read to a five-year-old at bedtime, but a real, heroic, fairy story. What are the key ingredients? I think it should have dragons. It should have at its heart a great heroic character, larger than life and not too politically correct! There should be at least one damsel in distress, probably stuck in a castle or some other gloomy location, and longing for her gallant hero to come and rescue her. There has to be a great battle, a glorious victory and a triumphant homecoming, and they must live happily ever after. Also, good fairy stories never take place in a republic—have you noticed that? You cannot possibly have a president in a fairy story! There have to be kings and princes and princesses. Maybe you grew up on those heroic stories; perhaps you still read them today. Perhaps you have secretly longed that the story was true, and that *you* could be the handsome prince or the beautiful princess.

The good news is that if you belong to Jesus, you do feature in a story like that. It is not a fairy story, but a *true* story. Revelation 19 is all about a noble hero riding out to battle, deadly enemies who are overwhelmed, a bride who is getting ready for the big day and a wedding that is coming soon. If you belong to Jesus, you are in it; you are the princess, and the story is going to end with those wonderful words: 'They lived happily ever after.' They will be true words from God (19:9). And if you don't belong to Jesus, you are in the story too, but your part is a different one. You *don't* live happily ever after—that is the straight truth of this chapter.

Heaven responds to the overthrow of Babylon (19:1–5)

As we move into these climactic final chapters of Revelation, the visions seem to grow ever more powerful, the language ever stronger. Now we meet our hero, the Prince, King Jesus himself, and we get a clear glimpse of his beautiful bride. In the last two chapters, we have looked at the overthrow of Babylon. By the end of chapter 18 she lies fallen, the woman pictured as devoured and deserted, and the city as burned, ruined and silent. Her story is over. Now we hear the response of heaven. John hears a huge crowd yelling, 'Hallelujah!' (that is, 'Praise God!'), 'He has condemned the great prostitute ... [and] has avenged on her the blood of his servants' (19:1–2). They praise God at the sight of the column of smoke rising into the skies, burning for ever; for Babylon, in the end, has been consigned to hell.

We have seen time and again in these last few chapters how God's judgement inspires a reaction in heaven. It is not a reaction of embarrassment or shame; rather, it is praise and worship that rise to the throne as the outrage of sin is punished at last. It is completely different from the mourning we found in chapter 18, where everyone who had benefited from Babylon and enjoyed her immoral luxury watches her destruction with utter dismay. In heaven, the response is diametrically opposite. And so in verse 4 we read how the twenty-four elders, representing all God's people, and the four living creatures, representing creation, together fall down in worship and again cry, 'Hallelujah!', for God has acted to set wrong to right—and that is wonderful.

The bride waits for the Bridegroom (19:6–10)

So Babylon's story is over; the prostitute's story is finished: now it is time for the bride to appear. Look at verses 6–8. This chapter is the only place in the New Testament where we find the word 'Hallelujah!', by the way, and it was these verses that inspired the 'Hallelujah Chorus' in Handel's *Messiah*. And the 'Hallelujahs', the cries of 'Praise the Lord!', erupt at this point for two reasons: first, because the final judgement has now begun at last; and secondly, because the church, the bride of Christ, is getting ready to meet her Bridegroom.

Scripture often compares God's love for his people with a marriage and all that surrounds it. The Old Testament prophets are full of this imagery of courtship and union—yes, and also of desertion and divorce; it is by no means always a happy picture, because it mirrors the waywardness and unfaithfulness of God's people. Think of how Hosea is called to reflect that unfaithfulness by going out to remarry his wife, who has been adulterous in the first place and who is very likely to be so again—all to show Israel how hopelessly they have failed to keep their marriage vows to the Lord (Hosea 3).

But it will not be like that any more! There is going to be a wedding between God's Son and the bride, and this time the bride is *not* going to be unfaithful; in fact she will not be flawed or imperfect in any way whatsoever. She has been redeemed by Christ and now, at the end of days, she will come to him perfected and glorious, and be united with him for ever, the loveliest woman in the world.

The woman who is different (19:6–8)

These chapters are really a tale of two women. Look at them side by side—the prostitute and the bride. How do they appear? On the one hand we have the woman in chapter 17, overdressed in her extravagant finery, glittering with jewellery, drunk on the blood of the saints, truly the ugliest woman in the world; and on the other the bride, dressed in beautiful simplicity—'fine linen, bright and clean'.

There is a slight difficulty in verse 8 with the word which the NIV translates as 'righteous acts'. The Greek word *dikaioma* usually means God's 'regulations' or his 'righteous decrees'. Occasionally it means his 'righteous actions'. But in the Bible it never means simply 'good works' that people do. It seems more likely that the word here refers mainly to the righteous action of God in declaring them justified, and the righteousness of Christ which they now possess as their own. So the point is not that the bride is adorned with her own good deeds, but that her clean and bright clothing, which, after all, has been 'given' to her, is that right standing with God which the Bridegroom himself has awarded her. That is why the bride looks so beautiful and why the Lord looks on you and me with such delight in his eyes—because he sees on us the perfect, pure and wonderful life lived by his Son. If he says we are beautiful, then we are![1]

So the prostitute is ugly; the bride is beautiful. The world loves the prostitute, but it hates the bride. The story of the last two chapters has been of the way the prostitute has successfully seduced people, the way that the city of Babylon has trapped and ensnared everyone into its web of greed and desire. It has been about the woman who promises satisfaction of every desire here and now, with no need to wait. 'You can have it all now,' she says. Many of us cannot even drive a couple of miles through our home town without seeing evidence of that spirit at work in our world. Babylon is this world's system; she is this world's rebellion against God. But what a contrast with the bride, the church, who has suffered and whom the world hates, the church who has had to wait such a long time for her rescue! Back in chapter 6 we heard the voices of the martyrs cry out from under the altar: 'How long, Sovereign Lord ... until you judge the inhabitants of the earth and avenge our blood?' And they were given a white robe, and told to wait.

The theme continues. 13:10 tells us, 'This calls for patient endurance and faithfulness on the part of God's people.' Again in 14:12 we are told, 'This calls for patient endurance on the part of the people of God who keep his commands and remain faithful to Jesus.' The waiting goes on, while the beast holds sway and does the work of Satan his master, while the false prophet speaks his lies and demands his worship. Meanwhile the church simply has to hang on and keep the faith.

How well John's first readers would have known this, those believers who, thirty years earlier, had seen Nero using Christians as human torches to light the palace gardens in Rome, and who now saw Domitian persecuting the church and exiling men like John! How well our brothers and sisters know it today, too—the cost of being one of the saints and being told to wait a bit longer, to endure patiently! That is hard to do, especially if you live somewhere like Iran or China, where the false prophets speak very loudly and it is hard to escape their clutches. It is hard to endure patiently, but that is what we are called to do—not to keep our heads down, not to dive for cover whenever trouble threatens, and not to strike back, but to wait and endure patiently and to keep the faith. In this picture, it is the bride who has to wait for the bridegroom to arrive, not the other way round! But arrive he will.

Again, what a contrast between the prostitute, who seduces

the world, gets all that she wants, but then spends eternity in hell, and the beautiful bride, who is chosen, redeemed, courted and loved by the Lord Jesus, and then spends eternity with him in glory! What a contrast! Once again the question has to be asked: which one do we identify with? Which one of the pictures represents *you*? There is no middle ground—you are either with the world or with Christ.

Those who are truly blessed (19:9–10)

The words are underlined for us: they are 'true'. In verse 9 an unknown angel speaks, possibly the one who introduced this series of visions in chapter 17. It is not that all the other words in Revelation are *not* true! The point is that this needs underlining because it is what we most need to know. There are so many times when it seems that it is the people in the world, the 'inhabitants of the earth' as Revelation calls them, who have the best of it. They seem to have the easy life: if anyone is blessed, it must surely be *them*. But the Lord says, 'No, don't you see what happens to people who stay in the world, the people who live in Babylon? No, *you* are the ones who are blessed, you who stay faithful to my name, however tough it is, because on your mantelpiece you have an invitation to the wedding.' We are not just the bride; we are the guest list as well!

John gets so excited about this that he wants to worship the angel and has to be prevented from doing so. The angel points out to John that they are just the same: they are both servants of the Lord and in their different ways they are both speaking his words. That rather difficult statement at the end of verse 10, 'The testimony of Jesus is the spirit of prophecy', simply means that *anyone* who knows Jesus is able to speak out for him, whether it is an angel, or an apostle like John—or for that matter you or I.

The hero rides forth to battle (19:11–16)

So the bride is ready and she awaits the appearance of the bridegroom. But, as the next scene opens, it is not a bridegroom that we see, but a warrior, because, like every good hero, this one has a battle to fight before he can settle down with his bride. She must wait just a little longer (19:11). Once more John sees heaven standing open, but this time it is not so that he can see in or enter himself: it is to allow the King of Kings to ride *out*. The portcullis is raised; the drawbridge is lowered; the gate is open, and out rides the white knight, our hero. In the next few verses, the descriptions tumble out in breathless succession, as though John himself were riding hard on one of the steeds which are following.

The rider on the white horse

The rider's identity is obvious. There are echoes of the words we heard in chapter 1 in the eyes which blaze like fire and the sharp sword which emerges from his mouth. This is a figure of power and authority. There are the titles he is given. He is called 'the Word of God' (19:13), which identifies him as God's active agent who, wherever he goes, carries God's character and will. He is called 'King of kings and Lord of lords' (19:16), the one who reigns, the Prince who inherits every earthly kingdom and is crowned as King. The heavens open for him, and this Jesus comes back to earth—no longer to experience tiredness and hunger and the taunts and accusations of men. In this, his *Second* Coming, he rides out in majesty to execute justice and to defeat his last enemies, to strike down the nations and to rule them with an iron sceptre.

By the way, you might recall that back in chapter 6 we saw another rider on a white horse, one of the so-called 'four horsemen of the Apocalypse', and some have thought that the two riders must be the same. But in fact the differences are much greater than the similarities: the horseman in chapter

6 was just one of a group, and he appeared to order when one of the seals on the scroll was opened by the Lamb of God himself. Moreover, the context of chapter 6 dictates that the four horsemen are all harbingers of disaster. But *this* horseman, this King Jesus, rides out in glory and majesty that is all his own. He comes to exert his own authority, to rule his own kingdom.

The robe dipped in blood

Ominously, he comes wearing 'a robe dipped in blood' (19:13). Many commentators see this as a reference to the cross. This is Christ's *own* blood, they say, pointing to the fact that the saints are seen here dressed in pure white garments, their own righteousness bought at the cost of the blood of Christ, the blood which still stains his robe as an eternal reminder of his sacrifice. Of course, it is wonderfully true that it is the blood of Christ that has freed us from the power of sin. But I think what John sees here is something different. This is an altogether darker picture: it is not about our salvation; it is about *judgement*.

The reason for taking this view is that the passage is full of allusions to the later chapters of Isaiah. Remember what we have seen right through this book: the key to understanding Revelation is the Old Testament. Compare this passage with Isaiah 63:1–6. The preceding chapter in Isaiah speaks beautifully of the Lord saving his people and rejoicing over them like a bridegroom over his bride. We are in the same territory. The blood on the robe of Christ is, therefore, the blood of his *enemies*. Verse 15, where we read of him treading 'the winepress of the fury of the wrath of God Almighty', takes us back to that haunting, dreadful picture at the end of chapter 14, where the grapes are harvested from the earth, and out from the winepress flows a river of blood that fills the land. Chapter 14 didn't tell us who was trampling the grapes of wrath, but now we know. Is that shocking—that the Prince of love, our hero, the one who is coming to claim us as his bride, is the same one who is portrayed here crushing God's enemies underfoot? Can it be?

The answer is that this is the mission of Christ, the Word of God—to deal with sin, through judgement. Either judgement is done *on* him at the cross, and sin is dealt with as he suffers in our place, or else, failing that, judgement is done *by* him as people's unforgiven sin sends them to hell. The reason this shocks us is that we have no grasp of the horror of sin. We just do not see how bad sin is. Our sin took the perfect, infinite, eternal Son of God and tortured him with the wrath of God on the cross. For the first and only time ever, it tore open the relationships within the Trinity. It brought the deathless one to death. That is what our sin did to Jesus—that is the measure of his staggering love for his people, that he became the glad and *willing* sacrifice for us, so that our sin is no more! But sin that is not dealt with on the cross has to be dealt with in eternity. There is no other way for God to be just.

The battle and its aftermath (19:17–21)

So the stage is set for battle. It is one we have heard of before—the battle of Armageddon in chapter 16, where the powers of this world are marshalled together to fight, and the battle at the end of chapter 17, where the beast and his forces take on the Lamb and his army, and are overwhelmed. This time we finally get a full view of the battle. It is heralded by an angel summoning the birds to a feast (19:17–18). Clearly this angel has no doubt whatsoever about the outcome: it is not going to be much of a battle. And sure enough, this is what happens (19:19–21). The battle is over in a flash—it barely merits a description. When the Lord finally appears, evil will not survive for an instant. The beast and the false prophet, those great partners in crime, end up as partners for ever in hell. The rest are portrayed as food for the vultures and the carrion birds which settle on the bodies in their hordes and gorge themselves on the dead.

This is just one more picture of the judgement that is coming. It is as if the Holy Spirit inspires one different, appalling vision after another to force home the devastating reality of what is coming. There is an endless battlefield, strewn with millions of corpses, where the only movement to be seen is the birds tearing at the flesh of the dead. There is a lake of fire, burning for ever, foul-smelling, to receive those destined for hell. There is a winepress where the grapes are spurting out blood. Judgement is real and horrifying, and it is coming. What lies ahead for people without Christ is terrible. No wonder so many try to write off the message of this book—not because it is too confusing, but because it is all too clear. No wonder they try to cut it out of their Bibles as unworthy of a God of love. But it is the Holy Spirit himself who inspired these words and made sure that they ended up in our Bibles. The God of unending love is also the God of justice. He does what is right.

The two suppers

This passage speaks of two feasts, two 'suppers' (19:9,17) —two parties, as we might say. There is 'the wedding supper of the Lamb' and there is 'the great supper of God'. The fact is that we are all going to end up at one or the other. It could not be clearer. Are you sure you know that you are headed for the right one?

We finish this chapter with two thoughts for believers.

1. Don't forget about hell

Think about the images of hell in this chapter. Many of us have beloved family members or close friends who are not saved. The temptation is to shy away from these pictures, these thoughts about hell, but we should not do that. Rather, we should turn them into prayer—renewed prayer for our loved ones; renewed prayer for a passion for the lost, that we should grasp a little of the horror of sin, even our *own* sin; and renewed praise for the one who has loved us and spared *us* from these scenes.

2. Look forward to the wedding

Our hero is coming back for us. When the last battle has been fought and won, when the white knight rides back through the open gates of heaven, then will come the wedding. Our hero, who laid down his life for us, snatched us from our dungeon, rescued us from our helpless position, destined for a lost eternity, will return to take us to himself and we shall be his chosen companion for ever and ever—beautiful, perfected and beloved. Our Lord Jesus is coming. Until then, we endure, we stand firm, and we look forward to the day.

To discuss or think about

1. What impact does the thought of hell have on you? Do you feel that you want to avoid thinking about it? Do you agree that your view will be different when you see it from the standpoint of heaven?
2. Think (or talk) about the return of Jesus Christ in his triumph. What will that day mean to you then, and what does it mean to you now?

19

No more tomorrows

Please read Revelation 20

Have you ever thought of writing your own life story? If we are honest, a lot of us have—especially, perhaps, when we were young and ambitious, thinking that one day we would be sitting in our slippers by the fire, scribbling away at our life history and sharing the secrets of our life with an eagerly waiting world. After all, plenty of autobiographies do get written and many of them make fascinating reading. I have always been interested by people who simply call their book *My life*, or *The story of my life*, as if no other hook or appeal were necessary—for instance, Marlene Dietrich, actress; Richard Wagner, composer; Moshe Dayan, Israeli general; Golda Meir, Israeli prime minister; Bill Clinton, US president; Oswald Mosley, British fascist; and Leon Trotsky, Russian Communist. Could it be that these are all people who share a sense of their own importance? They are all concerned that history might misjudge them.

The fact is, of course, that most of us will never write our life story. We abandon that idea some time by middle age, when we realize that our lives may not shake the world quite as much as we once planned! But, nevertheless, every single one of us is having our life story written. At this moment, our thoughts, feelings and actions are all being recorded in a book, far more accurately than we would ever do it for ourselves. One day it will be opened and read, in public, before a mass audience and in the presence of the greatest of critics. That is what Revelation 20 tells us. We have reached the point where we see all of humanity, great and small, standing before the throne of God to be judged. It is the time when every chance has gone, every last fact has been recorded in those books, every day of opportunity has passed, and there are no more tomorrows. It is an awesome scene which we shall all have to face—the scene that brings human history to an end and ushers in eternity, and beyond it all that remains is the glory of the new heavens and the new earth for God's people, and for the others eternal hell.

The thousand years (20:1–10)

But before we get to that Judgement Day scene, with its strong echoes of Daniel 7, we need to tackle the events of the first half of the chapter to see what happens immediately before—the time described here as the 'thousand years', or the *millennium.* This is easily the most controversial section of the book of Revelation. Whatever does it mean?

This is one point in the book where I will not claim great confidence, because when we come to the subject of the millennium, there are four major views which are held by Bible-believing Christians. They are views held with integrity and after careful study and thought. There has been much debate and not a little division over the nature of the millennium, especially in America. It is probably fair to say that Americans tend to worry about the issue too much, while in the UK we don't bother about it enough. I am not going to be dogmatic: I have to say that I find the level of certainty which most books on Revelation claim about the millennium quite staggering!

A summary of what takes place

First, we will look at what is described in verses 1–10. An angel is sent from heaven to seize Satan and put him away. He is locked in the Abyss for a thousand years, so that he cannot do his dirty work of deception, while elsewhere life goes on (20:1–3). Then, in verse 4, John sees the martyr church. Although he singles out those who have been killed because of their faith, it is likely that he means the whole church of faithful believers, everyone who refuses to wear the mark of the beast and who has suffered because of it. Remember that in Revelation everyone wears one of two badges, or marks: either the mark of the Lamb or the mark of the beast. These people John now sees living and reigning with Christ for a thousand years, never more to face death.

Then, at the end of the thousand years, Satan is briefly freed (20:7) and goes on the rampage. He gathers the nations for battle (20:8)—'Gog and Magog' is a reference to an obscure passage in Ezekiel 38–39, looking to the far future and prophesying that a figure named Gog will appear at the head of a great horde and attack God's people, who at that time will be living in peace. Magog is probably the land where Gog comes from. So Satan gathers his huge army; they sweep across the earth (20:9) and they attempt to assault God's people, but before anything can happen they are destroyed by fire from heaven. Then in verse 10, Satan is taken and thrown into the fiery lake, where his two henchmen, the beast and the false prophet, have already preceded him. Meanwhile the rest of the dead are raised to life (20:5) and, as we shall go on to see, everyone together then stands before the judgement seat of God.

So, there are a 'thousand years' during which Satan is bound;

he returns for a final, violent but futile fling at the end; then there is resurrection and judgement. But what *is* this period of a thousand years?

Some basic principles

Before we tackle this question of what the millennium actually is, let me make a few points in preparation.

Firstly, this passage clearly teaches the absolute sovereignty of God over Satan and sin. It is God through his angels who binds or releases Satan and ultimately sends him to his destruction.

Secondly, the fate of believers is clearly marked out as very different from that of unbelievers. The millennium culminates in the Day of Judgement, as we shall see.

Thirdly, given the way that we have seen that Revelation works, the thousand years we read of here is more likely to be a *symbolic* period of time than a *literal* period, just as the chain is not literally a metallic chain and the key is not the kind you use in your front door!

Fourthly, in view of the way that Revelation is structured, this passage might be a rerun of something that we have seen before. The fact that it follows chapter 19 does not necessarily mean that it happens afterwards. We have to work that out from what the passage itself says.

Four views on the millennium

Let us now sketch the four main views on the millennium.

The first and simplest view is called *amillennialism*, meaning '*no* millennium', though that is a something of a misnomer, as we shall see. Amillennialists believe that at the end of *this* age, the *church* age, Christ returns in glory, the dead are raised, the Last Judgement takes place and God brings in the new heavens and the new earth. It all happens at the same point. So on this view, the millennium is *now*. It is simply another way of describing the church age, and amillennialists point out that this particular description is found nowhere else in Scripture. After all, Revelation has often shown us the same scene, re-told the same story, from different angles. Here we see Satan's power severely limited ('bound') by Christ's death on the cross, and believers who die during this age live and reign with Christ in heaven until he returns, the dead are raised and the believers, the saints, receive resurrection bodies. This view is very popular today among evangelicals in the UK.

However, others are not convinced by this idea that the millennium is now. The remaining three views place it *in the future.*

Some believe that our current age will gradually see a massive increase in the influence of the gospel and the size of the church. As time goes by, under the growing influence of the church, the world becomes a better and better place and Satan's power grows weaker and weaker. The present age turns into the millennium, and *then* Christ returns. These people are *postmillennialists* because they think that the Lord will return *after* the millennium. Again, many Christians down the years have taken this view, including most of the Puritans; to me, however, it seems inconsistent with what the rest of Scripture teaches. We are repeatedly told, both by Christ himself and the apostles, that the world is going to become a tougher place for believers and a worse place generally before he returns in glory. Matthew 24; 2 Thessalonians 2; 2 Timothy 3, to name but a few key passages, are all very clear that tribulation will come and will get worse for us as the years go by. Today, as we look around the world, although the church is growing dramatically, evil is undoubtedly rampant and apparently increasing.

There are also many Christians who take a *premillennial* view, and that means they think that Christ will return *before* the millennium. On this view, chapter 19 describes Christ's Second Coming and chapter 20 the millennium. The current age continues with the church growing, but suffering and enduring tribulation, which gets worse rather than better. Then at the end of that period, Christ returns in glory, Satan is imprisoned and the Lord establishes an earthly kingdom of righteousness, justice and peace. The saints are raised to life and reign with him here, and *that* is the millennium. There will still be non-Christians in the world and not everyone will be happy to have Christ reigning here: some will turn to him and be saved; others will not, but he will rule them all the same. At the *end* of the millennium, Satan is allowed one more brief rebellion; he stirs up and gathers all the remaining rebels on earth and makes a final assault on God's people, but it all comes to nothing and he is utterly defeated. Then the rest of the dead will be raised and all will be judged, and after that comes eternity.Having said that, I now need to explain that there are two very different varieties of premillennialism. One is the 'traditional' or 'historic' variety that has been held by many Christians from the earliest days. This version is entirely consistent with the way that we have been reading the book of Revelation up to this point, including the repeated views of history and the widespread use of symbolic language. To be a little more technical, it is also consistent with mainstream Reformed theology and its view of God's covenants.

The second variety of the premillennial view appeared in the nineteenth century and is especially widespread today in the USA and in Africa. This is the view that inspired the *Left Behind* series of books and was held by influential popular writers such as Hal Lindsey. It is called *pretribulational premillennialism*, meaning that Christ comes secretly and snatches, or 'raptures', the church *before* the time of great suffering and trial at the end of the age, so that Christians do not have to pass through it. He then comes back *again*, seven years later, when the tribulation[1] is over, and sets up his millennial reign.

Now this view usually accompanies a distinctive approach

to the whole of Revelation. In particular, it tends to take the visions much more literally than I have done and sees them as taking place one after the other, in a line, not as repeated views of the same events. If you have read any of the *Left Behind* books you will recognize this at once. This view is standard among dispensationalist Christians, who generally take Scripture's prophecies about Israel very literally, rather than applying most of them to the church. They maintain that God still has a central purpose for Israel today and therefore tend to give almost unqualified support to the modern state of Israel. It therefore assumes very great *political* importance—though this is not the place to tackle such issues in any detail. But this view cannot be said to be consistent with Reformed theology, because it understands God's dealings with humanity through the covenants so differently.

However, I hope you will be convinced by now that this is not the best way to read Revelation. Nor does Scripture give any real support to the idea that the church is snatched out of the world before it becomes too unpleasant for us. Try telling the suffering believers today in Indonesia, Somalia, or any of fifty other countries, that everything is really all right, because the tribulation has not yet begun!

A personal assessment

As I see it, we are really left with two viable options—amillennialism or traditional premillennialism. Either the millennium is *now* ('We are already enjoying it', say amillennialists!), or else Christ will bring it in after he returns—and obviously that would be a very different *kind* of millennium. Everything that has been said so far is consistent with either of these two views; in fact they have a great deal in common. In terms of the way we live our Christian lives here and now, there is virtually no difference. *Both* these views teach us to expect a visible return of the Lord Jesus, which could happen any day at very short notice, and both teach that we shall then receive our perfect, resurrection bodies. Both teach us to expect that meanwhile the world will become a worse place and will be more and more hostile to the church. Of this much I am fully convinced.

But is it possible to decide between the two views? Is Revelation 20:1–10 another view of the church age—the amillennialist view—or another age which follows Christ's return—the premillennialist view? I have come to hold the second of these views for reasons I shall now explain.

Look at what happens to Satan in verses 2–3. He is bound with a chain and dropped into a deep pit which is then locked and sealed over him. It is a fourfold statement of imprisonment. The Greek is explicit about this: in fact, the closest parallel use of the word 'seal' is the sealing of Jesus' tomb. The whole force of this picture is that Satan has been completely removed from the scene for the duration of the thousand years. The amillennialist says that is *now* and that the binding of Satan referred to here is the same as that described in Matthew 12:29 and Mark 3:27 (other texts may also be quoted, but these two are by far the strongest for the amillennialist position): Satan's power is limited and he cannot prevent the gospel going out to all nations.

But can the imprisonment of Satan described in Revelation 20 really be squared with what we read in Scripture and see in the world today? In spite of the protestations of many commentators, I cannot bring myself to believe it. The rest of Revelation shows Satan as extremely *active*. When he is thrown out of heaven and down to the earth in chapter 12, he is not imprisoned in the Abyss.[2] On the contrary, we read that he is very angry and immediately sets off to destroy the church. He *still* deceives the nations (12:9 uses the same word, *planao*, for 'deceive' as 20:3, though this is not clear in the NIV). In chapter 13 we see Satan commissioning the beast and the false prophet. Going outside Revelation, the picture of Satan's activity becomes clearer still—see, for instance, 1 Peter 5:8 and, above all, 2 Corinthians 4:4. Satan is *still* deceiving the nations, in spite of the growth of the church and millions being saved. If we look at the world and think of the huge areas where people live in the clearly satanic grip of witchcraft, spirit worship or folk Islam, if we have any experience of the very real activity of demons in people's lives, even in the Western world today, we shall surely conclude that Satan is still very much part of the picture.[3] All this strongly suggests that his imprisonment still lies in the future.

What about the battle that Satan fights in verses 8–9? Surely, you may say, that is another repeat viewing of the final battle, described as Armageddon in chapter 16 and the battle of the rider on the white horse in chapter 19? Yes, it could be, especially as both chapter 19 and chapter 20 clearly refer to the *same* prophecy about Gog and Magog in Ezekiel 38–39.[4] This is an argument in favour of amillennialism, although 'Gog and Magog' have been broadened here to include *all* the nations (20:8). On the other hand, it is quite possible that Ezekiel's imagery is being used for a second time in Revelation 20 to describe the conclusion of unfinished business in a separate battle. And there is at least one clear indication that it might be a different one. Two of the chief characters are now missing—the beast and the false prophet! If this is the *same* battle we might expect them to appear, but actually they don't. On the other hand, if Satan was destroyed in the battle at the end of chapter 19, as amillennialists would say, it is hard to understand why John should mention only his henchmen and not the ringleader himself!

But if you take the premillennial view, this all fits together quite neatly. The beast and the false prophet are absent in chapter 20 for the excellent reason that they were captured and thrown into hell by Christ, the white knight, at the end of chapter 19. And in the millennium there will be no beast, no worldly tyranny; Christ will be the only ruler. There will be no false prophet, because false religion will have been abolished. Of the 'unholy trinity', only Satan will remain, but he will be bound. I believe there *will* be an earthly millennium, probably not literally of a thousand years—given that the entire church age has previously been represented as forty-two months, the millennium could even be much longer![5] That is when Christ will rule the nations with a rod of iron (19:15, quoting Psalm 2:9—otherwise, when does this happen?); that is when the glorious visions of Isaiah about a world of peace and harmony, and the nations submitting to God's rule, will be fulfilled; and that is when the saints will reign with Christ (20:6). Moreover, this view surely makes better sense of the references to 'coming to life', or 'the first resurrection' (20:5)—which amillennialists understand either as conversion (regeneration) or, more commonly, as passing into Christ's presence at death—and 'reigning with Christ' in verses 4,6.[6]

What difference does it make, and what is the point of such a millennium anyway? The point of it is the same as for everything else in God's purposes: to increase his glory. In his millennial reign on earth Christ, along with us, will display God's glory in a new way, a way which is not possible now. It will be another stage in seeing sin defeated and God declaring his rule over the powers of evil. We shall see many things happening that for now we can only long for—true, godly government, justice in the courts and between the nations, a world healed of ecological disaster, a church that is no longer abused and kicked around, but that truly begins to reflect the character of her Bridegroom. This is something else for us to look forward to!

But if you are still not convinced of the arguments for an

earthly millennium, I am not too concerned! Evangelical Christians should never divide over this issue. Here and now, we are to live in the daily expectation of Christ's return in glory, and to watch, pray and keep the faith as the world darkens. Whether the millennium is now, or is still to come, one thing is starkly clear: at the end of all things Satan will be thrown into the lake of fire to be tormented day and night for ever. At the end, there are no more tomorrows—only judgement and the great white throne.

The Day of Judgement (20:11–15)

The two books

Look at verses 11–12. The dead from every age, from every century and from every place where they have died, now stand, raised to life before the throne, before one whose stern and piercing gaze is such that even the earth and sky cannot endure it. They stand before a Judge who cannot be bribed, distracted, or confused, a Judge who knows and sees everything with perfect understanding, a Judge who has watched over history. We are all there standing before him. And now the books are opened. For every one of us, a book that records every deed of our lives, good or bad—the words you and I have said today, all that we have failed to do this year, last year, the year before. It is a perfectly accurate biography. Do you know what is in your book? I know some of the deeds in mine—plenty that I bitterly regret, plenty to make me tremble with fear at the thought of what the Judge will say when it is all read out. It is *damning* stuff: for once that word is literally true.

But there is another book! As I stand there and the story of my sinful life is exposed, someone is checking the entries that are written there. In this other book it just has my name written down, not my biography. It is the book of life—and *my* name is in the book! I look again at the Judge, and I see that he has nail-prints in his hands and, as he looks at me, his face is no longer stern, because he is also my Saviour. Nothing could be more vital than knowing that we shall be safe on that day.

Verses 14–15 show us once more the lake of fire. It is a picture, and pictures have their limitations, but the reality will certainly be worse. The lake of fire is real. The beast, the false prophet and Satan himself are already there; 'death and Hades'—that is, the grave—now join them. There will be no more death except 'the second death', the one that never ends, the death of eternal torment for those whose names are not written in the book of life.

We shall all be judged

It is sometimes said that Christians will not face judgement, but the New Testament makes it clear that we shall. Certainly, there is no *condemnation* for those who are in Christ Jesus, but Paul writes, 'We must all appear before the judgement seat of Christ, that each one may receive what is due to him for the things done while in the body, whether good or bad' (2 Corinthians 5:10). There is a judgement by works for everyone: the difference is that for those outside Christ, the outcome will be eternal rejection, while those who are in Christ are saved by his grace and there will be eternal rewards.

Again it is Paul who writes about this, in 1 Corinthians 3:10–15. The 'Day' is the Day of Judgement. We must ask ourselves the question: what will survive when *our* work for the Lord is tested with fire? What legacy are we going to leave? Will it be building work that will last for *ever*—people won to Christ, lives shaped and built up by faithful ministry, the support given to others to help them to serve him, persistent intercession, the patient, outstanding quality of a Christian life that has shone out like a star in the darkness of this world? There *will* be rewards in heaven. They will not be like Olympic medals, where every time someone goes faster, or scores higher, everyone else moves down a place and everyone hopes that the ones who come behind them are going to trip up! This is no competition. In fact we should all be busy encouraging one another to do better so that we can *all* win a greater reward! Hebrews 10:25 says, 'Let us encourage one another—and all the more as you see the Day approaching.'

Charles Wesley finished his great hymn with those memorable words:

> Bold I approach the eternal throne,
> And claim the crown, through Christ my own.

'Bold'? I don't know. Maybe Wesley was right, but as I think about that scene of Judgement Day now, I still tremble, even though I know that my name is in the book of life. Bold or fearful, however, we shall all be there, and may we all be found safe in Christ!

To discuss or think about

These equally memorable words were written in 1837 by the Scottish pastor Robert Murray M'Cheyne. I include them here to help us in contemplating the Judgement Day and how it should affect our lives today.

> When this passing world is done,
> When has sunk yon glaring sun,
> When we stand with Christ in glory,
> Looking o'er life's finished story,
> Then, Lord, shall I fully know—
> Not till then—how much I owe.
>
> When I hear the wicked call,
> On the rocks and hills to fall,
> When I see them start and shrink
> On the fiery deluge brink,

Then, Lord, shall I fully know—
Not till then—how much I owe.

When I stand before the throne,
Dressed in beauty not my own,
When I see Thee as Thou art,
Love Thee with unsinning heart,
Then Lord, shall I fully know—
Not till then—how much I owe.

When the praise of Heav'n I hear,
Loud as thunders to the ear,
Loud as many waters' noise,
Sweet as harp's melodious voice,
Then, Lord, shall I fully know—
Not till then—how much I owe.

Chosen not for good in me,
Wakened up from wrath to flee,
Hidden in the Saviour's side,
By the Spirit sanctified,
Teach me, Lord, on earth to show,
By my love, how much I owe.

Part IX
The new heavens and the new earth
(21:1–22:5)

20

The new world for ever

Please read Revelation 21:1–22:5

Advertisers sometimes exaggerate—true or false? Take, for example, the official tourist website for my home town. The Visit Bristol website goes into raptures about the city's merits, its 'gorgeous Georgian terraces', its 'incredible range of independent shops, cafes and restaurants', its history. Meanwhile the pictures they choose conjure up a compelling vision of cheerful, bustling inhabitants, permanently engaged in enjoyable boat trips round the harbour, celebrations of Brunel's anniversary and delightful picnics in the warm sunshine on the Downs. So what Bristol *is* this? Yes, I love this city. I am very proud of our associations with Brunel—not to mention Wallace and Gromit! But anyone who knows Bristol knows that, while there may be some truth in those descriptions, the view they present is somewhat one-sided.

What does Visit Bristol *not* tell us? As residents, we could add what we know about drugs, run-down streets and the notoriously poor performance of our schools, to name but a few!

Outside our church building you can see soft drugs being openly traded; on a really good day you can see squads of armed police breaking into houses to seize crack cocaine. Our city certainly has its downside, its hidden side that tourists never see. It is full of places of deprivation and its corners of quiet despair, and it always will be. And of course, Bristol is no different in this from hundreds of other cities in the West, never mind the rest of the world.

But we also know about another city—a city that doesn't appear on any road atlas, or on Google Earth. This place doesn't need a penny of regeneration money and has no need of an enthusiastic copywriter to trumpet its attractions; there are no drugs, no derelict homes, no failing schools. It is a city with no hidden downside or quiet corners of despair, yet it is a real place —and if we know Jesus, it is where we are going. It is called the new Jerusalem, and Revelation 21 is all about it.

In chapters 17 to 20 we have seen how, at the end of the age, Almighty God begins to bring everything to a close as one by one his enemies are brought down: first Babylon, the great city that stands for human rebellion; then the beast and the false prophet, and then Satan himself. After that we saw the awesome scene where humanity stands before the throne of God to be judged. On that judgement day all evil is banished for all time, never to return. The last enemy is death, and even death is finally destroyed. But, praise God, that is not the end of the story, because now at last we come to look *beyond* that judgement day; at last we can see what eternity holds for us. If we know and love the Lord then our names are in the book of life, and we shall surely arrive at Revelation 21 and the new heavens and the new earth (21:1,5).

The new heavens and the new earth (21:1–8)

The Bible has a lot to say on this theme. Isaiah looked forward to the new heavens and the new earth—you can find that in Isaiah 65.[1] Other prophets too looked forward beyond the Day of the Lord, the Day of Judgement, to a new world that lies far in the distance. Now here it is. We don't know just how different it will be from the world we live in today. There are Scriptures that stress the destruction of the old world. 2 Peter 3:10 speaks of the elements being destroyed by fire and the earth and everything in it being laid bare. There are many texts, including some in Revelation itself, that suggest the upheaval will be so great that we shall not recognize what is left.

But on the other hand, God declared that his first creation was very good, before sin came in and spoiled it. To abandon it completely and start from scratch would be a defeat for his purposes. Romans 8:21 speaks of creation longing for liberation from bondage and coming to share the freedom of God's children. Creation is looking ahead to *freedom*, not total destruction. So although we cannot be sure—and this is an area where Christians have disagreed—it does seem that the new heavens and the new earth will share much in common with this one, except that there will be nothing wrong with it, nothing at all.

Apart from the city, John doesn't give us many details. But he does tell us this: 'There was no longer any sea' (21:1). Now to us in Britain that sounds strange. After all, we love the sea. Our nation is famous for it: for centuries our ancestors ruled the waves, and even today there are probably no people on earth who are more fanatical about all aspects of the sea than we are! So why can't we have the sea? The answer, of course, is that this is imagery. When the Israelites (and therefore the Old Testament) thought of the sea, they didn't connect it with sandcastles, fresh air and fun. For them the sea represented evil. It stood for the primeval chaos that God had conquered at the creation of the universe. It was where sea monsters lived; and it was by sea that many of their enemies had arrived. In Revelation itself, the beast emerges from the sea. But now the sea is no more: there is no longer any wild, untamed evil on the *new* earth. 'No more sea' means no more rebellion, no more conflict; it means peace for eternity.

All this is just setting the scene. The rest of the passage is about the new Jerusalem, the city John sees coming down out of heaven. Verses 2–8 introduce the vision and then the remainder of chapters 21 and 22 open it up, as we see the city described in all its glory and measured out and we are shown what it will be like to live there. Just as when we speak of an earthly city, we may equally well be referring to the structures or to the inhabitants, John has both the environment and the community of the heavenly city in his sights. It is a vision of stunning beauty.

The new Jerusalem described (21:9–22)

1. How the city is announced (21:9–11)

These verses should remind us of something. Look back to the start of chapter 17, where John is introduced to the great prostitute, the ugliest woman in the world. The same angel takes him to see the view. The same introduction is used: 'Come, I will show you.' And in both cases John is taken away in the Spirit to see the sight. In chapter 17, it is the prostitute Babylon who entices people into her clutches and seduces them away from the Lord. Now, in chapter 21, it is the bride, beautifully prepared for her husband, the Lord Jesus—the woman who is also the new Jerusalem, the city of God. The contrast is both deliberate and pointed. Once again we are reminded of the choice: two women, two cities. But now the story of Babylon is over; she is destroyed, while the story of the new Jerusalem is only just beginning. The latter comes down out of heaven from God, uniting together heaven and the now-perfected earth. She is breathtaking, shining like a great jewel (21:11).

2. How the city is built (21:12–14)

It is a city with twelve foundations—probably we should think of great buttresses which support the structure, rather than underground foundations—and twelve gates, so that, as you go round the wall, you see: gate, foundation, gate, foundation, all the way round; name of a tribe, name of an apostle, name of a tribe, and so on. The Old Testament and New Testament people of God are united in the holy city—twelve plus twelve, recalling the twenty-four elders we met in chapter 4.

3. The size of the city (21:15–17)

Now see how big the city is. We should be well used to symbolic numbers by now, but even without taking the measurements too literally, this is clearly a vast city. 12,000 stadia, or 1,400 miles, would be roughly the distance from Britain to Greece. A city of that size could comfortably accommodate *billions* of people, even without considering that it is 1,400 miles high as well—this is the ultimate high-rise! That tells us that God is going to save a lot of people to populate the city, not just a handful here and there. There are in fact 'twelves' buried everywhere in this description—the number twelve standing for the complete people of God. Indeed, as the mathematically inclined may have spotted, since the city is a perfect cube, if the angel measures every edge of the city, the total length is 144,000 stadia—and where have we heard that number before?

4. The shape of the city (21:16)

It is emphasized that the city is a perfect cube, probably to remind us of the only other object in Scripture that we are told was that shape. Much smaller, with each side just thirty feet long, it was the heart of the temple, the Most Holy Place, lined with pure gold, where only the high priest was allowed to set foot, and that just once a year. And inside the Most Holy Place was the ark, and above the ark the dwelling place of God, the place of his glory. This was where the Lord had his presence in the midst of his people, and now that small square room expands to gigantic size, until it becomes this vast city, every inch of it the dwelling of God with his people. No wonder John says in verse 22 that he sees no temple there. God's presence fills the entire city with his glory and holiness. The Lord Jesus referred to his own body as a temple (John 2:19–22), and now that picture is fulfilled, for in this new, perfect Jerusalem it is his own physical presence that takes the place of a physical temple. Every single inhabitant lives there and enjoys his presence every day, for ever.

5. What the city is made of (20:18–21)

It is very clear in this passage that John is struggling for words to describe what he sees. He is reaching out for the most precious and beautiful descriptions he can find. He tells us about the brilliance of the light and the beauty of the building stones, which shine like polished jewels—we read the list in verses 19–21. Some we recognize; some we are not sure about, but that is not the point. This is stunning, indescribably beautiful, flawless, costly.

A few years ago my family visited Prague, a city famous for its Bohemian crystal glass. There are whole shops full of nothing else but these exquisite cut crystal figures of animals, castles and abstract shapes, all arranged under brilliant spotlights. And, as the light falls on the facets of the glass, it is broken and scattered into glorious colours so that you simply want to stand and stare and drink it all in. John's picture is a little bit like that, but far better. Here are pearls the size of a city gate, and pearls were the most precious of jewels, like diamonds to us; in other words, here are walls and gates built of indestructible gemstones. Then there is the gold. John shows us the streets made of pure gold like transparent glass. That is impossible in a literal sense—the laws of physics forbid a transparent metal! But in this city it exists—or at least that is its appearance. Glass in John's day was usually dull and cloudy; glass as clear as crystal was both rare and fabulously expensive—you might just have found it in a palace. Yet that is what this city is like. It is the most amazing place to live. And more amazing still is the fact that we shall not ruin it, because we shall be just as beautiful ourselves!

Life in the new Jerusalem (21:22–22:5)

So what will it be like to live in such a place? The rest of the passage tells us. There will be no need for sun or moon, because the entire city will be lit up by the glory of God and of the Lamb. So it will never be night; there will be no darkness and, unlike every city John knew, the city gates will never have to be closed. There will be no enemies left to threaten us, in any case. And in this light of God that permeates the city we can see crowds of people in motion (21:24,26). A racist would feel very uncomfortable in the new Jerusalem, for every race and nation will be there. Of course, these nations are not the nations as we know them today: they are the redeemed. But I take these verses to mean that nothing that is good, noble and honourable about today's world is going to be lost. It will be carried over into the heavenly city. Surely there will be music there. Here on earth, for thousands of years, men and women with God-given creativity have been 'thinking God's thoughts after him', as the great astronomer Kepler put it. Will all that be left behind? Or could it be that all the finest art, literature and science of the ages will somehow be made perfect and brought into the new Jerusalem to add their splendour to it? I think they will.

The story of the world began with a garden. It ends with a city, but it is a *garden* city (22:1–2). Again, this river appears in the Old Testament, especially in the wonderful vision in Ezekiel 47 of the river that flows from the temple, bringing life wherever it goes and lined with fruit trees that are described just like the ones in these verses. In fact this whole passage is so crowded with Old Testament references that we can highlight only a fraction of them. Like an epic novel, the Bible in these closing chapters is tying up all the loose ends, bringing all the themes and sub-plots to the right conclusion. These verses bring the fulfilment of the age-old longing to get back to Eden, back to that intimacy with God, to the tree of life from which Adam and Eve were barred when they fell.

The Bible contains a total of 1,185 chapters. Out of all those chapters, sin is present in every one except for the first two and the last two, running through every human action, dashing every human hope. Sin dominates the Bible's big story. But now at last there will be *no* more sin, *no* more curse. At last we shall be breathing clean air. 21:6–8 reminded us that sin has been left behind, outside the city; these promises are for the people who have overcome, who bear the name of the Lamb. Now at last we shall be fed from the tree of life, sustained by its fruit and its leaves, drinking from the stream of living water that flows direct from God's throne down the main avenue of the city.

There in the city we shall 'see his face' (22:4). Ever since Adam and Eve sinned and went to hide away from God, that has been simply impossible. No one can see the face of God and live, because sinful flesh cannot bear the holiness of God. But there it will happen. What Adam could not do, nor Abraham, Moses, David, Isaiah, Peter or Paul, we shall be able to do—see the face of the Lord and live. Look at 21:3–4 and see how these verses stress over and over again how close we shall be to him. He will dwell with us; he will live with us; we shall be his people; he will be our God; we shall see his face; he will be with us. Everything that has hurt us in this world will be gone. Contemplate this wonderful picture of a father stooping down and wiping the tears from the eyes of his child, until every last tear is gone. That child is you and me.

In this life, the tears always return. Whatever comfort there is now—and of course there is great comfort for the believer even in this life—there is still always hurt, always pain; it truly is the vale of tears. But not any more. The time is coming when all the suffering—over broken relationships, wayward children, bitter disappointments, suffering for the name of Christ, the nights sleepless from worry, stress and pain—is gone for ever as our heavenly Father reaches down and personally wipes all of it away.

This vision should make a difference to our lives in two ways—one about what we are looking forward to, the other about how we should live here today.

1. What we look forward to

This new Jerusalem is very solid and very real! We are used to talking about 'going to heaven' when we die. The picture we often have in our minds is about floating in the air somewhere, or sitting on clouds, and doing not very much for a very long time. I hope we have seen that heaven is not actually like that: heaven is about praising the Lamb, the Lord Jesus, and looking on while he rolls out God's plans and brings human history to a close. It is quite true that we shall go to heaven—*if* we die before Christ returns. But our ultimate destination is not heaven at all. What we are really waiting for is the new heavens and the new earth and the city that comes down and becomes our home. We shall be living in perfect resurrection bodies, and the souls in heaven are longing for that resurrection morning just as much as we are—more, in fact, because they understand it better. This vision of the new Jerusalem doesn't say anything about sitting on clouds and contemplating infinity. This new city may be built of rather unusual materials; it may be more beautiful than anything we can possibly imagine, but it is still a city—physical, solid and teeming with people.

That is where God's people are going to live. We shall eat, drink, walk about, explore, learn and, above all, enjoy spending our days with the Lord Jesus, the Bridegroom. As the centuries pass, we shall know him better and better and we shall go deeper and deeper into loving and enjoying him, and this will never grow stale while eternity endures. So let's not imagine that *this* is the real world and the place where we are going, if it exists at all, is vague, shadowy and ethereal. No, *that* is the real world, the full-colour version, perfect for eternity; *this* world, as C. S. Lewis put it so vividly, is the Shadowlands.[2] The best that we can ever enjoy in this life, the deepest joy, the highest thrill, is no more than a shadow, a pale copy, of what we shall know there—just as the very best earthly marriage is just a shadow of the great wedding of the Lamb and the bride.

2. *How we should live in the meantime*

Secondly, as we look forward to the new world, we should prepare for the wedding day! See how Peter writes about it in 2 Peter 3:11–14. Remember that this glorious heavenly city is a picture of the perfected church. So don't we long to see the church beginning to look like this now—spotless, blameless, a bride ready for Christ to take? Even now, we are being prepared for the wedding day—so thank God for every little sign that it is happening in our own local churches, every gleam of the light of the city breaking out among us. We cannot create her streets of clear gold, or walls of jasper, but we can begin by turning away from anything that spoils her beauty here and now. We don't have to sin. Sin belongs to Babylon, and we have seen how ugly she is and what happens to her in the end. As we gaze at this vision of the bride, amazed at the honour and glory that God will give us, let's set ourselves, with the Holy Spirit's help, to be as ready *now*, as worthy *now*, as it is possible for us to be.

To discuss or think about

1. What do you think are the most appealing features of the

heavenly city? Do you tend to think more about freedom from suffering or the presence of the Lord?

2. Have you tended to think of our eternal state as vague and disembodied (as many Christians do)? How has this chapter helped you?
3. Think of any signs of the character of the new Jerusalem that you can already see in your own local church. Look out for them, encourage them and praise God for them!

Part X

Epilogue: ‘Come, Lord Jesus!’

(22:6–21)

21
The Final Word

Please read Revelation 22:6–21

Imagine that it is 1944 in occupied Europe. In France, four long years of grim and oppressive occupation have passed since the Nazi *blitzkrieg* swept through. As those years have passed, life has got tougher and more restricted, everyday supplies harder and harder to come by. Many people have simply fallen in with the occupation—many, but not all. The occupation is fiercely opposed by small bands of brave fighters—the *Maquis*, or resistance. At frequent risk of their lives, these men and women stand out against the occupiers. Using whatever weapons and supplies they are able to secure, they wage a constant guerrilla war against their enemies—destroying military installations, sabotaging railway engines, spying out the enemy and generally stirring up trouble wherever they can.

Now they cannot *win* the war. They cannot bring about their own freedom. But they can wait; they can prepare, and they can keep the faith. They know for certain that this terrible occupation will not, *cannot*, last for ever. One day their enemies will be destroyed and liberation will come. They don't know exactly when it will happen; they can only look to see which way the signs are pointing. They have been told to expect coded radio messages which will inform them that it is about to begin. Sure enough, on 1 June 1944, the BBC broadcasts the first coded message, hidden in one of its regular bulletins—the message which means: 'Stand by; we are coming soon.' And just five days later, D-Day, the event which they have been longing for, finally dawns—liberation at last.

Now we are not standing by for coded radio messages! But we, the church, are a people living under occupation, an occupation that is illegal, cruel and evil. We are living in enemy territory, looking forward to the day of our final liberation. It will come, not when a fleet of warships appears off the coast, but when the Lord Jesus Christ appears through the skies, when, as he has told us, the Son of Man comes with his Father's angels to gather his people from the four corners of the earth. He has transmitted the message: 'I am coming soon!' We don't know exactly when it will happen, but, just like the French resistance in 1944, *our* task is to be ready for that day, to wait, prepare ourselves and keep the faith.

With this chapter we reach the end of Revelation. We have studied, come to grips with, and sometimes puzzled over, this astonishing book, which takes us behind the scenes of history, beyond this present world into the unseen realms of heaven, into the throne-room where God reigns and works out his sovereign will. But now, as we come to 22:6, the visions are over. All the way from the start of chapter 4, they have flowed thick and fast. John has seen *everything* now: the new Jerusalem was the magnificent climax to those visions. But now the sight of her fades away and John is left, no doubt dazzled by what he has just seen, blinking as he finds himself back with his accompanying angel. Maybe that accounts for his confusion as he once more attempts to offer worship to the angel who has showed him these astounding visions (22:8–9).[3] But the angel puts him off and directs him to the closing instructions for his book—the final word.

Why did I call this book *The Final Word*? Obviously, because Revelation comes at the end of the Bible—the last book to be written, the closing of the canon of Scripture. It was also because this book speaks about the final events of history, the close of this age and the dawn of the next. The early church rightly placed Revelation at the end of the New Testament because it looks ahead to the end of everything. But another reason I called it *The Final Word* was because of its main character. Although this book is full of *many* characters and scenes—the story of angels, Satan, the beast and all of human history—supremely the book of Revelation is the story of our Lord Jesus Christ, *God's* Final Word. We have seen him as the dazzling figure who first appeared to John in chapter 1 and who addresses the seven churches in chapters 2 and 3, the risen, ascended and glorified Son of Man, our man in heaven, who guarantees that we shall be there with him. We have seen him in chapter 5 as the Lamb who was slain, who approaches the throne of God and takes the scroll that no one else can open, and one by one he unlocks the seals, opens the scroll and unrolls God's purposes through history.

We have seen the Lamb surrounded by the vast throng of the redeemed in chapter 7 and again in chapter 14. We have seen his human origins depicted in chapter 12, the son of the woman clothed with the sun. In chapter 19 we saw him as our great hero, the all-conquering warrior who rides out at the head of heaven's armies to destroy the enemies of God. We have seen him as the King reigning in the millennium and judging the world in chapter 20 and then enthroned in the new Jerusalem in chapter 21. This is his story, and *he* is the final word. Now in these closing verses we hear him speak. It is a closing, rallying call to the embattled church on earth, still waiting longingly for the day of liberation when those final visions are fulfilled and she becomes the bride. On the last page of the Bible, before the canon of Scripture is closed for ever, Christ speaks one more time to his church, to *us*, reminding us of his identity, his return and his final summons to his people.

Christ's identity (22:13,16)

He is the First and the Last (22:13)

'Alpha' and 'Omega' are the first and last letters of the Greek alphabet. Christ is the A and Z, 'the First and the Last, the Beginning and the End'. We notice that these are divine titles. In 1:8 and 21:6 we see these names ascribed to God himself (note that there are a number of parallels between the first and last chapters of the book—in particular, both stress the person of Christ, the truth of his Word and the imminence of the events which are being described). Now, in chapter 22, this is unmistakably Jesus speaking—he has just referred to his return, so we know it is he—and claiming exactly the same titles. This is another explicit statement of his deity.

So in what sense *is* Jesus the first and the last, the beginning and the end? Clearly, he is the beginning and end of the book of Revelation. But it means more than that. He is the beginning and end of *creation*. He was at the Father's side when the universe was made. He has been sustaining it by his powerful word ever since, and after he returns the universe will be remade, renewed, and he will reign over it.

He is the beginning and end of our *salvation*. Genesis 3 looked forward to him, in the promise God gave just after the Fall, the promise of the woman's distant descendant who would crush Satan—the hope to which God's people looked forward for thousands of years. It is his cross that bought our freedom, his resurrection that guarantees our eternal life and his return that will bring the end of the age.

He is the Root and Offspring of David (22:16)

In verse 16 we are given more of his titles. 'The Root and the offspring of David' means that Jesus is both David's ancestor and his descendant at the same time. He is David's *ancestor* because he is the Creator of all mankind. He is David's *descendant*, of course, because in human lineage he comes from David's line. Jesus Christ is not only reigning now in heaven 'up there' and masterminding the plans of God in the world; he has himself been the pivotal element of the human story 'down here'. What David foreshadowed in a very incomplete and imperfect way, Jesus is in full. He is fully God *and* fully man.

He is the Morning Star (22:16)

What is the 'bright Morning Star' of the same verse? Literally, it refers to the appearance of the planet Venus before sunrise. When it appears it is quite unique—firstly, because it is by far the brightest 'star' in the sky and, secondly, because when it rises in the darkness above the eastern horizon, the dawn is never more than a couple of hours away. Before the morning star is high in the sky, the horizon will be ablaze with light as the sun begins to rise. The Lord Jesus is the herald of the dawn. He is the guarantee to us, in the dark night of this world, that the light is coming, that eternity is dawning and our liberation is not far away.

Have we grasped what Jesus is—how he possesses Godhood, how he fills history, how his presence runs through the whole story of our race, how he is our Saviour and he is bringing in eternity? He is so much greater than the Jesus of the Jehovah's Witnesses, who cut him down to a kind of cosmic Superman. He is so much more than the Jesus of the Muslims, who claim to honour him so highly but in fact don't have the first idea about his true identity, because they say he is just a prophet, and not even the greatest of those. This is our Lord Jesus Christ—the God-man who fills heaven and earth and eternity. The question is, does he fill our *hearts* like that? Is our confidence all in him, that he will keep us through this dark world until he comes for us at last?

Christ's return (22:7,12,20)

He is coming soon (22:7,12,20)

The cry of Christ's return rings as a refrain through these closing verses. But 'Soon?', we might ask. 'Lord, we have been waiting two thousand years—what kind of "soon" is that?' Even knowing that the word 'soon' could equally well be translated as 'quickly' doesn't help very much. 'Soon' to us means in a few minutes, or next week, or at the very most next year. But this is *God's* book, and these are *his* words. Peter tackles exactly this problem in his second letter (2 Peter 3:8–10). The Lord's perspective on time is very different. His return will be sudden. It will be unexpected—like the arrival of a thief on your doorstep, it certainly is not going to happen by arrangement with *you*! ('Excuse me, can I make an appointment to burgle your house at 1 o'clock tonight?') It will be dramatic. And it will happen when he wills it to happen.

The word 'soon' reminds us that we must always be ready. When we look out across our world we can see good reason to expect that he *will* come soon—what *we* call 'soon'. Not only is the world full of crises everywhere, both human and environmental, not only are there the 'wars and rumours of wars' that Jesus warned us would characterize our times (Matthew 24); more than that, we can also see two key signs of the end times coming to pass in our own days. Firstly, the powers opposed to the church are strengthening and growing. The beast and the false prophet are flexing their muscles and moving against God's people with unprecedented ferocity. Listen to the news; understand the times. And, secondly, the gospel of the kingdom is being preached to all nations, and men and women are being saved in great numbers. God is bringing in the nations who will populate the new Jerusalem. It is happening now as never before, in Africa, in South America, in great swathes of Asia and even in some measure in the Middle East. Yes, the darkness is growing deeper, but the light is shining brighter.

He is coming with his reward (22:12)

What men and women decide to do with Jesus seals their fate or wins their glory. The time is near when it will be too late to change, and the course people have chosen to follow will be fixed for ever—that is what the rather difficult verse 11 is about. The pointed question must be asked: 'What have we done with the Lord Jesus?' Is it eternal life or a sentence of eternal death that he will pronounce? If we are believers, our reward will depend on how we have served him and what we have done with the talents he entrusted to us.

Christ's summons (22:7,14–15,17)

Now, in the light of his identity and his return, Jesus issues his summons to faithfulness. Together we have glimpsed these amazing visions and seen how the Lord is working out his plans and bringing it all to a glorious climax. But we need to get on with living here and now. We look forward with longing to his return, to meeting Jesus and living in the new Jerusalem, but for now we still live in the vale of tears.

Jesus calls us to be faithful to his Word (22:7)

There are precisely seven 'blessings' in Revelation—one more example of the number of perfection. By the way, there are many more 'sevens' in this book than you might see at first glance.

For instance, the word ‘Christ’ appears seven times, as does ‘Lord God Almighty’, the announcement of Christ’s coming, the prophets and the word ‘Amen’, as well as the seven spirits, eyes, letters, seals, trumpets, bowls and thunders—all showing how skilfully this book has been woven together. Anyway, there are seven *blessings*; and in this verse we find number six.

Now look back to 1:3, where we find blessing number one. These two blessings are the same: ‘Read this book; take it to heart; do what it says.’ Together they bracket the whole book and tell us that the blessing from this book of Revelation is not in decoding it, nor in working out clever schemes and interpretations about the end of time, but is for those who are faithful to the Word. Time and again this chapter emphasizes that ‘These words are trustworthy and true’ (22:6); you are blessed if you keep them (22:7); the testimony comes from Jesus (22:16) and, finally, the solemn warning of verses 18–19.

Some have suggested this is nothing more than a warning to the early copyists of Revelation, painstakingly writing it out over and over again long before the days of printing: ‘Don’t slip up—or else!’ But this warning is nothing to do with accidental errors. It is addressed to anyone who deliberately distorts God’s Word. Although its immediate meaning is clearly just about Revelation itself, in practice the warning applies to the whole of Scripture. Far from being an appendix that we need to read only if we are especially keen, the book of Revelation summarizes the whole of Scripture: it retells the whole of Scripture’s story.

So these words warn people who say that this Bible is *not enough* for us and that we need extra books to add to it, like the Quran or the Book of Mormon. They also warn people who say that this Bible is *too much* for us and that we need to cut bits out of it, parts that we cannot believe any more, or that we don’t like the look of—the sort of message that is given even in some theological colleges and seminaries. ‘Don’t add to it; take nothing away from it.' It is also a reminder to *us* that the whole Bible is God's Word, not just the parts we like best.

But the warning here is even more basic than that. The key message of all Scripture is the gospel of Jesus Christ. Whether you endure the plagues, or enjoy the tree of life and the holy city, depends quite simply on what you do with the gospel of Jesus—do you accept it, or do you reject it? It is not so much a threat as a statement of bare fact. The message is that if you accept the gospel and stay true to God's Word, you are *blessed*; if not, you are *cursed*. He summons us to be faithful to his Word, to read it, understand it, learn it, study it, love it and live by it.

He summons us to be faithful to our calling (22:14–15)

Again we see the contrast between those *inside* the city and those left behind *outside*. Even here, right at the end, we have a reminder of the two camps that everyone is in, and the stark contrast between the two. 'Dogs' in this passage are not literal canines, of course; this is a pejorative term for people who are unclean, rejected because of their evil ways. But here in verse 14 is the seventh and final blessing to which all the others point. The picture of 'washing their robes' has already appeared back in chapter 7, where we read about the saints who had washed their robes in the blood of the Lamb. It is a picture of sins being washed away. The Greek word *plunontes* (a present participle) makes it clear that 'washing our robes' is an ongoing process, something we have to do repeatedly. We *still* sin; we still have to come back to the cross over and over again to deal with our sin; we still have to 'wash our robes'. The ultimate blessing—entering the city and inheriting what Adam lost—is for those who are faithful to the end, not for those who begin and then fall away.

He summons us to be faithful to our mission (22:17)

The invitation rings out. It comes to us first: the Holy Spirit and the bride, the church perfected as she will be, call us to join them, and we hear the call. We are part of the bride of Christ, filled with his Spirit. And then we too say, 'Come!' The mission Jesus has left us is just this: to offer the free gift of the water of life to whoever is thirsty and invite them to come to Christ and drink this water of life. We are not to cower in a corner while the world gets darker and we wait for Christ to come back and pull us out of it. We are not to be content to leave this world as Satan's kingdom while we keep our heads down. The Christian life is not about survival; it is about *mission*. And as we see people accept the invitation, beginning to drink the water of life, we are speeding Christ's return, because he returns when the mission is finally completed—and not one day before.

To sum up

This world is a tough place for a believer to live. How do we do it? There are churches that you can go to where they will tell you that if you only have enough faith, you will never have to suffer illness or pain; that if you only claim it confidently enough, you will have wealth instead of poverty; that God's will for you is that this life should essentially be a bed of roses—though they might not put it that way. But throughout this book, written to tell believers how to live when the world is against us, we find not one trace of that kind of teaching. It is a lie. The message of this glorious book is this: 'Yes, you *will* have trouble here, lots of it. You will suffer as the Lamb's people, *because* you are his people. But in the end, Jesus wins and his people are safe for ever; and what he has prepared for us is beyond our imagination. Meanwhile, be faithful.'

So John's heavenly vision comes to its end. He comes out of it and finds he is back on Patmos on a Sunday evening. The breeze is blowing and it is getting cold and dark, and he is still a prisoner. Does he weep to think that, after seeing all this, after seeing into heaven, conversing with angels and glimpsing the awesome future for God's people, he is still in exile on his barren island, he is still an old man with the aches and ailments of old age? After all the visions, this is today's reality, and he still has to live here. But then he remembers how it all finished. The Lord Jesus summons us to be faithful—to his Word, to our calling, to our mission. This is what John's churches had to hear, living as they were with the opposition of their culture, struggling under the persecution of the empire. And this is what *we* need to hear, because we don't live in the heavenly city yet. We still live in Babylon, the place of rebellion against our God. We are still living in enemy territory; we are the resistance, waiting for our final liberation. And it is coming.

This was the point of all the spectacular visions, to nail it down for God's people still living in this fallen world with all its suffering and pain: 'See, this is who your Jesus is, the Lord of your history, greater far than all your enemies, the beginning and the end, Alpha and Omega. This glorious Lord Jesus is coming again, and he is coming soon. So be *faithful*. Keep his words, be true to him.'

Amen. Come, Lord Jesus!

To discuss or think about

1. Do you think of yourself as a fighter in enemy-occupied territory? Do you find that a helpful illustration of what it's like for Christians as we await the return of Christ?
2. What can you do to invite people to 'take the free gift of the water of life'?
3. Are you looking forward to Jesus' return?

Notes

Introduction

1. The distance from Patmos to Pergamum, the most distant of the seven churches, is about 150 miles as the crow flies.

2. The futurist view is usually held as part of a wider view of Scripture called dispensationalism. This book is not the place to discuss dispensationalism in its fuller sense, but at least two of its distinctive beliefs are highly relevant to reading Revelation: (1) that all prophecy should be read as literally as possible. Since dispensationalists regard Revelation as primarily prophecy, this means that the imagery of Revelation is understood in far more literal ways than with the other views. (2) that the nation of Israel is still at the heart of God's purposes in salvation today, and that God has separate plans for Israel and the church up to the return of Christ and even beyond.

Chapter 1—The First and the Last

1. The seven blessings are found in 1:3; 14:13; 16:15; 19:9; 20:6; 22:7,14. In a very illuminating article, David Field has shown how the seven fit together, reflecting the deliberate literary composition of the book and pointing on to the seventh blessing, which is the privilege of entry into the heavenly city (D. Field, 'The Seven Blessings of the Book of Revelation—A Brief Exegetical Note', *Foundations* 53, 2005).

2. The Greek contains a grammatical 'mistake' at this point. It seems that John has deliberately decided not to modify the form of this title of God, as the rules of grammar would require here, out of reverence for his name.

3. Verse 19 is sometimes cited in support of the 'futurist' view of Revelation. On this understanding, the verse neatly splits the book into three parts. 'What you have seen' refers to the vision of Jesus in chapter 1; 'what is now' refers to the current state of the church, reflected in the letters to the seven churches in chapters 2 and 3; and 'what will take place later' refers to the rest of the book (chapters 4 to 22)—all of which, therefore, will happen in the *future*. I don't think this way of reading the verse is justified. A better way of understanding the verse is something like: '... everything you see, both what is going on now and what is going to happen in the future'. For a much fuller explanation, please consult one of the technical commentaries.

4. We shall discuss the identity of the 'angels of the churches' in our next chapter.

Chapter 2—Firm as a rock?

1. Premillennialists will understand this as a reference to the earthly reign of Christ with the saints in the millennium, while amillennialists generally see it as sharing in Christ's *present* kingdom and his authority to judge the world. We shall tackle this difficult subject when we reach chapter 20.

2. Compare Galatians 6:16.

3. The 'ten days' of 2:10 probably allude to the ten-day test to which Daniel and his three companions were subjected (Daniel 1:11–16). Like them, the believers at Smyrna 700 years later are faced with attempted seduction by the pagan world. By this reference to ten days, the Lord is saying, 'You are following in the steps of faithful Daniel, and I will see you through the test too.'

4. There is a clear allusion here to the description of Eliakim, son of Hilkiah, in Isaiah 22:20–24. Eliakim was one of Hezekiah's senior officials (see

2 Kings 18:18). He seems to be presented as a type of Christ, the truest and most faithful Servant.

Chapter 3—Good image or good heart?

1. John's first letter makes this connection explicit (1 John 5:4–5).

Chapter 4—The plot is not lost

1. *As You Like It*, Act 2, Scene vii.
2. These include a reference to the bronze 'sea' which stood in the temple courts and the idea that it is a symbol of humanity, but I think there are problems with both of these, as well as other proposals.
3. Some of the Church Fathers believed that these creatures represented the four Gospel writers, but as soon as they began to identify each one, any agreement quickly disappeared!
4. Verse 10 refers to the saints who will 'reign on the earth'. Depending on your view of Revelation 20, you will understand this primarily either as a reference to the earthly millennium, or to the new heavens and the new earth.

Chapter 5—Suffering and the end of the age

1. In effect, this is the option chosen by those who follow the theological path known as 'open theism'—the belief that God's power is limited, either because of his nature, or because he has chosen to limit himself, so that he works in history by thinking ahead and trying to make the best of the actions his creatures choose to do.
2. Quotations from the early chapters of C. S. Lewis, *A Grief Observed*, Faber & Faber, 1966.
3. The idea that John is the one addressed was supported by the Authorized/ King James Version, which added the words 'and see', but the manuscript evidence favours omitting these words.

4. These points are more relevant than the minutiae of the two different 'rider visions', such as the different words used for 'crown'.

5. There is also a strong correspondence, as we have already noted, between the first five seals and the earlier parts of Matthew 24 (vv. 4–14). Thus Wilcock can say, '... Christ is not only expounding the same subject, but expounding it in the same order, in both places. The two chapters engage at point after point like the two sides of a zip.'

Chapter 6—From every nation one voice

1. There is more to Zechariah's vision than we can deal with here. The point is that the imagery is very similar and it is these images and their basic meaning that give us so much of the background to Revelation.

2. In Revelation 11, as we shall see, Jew/Gentile language is applied to the church in the midst of a hostile world. However, those who do not accept that the crowds in Revelation 7 are both the same are unlikely to be convinced of this reading of chapter 11 either!

3. It may help to think of a telephone number. If your phone number is 0123 456789, that figure does not correspond to a total number of phones (though it does suggest that there are a lot of phones in circulation); it is a *symbol* which represents your particular phone. It is a number with a meaning, not a statistic.

4. A brief survey of the different ways Revelation has been read is given in the introduction.

5. It is interesting that the way John describes the nations of the world varies, but there are always four components, corresponding to 'four' as the number of the world. Moreover, an expression like this occurs seven times, A particularly helpful book for understanding the use of numbers in Revelation, and much else besides, is Richard Bauckham's *The theology of the book of Revelation*.

6. Greek, *thlipsis.*

Chapter 7—Prayer and the purposes of God

1. Greek, *hagios.*

Chapter 8—Warnings that go unheard

1. The Ukrainian *chornobyl* is actually a different though closely related plant.
2. The fact that the 'star' is said to have 'fallen' from heaven makes it very unlikely that it could refer to a good angel. Our God's providential control of history extends even to the activities of Satan.
3. C. S. Lewis, *The Problem of Pain,* Collins, 1977, p.81.

Chapter 9— The Word of God—sweet and sour

1. Commentators have debated whether the scroll of ch 10 is the same as ch 5. I don't think they are intended to be the same, because this one is described as 'a *little* scroll' and because it is destined, like Ezekiel's scroll, to be consumed and to become the prophet's message of judgement and salvation. However, if the two scrolls were the same, it would not make much difference to the meaning of this passage.

Chapter 10—The Word of God—unstoppable

1. Tempting as it may be to mix in here a reference to today's earthly city of Jerusalem, the book of Revelation gives us no warrant whatever for doing so.
2. The 'seven thousand' who are 'killed in the earthquake' may be meant to recall the seven thousand in Israel who had not bowed the knee to Baal. The seven thousand who die would then represent an exact retribution for the suffering of the faithful witnesses under Ahab's evil reign (1 Kings 19:18).

Chapter 12—The beast and his number

1. There are at least three interpretations of what the four beast-empires of Daniel 7 represent: (1) Babylonia, Media, Persia and Greece; (2) Media, Persia, Greece and Rome; and (3) Babylonia, Medo-Persia, Greece and

Rome. All have their proponents, but for the purposes of Revelation it does not matter which is correct.

2. In 1933, around 6,000 pastors broke away to form the 'Confessing Church', denouncing Nazism as a blasphemy. Those involved were from a range of theological persuasions; what they shared in common was the understanding that the church of Christ can never be subject to the dictates of an evil tyrant.

Chapter 13— The fatal division

1. We have not yet arrived at the new heavens and the new earth - that comes in chapter 21—so we can't actually say that this 'Mount Zion' *is* the new city. Rather, it represents that way that believers in the present age, even those in heaven, long for and aspire to the new age to come.

Chapter 14— The song of the winners

1. The NIV84 used the more literal expression 'testimony' for covenant law. The Greek is *marturion*, which is part of the word group for witness.

Chapter 15 —The fate of the losers

1. This verse contains the third of the seven blessings in Revelation (see chapter 1, note 1).

Chapter 17—The great escape

1. Revelation 2:10 probably alludes to Daniel's experience—see chapter 2, note 3.

2. The NIV84 was certainly wrong to include this verse in what the captains and seamen say about Babylon—they have neither the inclination nor the insight to invite us to rejoice over her fall. The NIV11 has corrected this.

3. For an excellent treatment of these issues, see Tim Chester, *Good News to the Poor*, IVP, 2004.

Chapter 18—Our hero

1. But we should not forget that righteous deeds are the necessary result of our justification, and it is right to think of the bride 'wearing' these also. Scripturally, good deeds performed by God's people in the power of his Spirit are beautiful! Beale has an extended discussion of this difficult verse (*The Book of Revelation*, pp.934–941).

Chapter 19—No more tomorrows

1. The period of trial that is said to arise between the 'rapture' and the Second Coming is labelled the Great Tribulation, a term taken from Revelation 7:14. However, as we noted there, the word translated 'tribulation' is simply the Greek word *thlipsis*, which is the standard word for trouble. I don't believe that Revelation supports the idea of a distinctively different 'great tribulation' in the final days, still less that Christians will escape it.

2. Beale suggests that there are actually strong parallels between Revelation 12 and Revelation 20:1–3, making them essentially depictions of the same scene, but these are not convincing. In particular, as Beale accepts, the 'short time' of 12:12 clearly applies to the period from Christ's death to his Second Coming, whereas the 'short time' of 20:3 describes the more limited time of Satan's rebellion in the final days.

3. To point out that God is still in the process of saving his elect from out of all the nations, in spite of all that Satan can do, is no answer to this argument, though it is a true and wonderful statement. The point is that Satan is *still active* as 'the god of this age' (2 Corinthians 4:4).

4. Revelation 19:17–18 recalls Ezekiel 39:4,17–20. Revelation 20 simply makes the connection more explicit (20:8).

5. In his excellent recent book defending amillennialism (*Kingdom Come: the amillennial alternative*), Sam Storms repeatedly insists that all premillennialists take the millennium to span a literal thousand years. This is simply untrue, and is certainly not a necessary part of the premillennial position.

6. Revelation 20:4–6 describe two resurrections: everyone agrees that the one referred to in the first part of verse 5 is a physical resurrection. Amillennialists argue that the 'first resurrection' of verses 4, 5b and 6 is a *spiritual* resurrection, usually coinciding with physical death. The problem is that this requires a radical change of meaning for 'resurrection' within the space of a single verse. While this is possible (Beale provides a suggested explanation—see his *The Book of Revelation*, pp.1005–6), it is certainly not the most natural reading. Moreover, it seems very odd to describe as 'resurrection' the process of physical death where the soul simply continues to live! The normal biblical use of the word is so much fuller and richer than that.

Chapter 20—The new world for ever

1. It is possible that some of the prophecies in Isaiah 65:17–25 will be fulfilled during the earthly millennium (see verse 20 in particular).
2. In *The Last Battle.*
3. Twice we have seen John attempting to worship an angel (the first occasion being 19:10). In each case the angel tells him to worship only God. We shouldn't miss the fact that this amounts to an explicit assertion of the deity of Christ, the Lamb. In 5:11-14 we find the whole of Creation worshipping him! Revelation asserts the deity of Christ as clearly as any other New Testament book.